The Heart of Hinduism

A Comprehensive Guide for Teachers and Professionals

Rasamandala Das

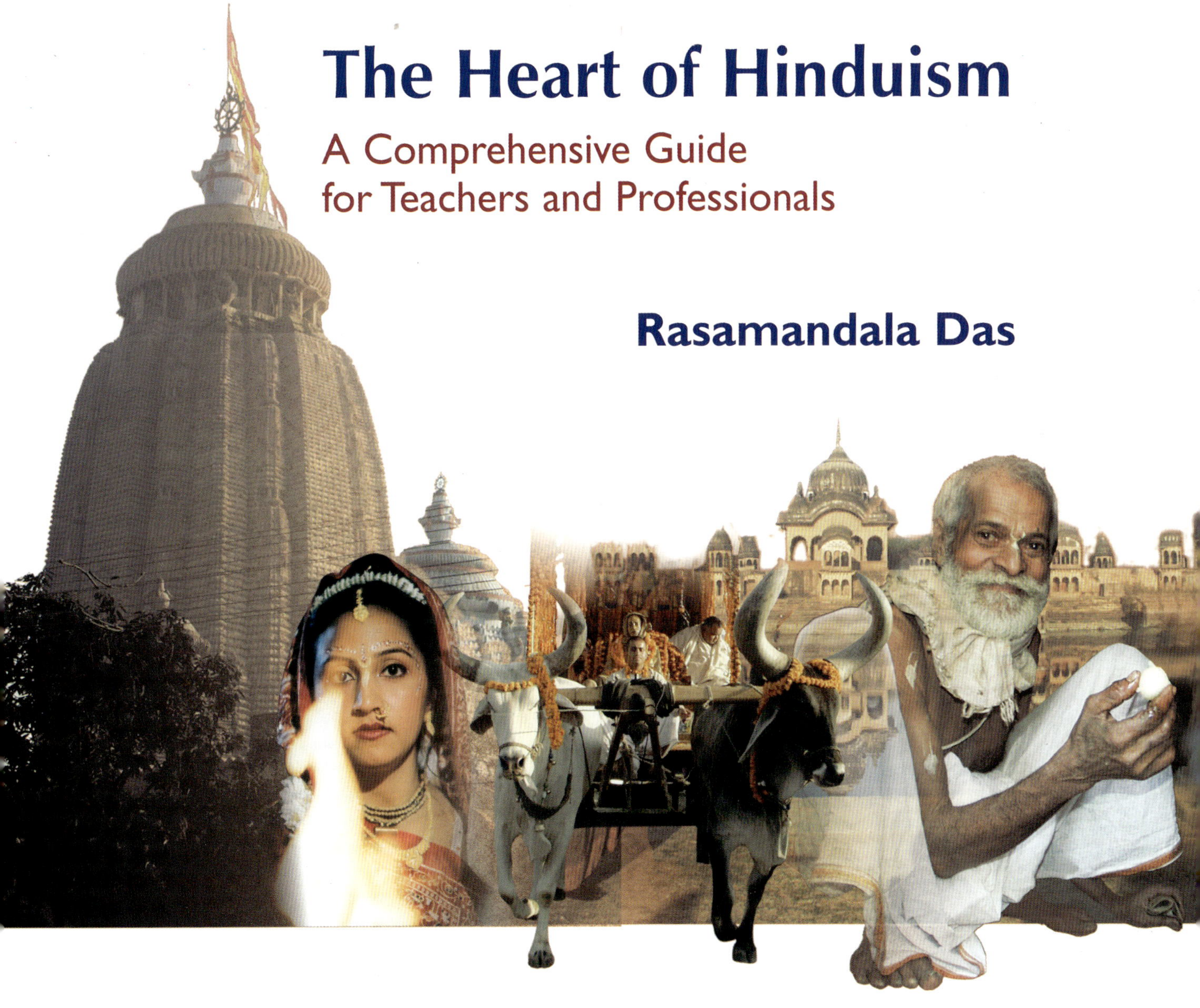

Acknowledgments

ISKCON Educational Services
Bhaktivedanta Manor, Hilfield Lane,
Aldenham, Herts. WD25 8EZ, England, UK.

Produced in cooperation with
Dharma Publications,
Chintamani, Wall Hall Cottages,
Aldenham, Herts. WD2 8AS.

ISBN 0-9522686-3-9

Illustrated by Sue and Steve Coote
Photography by Dave Evans and Yogendra Sahu
Edited by Indriyesha Das, Vandana Synghal, Tattvavit Das and Philip and Petra Lucien
Designed and typeset by Ajay Kumar, Nitesh Vaghadia
Layout by Ajay Kumar and Bhawesh Shah
Project Manager: Sita Rama Das
Printed in Great Britain by:
A.G. Printing & Publishing Ltd.,
797-799 Harrow Road, Wembley,
Middlesex, HA0 2LP, U.K.
Tel: 020 8904-5001   Fax: 020 8908-4004

Acknowledgments

This book is dedicated to the many teachers and other Religious Education specialists who kindly helped in the planning stage and in trialling the material. We'd especially like to thank the following people:

Re-Advisors/ Consultants and Specialists:

Jo Fageant (C. of E Diocesan Board for Oxfordshire), Pat Stevens (Harrow), Denise Chaplin (Lewisham), Lisa Kassapian (Hertfordshire), Sarah Smalley (Cambridgeshire), Gavin Craigen (North Wales) Joy White (Hope University, Liverpool), Veronica Voiels (Manchester), Lynn Broadbent (Brunel University), Bill Gent (Redbridge), Julian Stern (Brunel University), Mark Brimicombe (Devon),Cathy Bowness (Plymouth).

Teachers:

Elizabeth Wayne (Soar Valley, Leicester), Wendy Meldrum (Watford Grammar School for Girls), Catherine Jupp (Sir Frederick Osborn W.G.C), Frances Cooper (Forest Hill, London), Michael Wilcockson (Eton College), Kirtida Dasi (ISKCON Newcastle) Sue Coote (Woking), Delyth Clarke (Henrietta Barnett School), Dhirashanta Das (ISKCON Plymouth), Nikki White (Danbury Park County Primary), Freda Ross (Longford Primary, Cannock), Liz Bassett (Mayfield School, Cambridge), Lisa Williams (Garden Suburb Infant School), Margaret Slater (Wood End JMI), Lorraine Beal (Hawthorns, Bletchingly), Lynn Ridley (The Kendrick School, Reading), Morris Twigg (Harwarden High), Anne Evans (Beacon Community College, Crowborough), Linda Stevens (Breakspeare Junior), Simon Bennett (Tudor Grange, Solihull).

The publishers would also like to thank the following people for permission to reproduce copyright material

Heinemann Educational for "the Body Club Strike" (poem) from Beliefs, Values And Traditions by Ann Lovelace and Joy White. Ahimsa Books for "The Sadhu's Blessings" and "The King's Finger" from Vedic Stories from Ancient India. CEM (now Christian Education) for the article, "Visiting Faith Communities" from RE Today. The SHAP Working Party for permission to reproduce the article "Hindu Notions of Time" from The Shap Journal (2000/2001). Sakshi Gopal for permission to reproduce his poem, "The Bird in the Cage". Oneworld Publications, for the quotes from "The Wisdom of Hinduism" by K.K. Klostermaier.

We would also like to thank the following for permission to reproduce photographs and illustrations:

Gwyneth Little and Christians Aware – pages 25, 33, 80 (bottom), 86. Robert Jackson and Dr. Eleanor Nesbitt of Warwick University for the photos from "Listening to Hindus" (p.63, 74,77, 136). Ranchor Prime and Friends of Vrindavana - pages 88,110. The Bhaktivedanta Book Trust (p. 10, 34, 39, 40, 48, 52, 53, 77, 99, 101, 118, 120, 121, 122, 124, 125, 127-130, 139, 143), Mandala Media (p. 30, 48, 49, 90), Peter Hayes (111), Torchlight Publishing (p. 131), Ajamila Das and Goloka Books (p. 9, 15, 21, 36, 41, 82, 91, 102, 117, 126, 127, 146, 147), Sewa International (p.88), The Swami Narayana Mission (p. 61), Franklin Watts for the photograph on p. 91 (photography by Chris Fairclough), Hare Krishna Food for Life - (p.88, 108, 109). Transcendental Meditation (p. 145), Gayathri Matha Temple, London (p. 132, 146), the Vishva Hindu Parishad (p.73, 78), the Vedic Academy (p.101), David Rose (p.67).

A special thanks to:

The Oxford Centre for Vaishnava and Hindu Studies, 13-15, Magdalen Street, Oxford OX1 3AE for acting as our consultants and for the academic advice provided by:

Dr Eleanor Nesbitt (University of Warwick), W. Owen Cole (Chichester), Prof. Narasimhacharya of Chennai (Madras) University, Dr. Guy Beck of Tulane University, New Orleans

We are most grateful for the feedback and suggestions from the following Hindu organisations:

Atmasvarupa Swami, the Swami Narayana Mission, Neasden, London. Dilip Lakhani, The Vivekanand Centre, London. Dr N. Prinja, the Visva Hindu Parishad, Cheshire. Vipin Aery, The National Council for Hindu Temples & The Hindu Council.

Thank you to all others who helped, including:

Satvinder Heer, Reeha Patel, Vijay Hirani, Mehul Patel, Raj Gope, Sunit Patel, Deepak Vohra, Ramesh Kallidai, Prema Sankirtan Das, Rakesh Dhamecha, Manisha Kotecha, Nilesh Patel, Naina Parmar, Shrutidharma Das, Subhangada Dasi, Jaya Patel, Donald and Sudha Fisher, Urvasi Bharadia, Naina Bhika, Arya Dasi, Nandini Sodha, Ranchor Prime, Abala Dasi, Jagannatha Suta, Pete Booker, Pradip Gajjar, Vibha Ruparelia, Bret Townsend, Shamita Kumar.

Contents

What is Hinduism?

Hinduism is perhaps the oldest of all religions and yet endures today as a healthy, colourful and exuberant tradition. It has intimate links with India, but its influence visibly extends throughout Britain and across the globe. It is conspicuous through its art, food, dress, music and philosophy. It is classified as one of the main world religions, and the source of other Eastern traditions such as Jainism, Sikhism and Buddhism.

Scholars suggest that the term 'Hindu' was first used around the eighth century CE, by Persian invaders to refer to the people on the far side of the River Indus. The early connotations weren't specifically religious but more cultural, political and geographical. Only later, when outsiders tried to impose their own doctrines on India, did Hindus try to define their tradition as a separate, autonomous whole, a religion similar to other world faiths. Many scholars today prefer to call Hinduism 'a family of religions', with each member unique but bearing distinctive family features.

How we explain this family likeness is a challenge. Definitions of the words 'Hindu' and 'Hinduism' remain somewhat arbitrary. Whatever definitions we choose, we will find someone claiming to be Hindu – or whom others consider Hindu – who falls outside the bounds of such criteria. For example, some suggest that being a Hindu is based solely on birth, but there are now many 'white Hindus'. Others perceive Hindus as those who comply with the Vedic literature (the Vedas and their supplements). Still others identify Hinduism with Sanatana-dharma, and notions of universal and eternal truths that transcend any specific texts. Caste practice is a persistent feature of the tradition, but many claim it has nothing to do with the religion itself. Others claim that caste is an aberration of the ancient *Varnashrama-dharma* system, referred to in the Rig Veda and thus central to the tradition. We cannot resort to defining the tradition solely on belief – a term little used by Hindus themselves – for not all subscribe to the same teachings, or even key concepts such as karma and reincarnation.

For teachers, the tradition poses specific challenges. It has no single founder, no one scripture, no common creed, and no universally-accepted code of conduct. It features numerous leaders, diverse doctrines, hundreds of holy books, and widely variant practices. Most Hindus believe in one God but venerate one or more of a multitude of deities. And, to challenge us further, we cannot say with any certainty when the tradition began. Followers themselves often claim it is eternal!

What is certain, though, is that trying to squeeze the tradition into a purely Western framework is problematic. As far as possible, we need to view the tradition through its own eyes - to empathise with its particular mood, grasp its unique world-view and get a whiff of its distinctive fragrance. This requires authentic resources, born of both personal commitment and a reflective, critical and educational approach; material from practitioners who have imbibed their tradition and, simultaneously, can make it accessible to others. We hope that this book, and the attendant material in the teachers' pack, will serve your purposes. Despite the complexities of the tradition, it can be categorised and explained, as we have tried to do here. Moreover, it exudes a universal and timeless charm that can only enrich our study of religion.

Sanskrit and Hindi notation

We have not employed diacritics for Indian words in this book. We have largely used the Sanskrit versions of words, adding the final 'a', which may or may not be pronounced. Thus, we have written Rama rather than Ram. In some words 'v' and 'w' may be interchanged, as in Diwali or Divali, since the pronunciation may fall somewhere between the two letters as pronounced in English. Sanskrit and Hindu words are italicised except for words that have entered the English language, such as guru & ashram. Some words may be spelt in both traditional & anglicised forms. (e.g. brahmana & brahmin). For a spoken demonstration of how words are pronounced, consult the audio glossary on "The Heart of Hinduism" CD-Rom.

Representing Hinduism

There are distinct advantages to Hindus speaking on behalf of their own tradition. Nonetheless, there are potential drawbacks. For example, there may be a tendency to promote one group at the expense of others. We have consciously tried to avoid this, though our own experience as members of the Vaishnava tradition, and our access to resources (such as photographs) may somewhat slant our portrayal of the tradition as a whole. We are also aware that some Hindus might disagree with some of our statements and sentiments. This is to be expected and welcomed, though we sincerely hope that we do not offend anyone.

Part 1 - Concepts & Values

 ## Chapter 1 – Key Concepts

 ## Chapter 2 – Core Values

These two chapters are essential in helping us understand the Hindu worldview – how Hindus see and respond to the world. Religious phenomena make greater sense when examined in the light of the rationale and purposes behind them.

Some readers might denote these chapters core beliefs. However, the notion of religion as a belief system is alien to most Hindus, who talk of their tradition, *Sanatana-dharma*, as a universal science. Indeed, the tradition has largely managed to blend religious commitment with a spirit of philosophical inquiry. We might more accurately denote this section Hindu ideals, expressed as philosophical concepts (Chapter One) and personal values (Chapter Two). This second chapter is distinctive, since it explores Hindu values directly, rather than implicitly or thematically through ethical issues. Nonetheless, this material is most effective when used in conjunction with the auxiliary book, "Moral Issues in Hinduism" (see page 149)

Chapter 1
Key Concepts

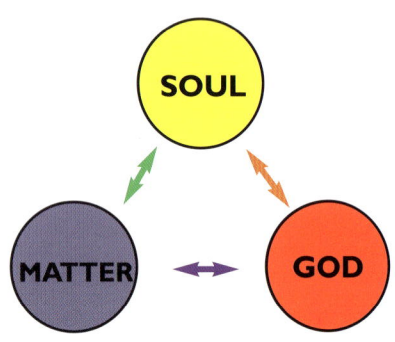

Above: This simple diagram shows the three basic 'concepts', which form the basis for Hindu thought. Different schools present various opinions on the nature of each 'concept' and the relationships between them.

Below: There are two main schools of thought within Modern Hinduism.

Key Points

- Hinduism is diverse; no single doctrine (or set of beliefs) can represent its numerous traditions.

- Nonetheless, the various schools share several basic concepts, which help us to understand how most Hindus see and respond to the world.

- The concepts we discuss here are largely based on Vedanta, and accepted by most modern traditions (but, keep in mind, not all!).

- Hinduism begins simply by differentiating between matter and spirit.

  Spirit is understood within two main categories, namely

  (1) the individual self, or soul (the atman)
  (2) the Supreme Self, or God (the paramatman).

- Hence, there are these three main truths (see left) , which form the basis for theological discussion.

- These three truths have been expanded here into 12 concepts. These twelve are interwoven into a useful overview of Hindu thought (given below).

Two Main Schools of Vedanta

Within Vedanta there are several doctrines. The main contention is about the nature of the Supreme, and in defining the relationship between God and the soul (represented by the orange arrow above)

(1) The *advaita* (monist) schools entirely equate the soul with God.

(2) The *dvaita* (monotheistic) schools tend to emphasise the distinction.

Many theologies synthesise these two elements. In this section, where relevant, we present the opinions of both these schools.

Overview of Hindu Theology

Almost all Hindus believe that the real self *(atman)* is distinct from the temporary body made of matter *(prakriti)*. The eternal soul identifies with matter and is entrapped by *maya* (illusion). Impelled by lust, greed, anger, etc., he undergoes *samsara* (the cycle of repeated birth and death). Each soul creates its unique destiny according to *the law of karma* (the universal law of action and reaction). Under the influence of eternal **time** and the three *gunas* (material qualities) he moves throughout the **creation**, sometimes going to higher planets, sometimes moving in human society, and at other times entering the lower species. The goal of most Hindus is *moksha*, liberation from this perpetual cycle, through re-identification with the eternal *brahman* (Supreme). Hinduism accepts **different paths towards this common goal** (union with God). Nonetheless, it stresses strict adherence to universal principles through the practice of one's *dharma* (ordained duty) as revealed through authorised **holy books** and usually received through the *guru* (spiritual mentor).

The following chart shows the twelve main concepts within Hindu thought. We have put them in a logical sequence (though the last two are more or less tagged on at the end). The notion of the soul (atman) is placed first as it is essential to grasp before moving onto other ideas. We especially recommend that you work through the basic concepts before trying to tackle the more complex, such as Hindu ideas of God. Nevertheless as you move through each concept, do not feel it imperative to read the entire double-page spread. You may choose only to read the main text and note the key points. Further details of the layout for this chapter are shown at the foot of this page.

Key Concept	Key Questions
1. The Atman (the Soul)	*Who are we? What is the real self?*
2. Reincarnation and Samsara	*What happens after death, before birth?*
3. The Law of Karma	*Why is there suffering?*
4. Prakriti (Matter) and Guna	*How does the world work?*
5. Maya (Illusion)	*Why do we get into difficulty in this world?*
6. Moksha (Liberation)	*What is the goal of life?*
7. God (Brahman / Ishvara)	*Is there a God? If so, what is He/She like?*
8. Dharma (religious duties)	*Which is the right way to act?*
9. One Goal, Different Paths	*How can we explain Hindu diversity?*
10. Scripture & Guru (Authority)	*How are the teachings preserved?*
11. Time	*When did it all start and when will it finish?*
12. Creation	*How and why was this world made?*

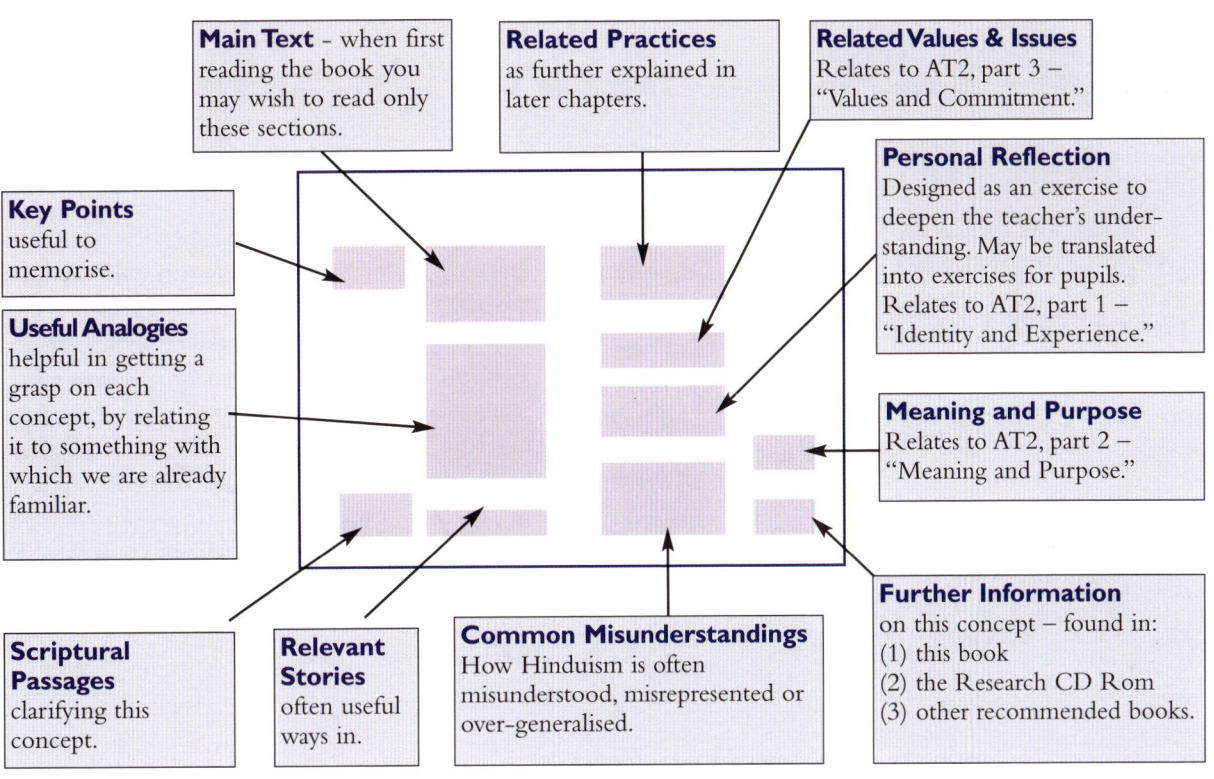

Main Text – when first reading the book you may wish to read only these sections.

Related Practices as further explained in later chapters.

Related Values & Issues Relates to AT2, part 3 – "Values and Commitment."

Personal Reflection Designed as an exercise to deepen the teacher's understanding. May be translated into exercises for pupils. Relates to AT2, part 1 – "Identity and Experience."

Key Points useful to memorise.

Useful Analogies helpful in getting a grasp on each concept, by relating it to something with which we are already familiar.

Meaning and Purpose Relates to AT2, part 2 – "Meaning and Purpose."

Scriptural Passages clarifying this concept.

Relevant Stories often useful ways in.

Common Misunderstandings How Hinduism is often misunderstood, misrepresented or over-generalised.

Further Information on this concept – found in:
(1) this book
(2) the Research CD Rom
(3) other recommended books.

1. Atman (the soul; the real self)

Key Points:

- The real self (*atman*) is distinct from the temporary body.
- Material designations do not apply to this eternal soul.
- The atman is spirit (*brahman*)- unchanging, eternal and conscious.
- Consciousness, as spread throughout the body, is a symptom of the soul.

In order to understand the Hindu world-view it is essential to grasp this first and foundational concept. *Atman* refers to the non-material self, which never changes. It is distinct from both the mind and the external body. This real self is beyond the temporary designations we normally ascribe to ourselves, in terms of race, gender, species and nationality.

Ideas of reincarnation, explained in the next spread, are natural extensions of this preliminary concept. Consciousness, wherever it is found, is considered a symptom of the soul, and without it the body has no awareness. This life-giving soul is considered spirit (*brahman*), differentiating it from inert matter. Belief in the soul is not just theoretical or the property of theologians, but is a world-view expressed by Hindus in all walks of life.

To work a car needs:
(1) to be mechanically sound (2) a driver

"You hit me"

The driver often identifies with the vehicle and thus feels pleasure and pain

"There goes the President"

We may identify others externally, without seeing the 'real them'.

"caravans!"

SWIFT DELIVERY

We may even discriminate based on the vehicle others and we possess

A Useful Analogy:

The driver in the vehicle

The body is compared to a vehicle and the soul to the driver.

- A car cannot run without a driver. Similarly, the body will not work without the presence of the soul.
- Just as a young child may not realise that each and every car needs a driver for it to move, those without developed knowledge perceive the body but fail to see the soul within.
- The driver may tend to identify with his car and even feel kinship with drivers of a similar model. Similarly feelings of friendship or enmity arise from identifying with the body.
- The driver develops a deep attachment to the car, so in an accident he commonly cries out "You hit me!" If the soul identifies with the body in the same way, then - preoccupied with the body's condition - he becomes caught in a web of distress and happiness.
- The driver is not satisfied maintaining the car alone without looking after his own needs. Similarly, looking after only the body cannot satisfy the soul.
- Although the driver is not the vehicle, he will move according to the nature of the car, namely fast, slow, etc.
- The same driver can get out of one vehicle and drive another. Similarly, the soul leaves one body and enters another.

Scriptural Passages

". . . all living beings, are seated as on a machine made of the material energy."

Bhagavad Gita 18.61

Related Stories

"The Bird in the Cage" (STO-101)
    -*A poetic tale about the need for spiritual nourishment.*
"Liquid Beauty" (STO-102)
    -*How beauty lies within.*

Related Practices:

All forms of yoga and spiritual discipline are aimed at realising the true self. Only when one stops seeking external happiness and looks within, can one perceive the true self. According to the Bhagavad Gita, this can be achieved not only through study, meditation and renunciation but also by active and selfless performance of one's duty.

Indeed, just prior to the great battle of Kurukshetra, Krishna encouraged Arjuna to develop his self-realisation by fighting *(right)*.

Related Values/Issues

The notion of the unchanging self and the ultimate need for self-realisation are at the root of Hindu attitudes towards many important issues:

- respect for life.
- shared values.
- tolerance (of duality), patience, forbearance.
- austerity and renunciation.
- empathy and compassion for others.
- wealth and poverty.
- transience.

Personal Reflection

- How can a criminal be punished after a crime if he or she is 'not the same person'? What is the scientific or philosophical basis for such continuity of identity?
- Is matter ever unchanging? Consider even the smallest quantity over the shortest of time periods.
- Do we feel a sense of continuous identity or are we changing? What is it that is changing? What does not change? Who am I really?
- What is the difference between a living body and a dead body? Why do I react to them so differently?
- Whilst eating a meal ask yourself, "If I am this body, then at what point does the food cease to be 'not-me' and become 'me'?"

Common Misunderstandings

"Hindus believe that they possess a soul."

On the contrary, Hindus believe that we, like all living beings, are the soul and possess a body

"Hindus believe that atman = brahman."

Whereas practically all Hindus hold that the soul is brahman (spirit), this equation can be misinterpreted to conclude that all Hindus believe that the soul and God are equal in all respects.

Scriptural Passages

"Never was there a time when I did not exist, nor you, nor any of these kings; nor in the future shall any of us cease to be."

Bhagavad Gita 2.12

" … that which pervades the entire body is indestructible"

Bhagavad Gita 2.17

See also:
Bhagavad Gita 2.16, 2.20, 2.23, 5.18, 13.27, 13.34, 15.7

Meaning and Purpose

Who am I? What is my real identity?

2. Reincarnation and Samsara

Key Points:

- At death the soul passes into another body.
- It is carried within the subtle (astral) body.
- The next body is determined by the state of mind at death, and by the soul's desires and deserts.
- The nature of the soul is the same, regardless of which body it resides in.
- Samsara - passing through the six categories of lifeforms - is considered painful for the eternal soul.

As the real self (*atman*) remains unchanged throughout life, it likewise continues after death. This soul is carried within the subtle (astral) body to its next destination. The precise nature of the new body is determined by the state of mind at death and is specifically influenced by (1) the person's desires, and (2) his karma *(see next spread)*.

Samsara refers to the process of passing from one body to another throughout all species of life. Hindus believe that consciousness is present in all life forms, even fish and plants. However, though the soul is present in all species, its potential is exhibited to different degrees. In aquatics and plants it is most 'covered', practically asleep, whereas in humans it is most alert. This progression of consciousness is manifest throughout six broad 'classes of life', namely (1) aquatics, (2) plants, (3) reptiles & insects, (4) birds, (5) animals and (6) humans, including the residents of heaven. Most Hindus consider *samsara* essentially painful, a cycle of four recurring problems: birth, disease, old-age and death.

A Useful Analogy:

Replacing old clothes with new

As the body wears clothes, the soul 'wears' the body.

- We discard clothes when they become old and useless, and buy and put on new ones (or, continuing the analogy from the previous spread, we buy a new car when the old one breaks down beyond repair).
- We buy clothes on the basis of (1) what we want, and (2) what we can afford. Similarly, we get our next body according to (1) our desires and (2) our *karmic* credits *(see the next spread)*.
- Just as a person wears layers of clothing, the soul wears a number of material coverings. They are primarily two:
  1. the subtle body, also called the astral or ghost body. It consists largely of the mind and usually remains with the soul as it quits the gross body.
  2. the gross or external body, which the soul (with the subtle body) discards at death

Glossary Terms

Samsara - *the perpetual cycle of repeated birth and death.*

Related Stories

"Story of Maharaja Bharata" (STO-103)
        -*A story about reincarnation.*
"The Life and Death of Ajamila" (STO-104)
        -*The time of death.*

Related Practices:

The Hindu rites of passage at death, during and after the funeral ceremony, are to ensure the peaceful passage of the soul. They aim to prevent the person being 'held up' in his or her spiritual evolution, and particularly to avoid the possibility of remaining in subtle form as a ghost (as yet without a new body).

In fact, many Hindus consider all rites of passage and other spiritual practices as preparation for inevitable death.

Related Values/Issues

The notion of a soul within all bodies is particularly relevant to the following issues:

■ abortion.
■ animal welfare/rights.
■ negative discrimination of all kinds (racism, ageism, sexism, nationalism, religious sectarianism, etc.).
■ empathy for others.
■ non–violence (*ahimsa*).
■ questions of identity.

Personal Reflection

■ We could explore our feelings towards animals. What similar features do they share with humans? What are the differences?

■ Could reincarnation relate to the phenomon of those about to die seeing their entire lives passing before their eyes?

■ How can we explain out-of-body or near-death experiences, and spontaneous 'past-life memories.'

Scriptural Passages

"As the embodied soul continually passes in this body from boyhood to youth to old age, the soul similarly passes into a new body at death."

"Whatever state of being one remembers when he quits his body, O son of Kunti, that state he will attain without fail."

"The living entity, thus taking another gross body, obtains a certain type of ear, eye, tongue, nose and sense of touch, which are grouped about the mind. He thus enjoys a particular set of sense objects."

Bhagavad Gita 2.13, 8.06, 15.9

See also:
Bhagavad Gita 2.22, 8.06, 15.8-10

Common Misunderstandings

"Hindus believe that in the next life the soul becomes a different person or even an animal."

No, the soul retains its identity, and the same 'real-self' passes into a new body. Any differences between the body we now have and that which we receive in the next life reflect the subtle (psychological) changes undergone in this chapter of life.

Meaning and Purpose

Why are we not born with equal opportunity despite attempts to accomplish this through social reform?

3. The Law of Karma

Key Points:

■ The universal law of karma (action and reaction) determines each soul's unique destiny.

■ Karma is generated only in human life.

■ The lower species are burning up 'bad karma', and gradually rising towards a human birth.

■ The residents of the heavenly planets are using up 'good karma', before falling again to human life on earth.

The law of *karma* underpins the process of transmigration of the soul. *Karma* literally means 'action,' but more often refers to the accumulated reactions to activities. Thus we talk of 'good karma' and 'bad karma' which are stored reactions that gradually unfold to determine our unique destiny.

The self-determination and accountability of the individual soul rests on its capacity for free choice. This is exercised only in the human form. Whilst in lower species, the *atman* takes no moral decisions but is instead bound by instinct. Therefore, although all species of life are subject to the reactions of past activities, such karma is generated only while in the human form. Human life alone is a life of responsibility.

The Bhagavad Gita categorises karma, listing three kinds of human actions: (1) *Karma*: those which elevate, (2) *Vikarma*: those which degrade and (3) *Akarma*: those which create neither good nor bad reactions and thus lead to liberation.

Useful Analogies:

Going on Holiday/Going to Prison

Attaining a heavenly destination is like going on holiday; a lower birth like going to prison.

■ By performing pious activities, one accrues good *karmic* credits and attains a higher birth in which one can enjoy without any difficulties. However, when one's pious credits are exhausted, one falls again to earth, just as one must return from holidays to the regular routine of work when one's well-earned funds are exhausted.

■ The residents of heaven can perform sinful actions, but generally do not, as they have all facilities of life.

■ For transgressing universal and God-given laws the soul is degraded to the lower species. Then, through gradual purification (by suffering), he rises again to the human platform. Once in the lower species the soul cannot exercise free will and is more or less condemned to a 'sentence.' This is very much like a criminal who illegally tries to enjoy life by circumventing the law rather than following it.

Quote:

*"Only the actions of the just
Smell sweet and blossom in the dust."*
                                    James Shirley

Related Stories

"The Sadhu's Blessings" (STO-105)
        -A story illustrating Karma.
"Death in Baghdad" (STO-106)
        -Trying to avoid our destiny.

Related Practices:

Pious activities such as charity, penance and pilgrimage, especially when performed in anticipation of material benefits, such as a higher standard of living on earth or an elevated birth on the heavenly planets.

Avoidance of impious acts, considered to bring misfortune and degradation. These includes the neglect or abuse of five sections of society, namely **women**, **children**, **animals** (especially cows), **saintly people**, and the **elderly**

Personal Reflection

- Explore common notions of karma – e.g. sayings such as, "He had it coming to him!"and "What goes around comes around."
- How much free will do we feel we have in life? What should we strive to change and what should we be content to accept?

Scriptural Passages

"In proportion to the extent of one's religious or irreligious actions in this life, one must enjoy or suffer the corresponding reactions of his karma in the next."

Bhagavat Purana 6.1.45

Common Misunderstandings

"Hindus don't eat meat because they think that they will then be reborn as an animal."

This statement suggests that Hindus perform pious activities largely out of fear and selfishness. It neglects the finer sentiments behind vegetarianism, such as empathy for fellow living beings.

"A good dog may become a human in the next life, whereas a bad dog may become a bird or insect."

The soul passing through lower species doesn't create any new '*karma*'. He only works off the *karmic* reactions generated whilst in the human form and gradually rises towards another human birth.

"Hindus blame suffering on karma."

Not usually. Blame and responsibility are different. Karma entails understanding that we are all ultimately responsible for our own lives. Belief in karma does not automatically create indifference to the suffering of ourselves or others (as the above statement may imply), but underpins sentiments of "helping others to help themselves".

"Hindus do not have to reconcile the idea of evil with the notion of an all-loving, omnipotent God."

No, many Hindus believe in a personal, all-loving and omnipotent God, and do indeed face this challenge, atleast on a personal level admittedly, with the development of theistic doctrines, any apparent contradiction has not remained an ongoing theological problem.

Meaning and Purpose

Why is there suffering if God is all good and all powerful? Why do bad things happen to apparently good people? Why are there inequalities at birth?

Free will and determinism: how much free will do we actually exercise?

Glossary Terms

In common usage:
Punya - *means pious activities.*
Papa - *means sinful activities (and is usually pronounced to rhyme with 'carp', the final 'a' being dropped).*

4. Prakriti *(matter)* and Guna

Key Points:

- Matter is inert, temporary and unconscious.
- It is composed of three qualities *(gunas)* corresponding to creation, sustenance and destruction. They are:
- **sattva (goodness)** – pure, elevating, enlightening
- **rajas (passion)** – motivates us to create, acquire and enjoy
- **tamas (ignorance)** – dirty, degrading, deluding and destructive
- Each *guna* is controlled by one of three main deities – Vishnu, Brahma and Shiva respectively *(see pg. 48)*

Quote:

"There's not one atom of yon earth
But once was living man;
Nor the minutest drop of rain,
That hangeth in its thinnest cloud,
But flowed in human veins."

- Percy Shelley

The eternal *atman* is entrapped within successive temporary bodies made of matter *(prakriti)*. Everything made of matter undergoes three stages of existence – (1) it is created, (2) it remains for some time and, (3) it is inevitably destroyed. These three phases correspond to the three *gunas,* that is, qualities or modes of material nature. Passion *(rajas)* creates, goodness *(sattva)* sustains and ignorance *(tamas)* destroys. These three are ranked hierarchically, with ignorance considered the lowest and goodness the highest. Each member of the Hindu *trimurti* represents one of the three *gunas*.

All material phenomena can be analysed in terms of the *gunas*. According to the soul's preference for a particular mode, it takes on a corresponding body. A person influenced mainly by goodness will be elevated to the heavenly planets at death. Those largely in passion stay in human society, and those infected with ignorance enter into the lower species. Only pure souls, transcending even *sattva-guna*, attain liberation *(see page 18)* and escape the entanglement of matter.

A Useful Analogy:

The three primary colours

– yellow, red and blue
From these three pure colours a whole palette can be created.

- By mixing three primary colours we obtain the three secondary colours – orange, green and purple. By further mixing we create an almost infinite range, such as we see in a colour chart for paints. Similarly, from the interaction of the three *gunas* emerges the entire range of life forms.

- On a colour chart, there is a section consisting of various reds, one largely of yellows, another mainly of blues, etc. Similarly, human society is mainly influenced by passion (the red section). The residents of the 'higher planets' live mainly under the influence of goodness (represented by yellow), and the animal species are principally under the jurisdiction of ignorance (the blue section).

- Just as there is diversity within each section of colours, similarly within human society the three *gunas* create a range of individuals, each with distinct characteristics according to their specific mix of *gunas*. Some will be relatively more influenced by goodness (yellow), others by passion (red), and the remainder by the quality of ignorance (blue).

Related Stories

"Three Men Enter the Forest." (STO-107)
    -How we perceive things according to the gunas.
"The Story of Brighu Muni." (STO-108)
    -The qualities associated with gunas: the Trimurti.

Related Practices:

The social system of Varnashrama-dharma is based on an understanding of how matter conditions the soul. Some claim that the original system enabled mobility between the social classes *(varnas)* and was based not on birth but on personal character and inclination for a particular type of work. The members of the four *varnas*, such as the *kshatriyas* *(see right)* were ascertained by the predominant influence of one or more *gunas*, as shown below:

Brahmanas	(priests, teachers and intellectuals)	– goodness
Kshatriyas	(police, soldiers and administrators)	– passion & goodness
Vaishyas	(farmers, traders and merchants)	– passion & ignorance
Shudras	(workers, labourers and artisans)	– ignorance

Related Values/Issues

All behaviour can be analysed according to this threefold *guna* model and which can be applied to many personal, social, moral and health issues. Especially relevant might be:

- the environment.
- health and diet.
- lifestyle.
- sustainability *(sattva)*.
- sex impulse *(rajas)*.
- drug abuse *(tamas)*.

Scriptural Passages

"From the mode of goodness, real knowledge develops; from the mode of passion, greed develops; and from the mode of ignorance develops foolishness, madness and illusion."

Bhagavad Gita 14.17
See also: Bhagavad Gita 14.5-20.
Also many verses in the
17th & 18th Chapters.

Personal Reflection

- Can we identify our own behaviour in terms of these *gunas*? Do we notice different qualities in, say, the different times of day?
- For a table showing the characteristics of each *guna* and a personality test, please consult the CD-ROM in the Heart of Hinduism Teachers' Pack.

Related Content

In the system of *sankhya*, matter is divided into different elements, both subtle and gross. The five gross elements, corresponding to the five senses, are:

1. **Earth**   2. **Water**   3. **Fire**   4. **Air**   5. **Ether**

Meaning and Purpose

Why do people act and respond differently?

5. Maya *(illusion)*

Key Points:

- Maya means 'that which is not' (illusion).

- It refers to accepting the temporary as having lasting value, and looking for enduring happiness in this world.

- Through cultivating the quality of goodness the soul may rise to transcendence and escape the clutches of maya.

Quote:

*"Savage, extreme, rude, cruel, not to trust.
Enjoyed no sooner but despised straight,
Past reason hunted, and no sooner had,
Past reason hated as a swallowed bait
On purpose laid to make the taker mad:
Mad in pursuit, and in possession so,
Had, having, and in quest to have, extreme,
A bliss in proof, and proved, a very woe,
Before, a joy proposed, behind, a dream."*

*William Shakespeare
Sonnet 129 (on lust)*

Under the influence of the three *gunas*, the soul is (1) misled by matter, and (2) subsequently entangled and entrapped. This tendency is termed *maya* (illusion).

Under *maya's* influence, the *atman* mistakenly identifies with the body. He accepts such thoughts as "I am white and I am a man," or "This is my house, my country, and my religion." Thus the illusioned soul identifies with the temporary body and everything connected to it, such as race, gender, family, nation, bank balance and sectarian religion. Under this sense of false-ego (false-identity) the soul aspires to control and enjoy matter. However, in so doing he continuously serves his enemies in the form of lust, greed and anger. In frustration he often redoubles his efforts and, compounding mistake upon mistake, only falls deeper into illusion.

In ignorance (*tamas*), he is fully convinced that right is wrong and wrong is right. In passion he is unsure, hesitant, sometimes enjoying and at others times repenting. Only in goodness does the soul begin to develop wisdom – to see things in the real light. Thus enlightenment means moving away from *tamas* towards *sattva (see previous spread)*. By so doing, the soul gradually escapes the clutches of *maya* and moves towards liberation.

Useful Analogy

Pursuing a mirage in the desert

- If one pursues a mirage of an oasis in the desert, one will not find water but will be misled. Similarly, this world provides no real happiness, which exists only as an elusive dream.

- The mirage indicates the presence of a real oasis, of real water. Similarly, our desire for happiness, though frustrated, implies that real pleasure does indeed exist.

Useful Example

Mistaking a rope for a snake

- *Maya* literally means "that which is not". In the twilight, in countries such as India, one may easily mistake a rope for a snake. In so doing, we feel fear. Hence fear and other emotions may often be based on illusion, an incorrect perception of reality.

Related Stories

"The Yogi's Cloth." (STO-109)
    -About the entanglement of material life.
"The Guru Embracing the Tree." (STO-110)
    -Describing the nature of Maya.

Related Practices:

All forms of enlightenment, particularly methods of *controlling the mind and senses*, so as to avoid being misled. Different paths involve the *regulation* of material activities, developing *wisdom*, performing *austerities* and *serving God*, instead of trying to enjoy and control the world.

Some traditions suggest *retirement* from materialistic society to avoid the temptations it offers. Accepting *good counsel* (e.g. from a *guru*) is usually considered essential. Perhaps most important is the role of *education* in training children so they can suitably respond to life, its opportunities and its allurements.

Related Values/Issues

- Becoming a responsible citizen — seeing the consequences of our actions. Learning from our mistakes.
- Avoiding immediate gratification with its possibly dangerous consequences (sex, drugs, etc.)
- Consumerism / advertising.
- Greed / compulsive shopping.
- Seeking guidance from others.
- Learning how to say "no."

Personal Reflection

- Our own experience of being illusioned — perhaps when a plan that promised happiness turned sour.
- What emotions tend to sweep us into difficult situations?
- Have we ever rectified one mistake with another?

Common Misunderstandings

"Hindu responses to good and evil . . ."
Though these concepts exist in Hinduism, more commonly discussed are the tensions between 'knowledge' and 'ignorance'. Ignorance is usually considered a matter of personal choice, and some scholars note the term's connection with the verb 'to ignore'.

It is wrong to think that Hinduism uses exactly the same conceptual models as other religious traditions.

"Hindus consider the world to be false, an illusion."
Some schools do. Others consider it real, but illusory in so much as it is temporary.

"Hinduism is world denying."
Although Hinduism tends to be ultimately 'world renouncing', it places much emphasis on accepting our temporal needs and meeting them in a dignified fashion, rather than denying them.

Scriptural Passages

"On the basis of this misconception which ties together the hearts of the male and female, one becomes attracted to his body, home, property, children, relatives and wealth. In this way one increases life's illusions and thinks in terms of 'I and mine.'

Bhagavat Purana 5.5.8

"If one clings to his attachments, refusing to let go, sorrows will not let go their grip on him."

Tirukkural 35.347-348

See also:
Bhagavad Gita 2.60–63; 16.3–18, 21.

Related Proverbs/Sayings

"All that glitters is not gold."
Being *"Led up the garden path"*
"A wild-goose chase"
"Failure is the pillar of success"
"The grass is always greener"

6. Moksha *(liberation or salvation)*

Key Points:

- For most Hindus, moksha is the highest goal.
- Moksha means release from samsara.
- Moksha is achieved through union with God.
- Such union is understood in different ways, primarily two:
1) complete union of identity
2) unity of purpose.

Most Hindu traditions consider *moksha* the ultimate goal of life. The other three goals *(see Concept 10, page 30)* are considered temporary but necessary stepping-stones towards eternal liberation.

The main differences of opinion centre on the precise nature of *moksha*. Although practically all schools consider it a state of unity with God, the nature of such unity is contested. The *advaita* traditions say that *moksha* entails annihilation of the soul's false sense of individuality and realisation of its complete non-difference from God. The dualistic traditions claim that God remains ever distinct from the individual soul. Union in this case refers to a commonality of purpose and realisation of one's spiritual nature (*brahman*) through surrender and service to the Supreme Brahman (God).

Useful Analogy 1:

The drop of water in the ocean

The soul is compared to a drop of water and liberation to its merging into the vast ocean which represents the Supreme Soul (God).

- According to the *advaita* schools, the soul and God are equal in every respect, and liberation entails realisation of one's Godhood. Thus, one's mistaken sense of individuality is dissolved, and one merges into the all-pervading Supreme.

Useful Analogy 2:

The green parrot in the green tree

The individual soul is compared to a green bird that enters a green tree (God). It appears to have 'merged', but retains its separate identity.

- The personalistic schools of thought maintain that the soul and God are eternally distinct and that any 'merging' is only apparent. 'Oneness' in this case refers to:

    (1) unity of purpose through loving service.
    (2) realisation of one's nature as *brahman* ('godly') but maintenance of one's spiritual individuality.

- Liberation involves entering God's abode, though many schools teach that those souls who have become free from material contamination are already liberated, even before leaving the material body

Scriptural Passages

"O best amongst men (Arjuna), the person who is not disturbed by happiness and distress, and is steady in both, is certainly eligible for liberation."

Bhagavad Gita 2.15

Related Practices:

Many religious practices and rites of passage are aimed at liberation. Particularly relevant are those designed to remove our attachment to this world and its transient pleasures.
Renunciation, especially in old age, is an important feature of Hinduism. Without conquering qualities such as lust, anger and greed, and without control of the mind and senses, there is no question of being liberated from the entanglement of the material world.

Related Values/Issues

- happiness – where is it to be found?
- salvation - by grace or personal endeavour?
- freedom – personal, social, political?

Personal Reflection

- Do you ever feel like dropping everything and making a clean break? Will it work, or will you again feel entangled? Would it be responsible? On the other hand, can claims of being responsible be excuses for not moving forward? Why do we sometimes remain attached to situations that give us pain?
- Do you ever feel that you are not really free, even when you are apparently enjoying yourself? What is the nature of freedom?

Common Misunderstanding

"Hindus believe that liberation is entirely dependent on personal spiritual endeavour."
Hindus have debated extensively the 'grace versus works' polemic and developed many sophisticated theologies acknowledging the role of God's grace. At the same time, they don't, on the whole, totally exclude the role of personal endeavour.

"Hindus consider liberation to be the highest good."
Many do, but not all. For example, some *Vaishnavas* consider the desire for liberation to be selfish and advocate a 'fifth goal of life'. This they describe as *prema* (love of God) or *nitya-lila* (entrance into the eternal pastimes of the Lord)

"Hinduism is world denying."
(see page 17)

Scriptural Passages

"Though engaged in all kinds of activities, My pure devotee, under My protection, reaches the eternal and imperishable abode by My grace."

Bhagavad Gita 18.56

"Perfection is characterised by one's ability to see the self by the pure mind and to relish and rejoice in the self. In that joyous state, one is situated in boundless spiritual happiness, realised through transcendental senses. Established thus, one never departs from the truth, and upon gaining this he thinks there is no greater gain. Being so situated, one is never shaken even in the midst of greatest difficulty. This indeed is actual freedom from all miseries arising from material contact."

Bhagavad Gita 6.20-23

see also:
Bhagavad Gita 4.9, 5.19, 5.24, 8.05

Meaning and Purpose

What is the purpose of life?
What is the goal of religion?

7. God (Part 1) Perceived in Three Ways

Key Points:

■ God has three main aspects:

(1) as the all-pervading **Brahman**

(2) as the Lord within the heart (**Antaryami**)

(3) as the Supreme Person (**Bhagavan** or **Ishvara**) living within the spiritual abode

Scriptural Passages

"That Brahman is in front and in back, in the north, south, east and west, and also overhead and below. In other words, that supreme Brahman effulgence spreads throughout both the material and spiritual skies."

Mundaka Upanishad 2.11

"The Supreme Lord is situated in everyone's heart. O Arjuna, and is directing the wanderings of all living entities."

Bhagavad Gita 18.61

"Bhagavan is He who possesses without limit the six types of opulence - strength, fame, wealth, knowledge, beauty and renunciation."

Vishnu Purana
See also:
Bhagavad Gita 9.4-6

Many Hindus describe God as **sat-cid-ananda**, full of eternity, knowledge and bliss. These correspond to three main features of the Supreme:

(1) *Brahman* – residing everywhere

(2) *Antaryami* – residing within

(3) *Bhagavan* – residing outside, beyond

1. **Brahman** refers to the all-pervading aspect of God, often called 'the all-pervading world-soul.' Since everything comes from God, it is non-different from Him. Scripture states "everything is Brahman." This **sat** (eternal) aspect of God is realised by understanding one's own eternal nature as *atman*.

2. **Antaryami** means 'the controller within' and refers to God residing within the hearts of all beings. He is sometimes called the Supersoul, *Paramatman*. The *Katha Upanishad* likens the soul and the Supersoul to two birds sitting within the same tree (i.e. the heart). The Supersoul is initially perceived in various ways, through memory, instinct, intelligence, inspiration, and exceptional ability. He is the object of meditation for many mystic yogis. This feature of God represents his **cit** (knowledge) aspect.

3. **Bhagavan** means 'one endowed with unlimited opulence' and refers to God who lives beyond this material world. *Bhagavan* is personal and the individual soul can enter into a direct relationship with him, thus experiencing **ananda** (spiritual pleasure).

Most traditions accommodate these three aspects of God, but will understand the relationships between them differently. They often stress one feature as more important than the others. They also differ as to the exact identity of God and their understanding of the many gods and goddesses (*see next section*).

Useful Analogy:

The Sun

The Sun, sunshine and sun's reflection are one but also different.

■ All-pervading sunshine is non-different from the sun. Both are heat and light, yet the Sun retains its form and identity as the source of everything.

■ Just as the sun may be reflected in numerous pots of water, so the same one God is reflected in the hearts of all living beings as the antarayami.

Related Stories

"The story of Prahlad." (STO-111)
- God appears from a pillar.

Related Practices:

Ways of perceiving the presence of God in various features.
Initially, God's **Brahman** nature is realised by philosophically understanding the eternal and unchanging nature of one's self. The mystic yogis, who initially perform the *hatha-yoga* exercises, often meditate on **Antaryami**, the Lord within the heart (*see right*). The process of *bhakti* (devotion) is aimed at worship of the Lord as a divine person, *Ishvara*, or as the Supreme Person (**Bhagavan** or *Param-Ishvara*), situated in his spiritual abode.

Related Values/Issues

■ Conscience – following or ignoring 'the still, small voice within.'

Personal Reflection

■ What evidence is there to support the idea that the real self is eternal or temporary?
■ Reflect on the ways in which you, if at all, perceive the divine. How do we account for exceptional ability in people? What is conscience? What is inspiration? How can you explain instinct?
■ Can God be a person? What must He/She be like?

Common Misunderstandings

"Hindus believe in brahman, the all-pervading world soul."
Although largely true, such statements often neglect the other two aspects of God – within the heart and without, as a person. Even when God's personal form is mentioned, it is often considered expedient or imaginary, to help the worshipper focus on the invisible and inaccessible Supreme. This represents one main school of thought (*advaita*), but there are others which hold that the personal feature of God is equally important or higher.

"God is personal in immanence but impersonal in transcendence."
Some prominent Hindu traditions consider transcendence to be personal - or, more commonly, both personal (*saguna*) and impersonal (*nirguna*).

Glossary Words

Brahman – *spirit, the Supreme*
Antaryami – *the Lord within*
Bhagavan – *God as a person*
Paramatman – *the Supreme Self, God*
Ishvara – *"controller" often used of God, or a god or goddess*
Ishvari – *a female deity*
Parameshvara – *the Supreme Deity (God)*
Purushottama – *the Supreme person*
Deva – *God*
Devi – *Goddess*

Note: the various traditions tend to use somewhat different terms. Vishnu is often termed 'Bhagavan', whereas Shaivites call Shiva 'Ishvara'. Shakti is often called 'Bhagavati', the feminine of Bhagavan.

Meaning and Purpose

Questions concerning the existence of God: If there is God, then why can we not perceive him? Where does God reside?

7. God (Part 2) Two Main Understandings

Key Points:

- There are many notions of God within Hinduism but two are most prominent.
1. **Monism** (advaita) - God is impersonal without qualities or form.
2. **Inclusive monotheism** (dvaita) God is personal, exhibiting qualities, displaying a form, and performing activities.

   Note: we use the term Dvaita to refer to anyone who considers the soul distinct from God. Some use it to refer specifically to the followers of Madhva (see pages 137-138)

The previously explored concepts are shared by most of the theologically developed strands of Hinduism. It is when we get to the nature and identity of the Supreme that the tradition appears complex. In the broader sense, Hinduism might well encompass every notion of God there is, including more primitive forms of polytheism. Within the more sophisticated schools of thought, particularly *Vedanta*, there are two main doctrines, each with many variations and each emphasising that there is one God. These are **monism** and **monotheism**.

The *advaita* (non-dual or monistic) schools consider the soul one with God in all respects. The numerous deities are considered more or less imaginary, representing aspects of the formless, all-pervading world-soul (*Brahman*). For *advaitins*, God is therefore entirely impersonal, though represented anthropomorphically for our own understanding. He is *nirguna* (without qualities).

The *dvaita* (dualistic/monotheistic) schools consider the soul and God be to eternally distinct even though both are *Brahman* (spirit). God is *saguna*, possessing spiritual attributes such as form and personhood, and activity. The *dvaitins* usually attribute different positions to the various deities. Their stance is usually theomorphic – i.e. holding that the human form is shaped on God. For its inclusion of other deities (gods and goddesses) it has been termed 'inclusive monotheism' (some might call it henotheism).

Useful Analogy 1:

Light passing through a prism

White light is broken down into different colours after passing though a prism (the monistic stance).

- As the different colours, the constituents of light, are shown through a prism, so the different aspects of the all–pervading God are illustrated through the various deities.

Useful Analogy 2:

The government with one prime minister

The government has many ministers and other officials but only one prime minister (the monotheistic stance).

- Though there are many ministers, there is still only one prime minister to whom all others are subordinate. The ministers depend on the prime minister for their power and authority.
- Approaching an MP, or a cabinet minister, is in one sense approaching the government. So worshipping the demigods is an indirect way of approaching God.
- The influence of the government and its leader extends throughout the state. Similarly, God and his authority extends everywhere, even though he retains his personal form and residence beyond this world.

Related Stories

"The Thread and the Blanket" (STO-112)
   -A debate about the nature of God.

Related Practices:

Types of worship, especially of the murti (sacred image), aim at perceiving the presence of God and developing a relationship with Him. This relationship is often compared to a family relationship, being sweet, loving and devoid of fear and awe. God may even take an apparently equal or inferior role, as a servant, child or beleaguered lover. This *murti (right)* is of Bal Krishna (Baby Krishna), acting as the butter thief, worshipped by members of the *pushti-marg (see page 144).*

Related Values/Issues

- The nature of God.
- Image worship/idolatry *(for more information, see page 55).*

Personal Reflection

- Have you misunderstood the Hindu ideas of God? What does monotheism mean, and how does it differ from monism? Do you see the same ideas in the Semitic traditions?
- Can I accept the idea of deity worship? Do I have problems with it? Why? Does all image worship constitute idolatry?
- Must all personalistic concepts of God be anthropomorphic?

Common Misunderstandings

"The Hindu concept of God is ultimately impersonal, and any personhood is anthropomorphic. The various gods and goddesses, and the stories about them, are merely ways by which Hindus relate to an impersonal Supreme."

There are many schools, mainly *Vaishnavas* but also within *Shaivism* and *Shaktism,* who believe that God possesses personality.

"Sacred images are not worshipped as such but are merely meditational aids to help focus on the all-pervading world-soul (Brahman)."

Again, not all Hindus believe exclusively in the impersonal feature of God. Many consider that he not only has form but appears as the *murti* to accept worship.

"The monotheistic traditions . . ."

This phrase, as used to denote the Semitic religions, wrongly implies that monotheism is absent from the 'Eastern religions', including Hinduism.

"Hinduism is entirely inclusive and tolerant"

There remain theological controversies as to the nature and identity of God, and there are documented instances of sectarian intolerance. Nonetheless, the notion of *Sanatana-dharma* makes the tradition relatively inclusive.

Scriptural Passages

"Everything is Brahman."
Chandogaya Upanisad 3.14.1 2.

"Just as the illumination of a fire, which is situated in one place, is spread all over, the energies of the Supreme Lord, Parabrahman, are spread throughout the universe."
Vishnu Purana 1.22.53

Meaning and Purpose

Is there a God? Why? What is God like? Is he male or female (or neither, or both)? Is he within or without? Does God possess a body or form? Is God simply a concept or a reality?

Glossary Terms

Inclusive monotheism - *belief in one supreme Deity and the existence of many subordinate deities.*
Monism - *belief in one impersonal supreme, equally represented by many deities.*

(i) **For more information see:**
Pages 46-53, 133, 137.

8. Dharma (a)-Sanatana-dharma

Key points:

- Dharma – 'duties that sustain us according to our intrinsic nature.'
- Two main types:
  – *Sanatana-dharma*
  – *Varnashrama-dharma*
- Sanatana-dharma refers to 'the eternal law' which is universal.
- Basic moral codes are called sadharana- dharma.

*D*harma is often translated as 'duty', 'religion' or 'religious duty' and yet its meaning is more profound, defying concise English translation. The word itself comes from the Sanskrit root *'dhri'*, which means 'to sustain'. Another related meaning is 'that which is integral to something'. For example, the *dharma* of sugar is to be sweet and the *dharma* of fire to be hot. Therefore, a person's *dharma* consists of duties that sustain him, according to his innate characteristics. Such characteristics are both material and spiritual, generating two corresponding types of *dharma*:

(a) *Sanatana-dharma* - duties which take into account the person's spiritual (constitutional) identity as *atman* and are thus the same for everyone.

(b) *Varnashrama-dharma*, duties performed according to one's material (conditional) nature and specific to the individual at that particular time *(see next spread)*.

According to the notion of *Sanatana-dharma*, the eternal and intrinsic inclination of the living entity (*atman*) is to perform *seva* (service). *Sanatana-dharma*, being transcendental, refers to universal and axiomatic laws that are beyond our temporary belief systems. Most adherents prefer to call their tradition *Sanatana-dharma* rather than using the more recent term, 'Hinduism', which they consider has sectarian connotations. (Sometimes another category is added, called *Sadharana--dharma*, general moral rules for everyone.)

Useful Analogy 1:

The sun and its various names

The same sun is called by different names in different countries.

- The sun is called by different names but remains one no matter how widely we travel. Similarly, God is above such designations as 'British' or 'Indian', 'Christian' or 'Hindu.' The soul also transcends such temporary labels. Real religion, which involves re-establishing and acting in one's eternal relationship with God, is above worldly and sectarian designations.

Useful Analogy 2:

Different Universities

Various universities teach the exact same subject.

- A related metaphor, which endorses the autonomy of the different religious traditions, compares religion to a science. Students may attend different universities – and the autonomy of each is to be respected – but the subjects are universal. For example, mathematical laws remain the same, whether in India or in Britain. Similarly, one may accept a particular authorised religious tradition, but the subject is the same. Many Hindus would therefore also include members of other authorised religious traditions under the banner of *Sanatana-dharma*, though they may have a natural preference for their own particular 'school.'

Related Practices:

All types of religious vows, rituals and practices aimed at service to God, *Sanatana-dharma.*

A generally inclusive stance towards other autho-rised religions. Hindus will often take stories from other traditions and accept and assimilate them into their own. They place relatively little emphasis on expressions of alle-giance to a particular creed. This painting *(right)* on the ceiling of a temple in Leicester shows the founders of various religious traditions, all considered within the fold of *Sanatana-dharma* (duties based on universal truths and values). Some groups, obviously connected with '*The Vedic tradition*', are reluctant to call themselves Hindu because of its possibly sectarian connotations *(see page 145).*

Related Values/Issues

- Equality – the notion of *Sanatana-dharma* as a basis for spiritual unity.
- Interfaith dialogue and inter-religious understanding.
- The relationship between faith, truth and opinion.
- Could Vedic philosophy have preceded the Greek? Are we patronising towards non–European cultures?

Further Related Topics

Some groups are reluctant to call themselves Hindu, largely because of its misleading and sectarian connotations. Other groups are happy to use the term, while even others use the expression "Hindu dharma."

Personal Reflection

- In what ways are religions the same and in what ways different? Which differences are desirable and which divisive? Is religion or spirituality the problem, or something else?
- Why does religion often have a bad name?
- In what ways does emphasis on expressions of allegiance to a particular creed differ from the notion of Sanatana-dharma?
- In what ways is the *dharma* of service to God inescapable even though we try to oppose it?

Quote

"Dharma is sometimes translated as 'religion' but that is not exactly the meaning. Dharma actually means 'that which one cannot give up' and 'that which is inseparable from oneself.' The warmth of fire is inseparable from fire; therefore warmth is called the dharma, or nature, of fire. Similarly, sad-dharma means 'eternal occupation.' That eternal occupation is engagement in the tran-scendental loving service of the Lord."

A.C. Bhaktivedanta Swami

Scriptural Passage

"The supreme occupation [dharma] for all humanity is that by which men can attain to loving devotional service unto the transcendent Lord."

Bhagavat Purana 1.2. 6

Meaning and Purpose

Is there one truth or many? Is truth relative or absolute? Why do religions appear to differ in answering life's ultimate questions?

ⓘ **For more information see:**
   Page 81

8. Dharma (b)-*Varnashrama-dharma*

Key Points:

- *Varnashrama-dharma* – duties performed according to the system of four *varnas* (social divisions) and four ashrams (stages in life).

- Focus is on responsibilities (which naturally fulfil the rights of others).

- Four *varnas* – **brahmins** (priests, teachers and intellectuals), **kshatriyas** (police, army and administration), **vaishyas** (farmers, merchants and business people), **shudras** (artisans and workers).

- Four ashrams – **student life, household life, retirement** and **renunciation.**

Erratum
In text, above-right, line 12: 'animal sacrifice' should read 'non-violence, which includes refraining from animal sacrifice,...'

According to Hindu texts, *Varnashrama-dharma* is not a man-made system but refers to natural classifications that appear to various degrees in all human societies. Individuals have different innate tendencies for work and exhibit a variety of personal qualities. There are also natural phases in life, when it is easier and more rewarding to perform certain activities. Hinduism teaches that individuals best realise their potential by taking into account such natural arrangements, and that society should be structured and organised accordingly.

Each *varna* and *ashram* has its own specified *dharma*. What may be desirable for one section of society may be degrading for another. For example, absolute animal sacrifice is essential for the priestly class but considered wholly unworthy of a *kshatriya* (warrior). Generating wealth and producing children are essential for householders, but intimate contact with money and women is spiritually suicidal for the renunciate. Underlying all these apparent differences is the common goal of advancing in spiritual life based on *Sanatana-dharma*. without the spiritual equality and sense of service inherent in *Sanatana-dharma*, *Varnashrama-dharma* tends to degrade into the rigid and exploitative caste system.

1. Vision
   Thinking
   Listening
   Advising

2. Protecting
   Fighting
   Administrating

3. Nourishing
   Producing

4. Supporting
   Transporting

Useful Analogy:

The Social Body

The social body and its components are likened to the human form.

- Society is compared to a body with the *brahmanas* as the head, *kshatriyas* as the arms, *vaishyas* as the belly (or thighs) and the *shudras* as the legs

- Social functions are determined according to this analogy. For example, the *brahmanas* are the eyes and mouth of society. They provide a spiritual vision for society and teach people accordingly. Just as the arms are raised to defend the body, the *kshatriya's* main duty is to protect society. The *vaishya's* main duty is material nourishment, and the *shudra* supports all other sections of society.

- The *ashrams* are sometimes related to the same metaphor, with the successive stages of student life, household life, retirement and renunciation represented by the legs, belly, arms and head respectively.

Related Stories

"Gautama's Disciple."
    -*How varna is truly determined.(see page 102)*

"The Brahmin and the Cobbler." (STO-113)
    -*How character is more important than status.*

Related Values/Issues

- The notion of a classless society.
- Rights and responsibilities.
- All types of inequality.
- *Varnashrama* as a basis for categorising diversity in human society.

Personal Reflection

- Is it desirable to divide society according to each person's natural tendency for a particular type of work, and form educational, political, trade or labour associations for cooperative and mutual support?
- Do teachers need personal and professional qualifications, or should anyone be able to take the job? Is a person qualified as a teacher simply because his father and mother were both teachers? Does he generally have a better chance?
- Do natural classifications exist and can they be useful? Are they all merely man-made and exploitative?
- How does your school apply *Varnashrama-dharma* principles? Are there various year groups, for example? And within each year, are all students required to study the same subjects?

Common Misunderstandings

"Caste and Varnashrama are synonymous."
Mahatma Gandhi, the most famous opponent of caste abuse, actually believed in the original principles of *Varnashrama-dharma.* The system of four *varnas* (with subdivisions) was based on mutual support and service, allowing for upward and downward mobility. The caste system, as it has now become, is rigid and hereditary, often motivated by exploitation and a desire to maintain the status-quo. *(see page 141 for more information on Gandhi; also page 104)*

Scriptural Passages

"According to the three gunas and the work associated with them, the four divisions of human society are created by Me."

Bhagavad Gita 4.13

Meaning and Purpose

Is the universe naturally hierarchical? What are my duties as a human being?

Quote

"The distinction between varna and caste is well known to anthropologists ... even if it is ignored by some authors ... (who) use the word caste when what they mean is clearly varna"

Dr. D. Killingley

ⓘ **For more information see:**
Pages 81-87, 102-104, 139-141

9. One Goal, Different Paths

Key Points:

- Hindu scriptures say there are four goals in civilised religious life:
  1. dharma – righteousness
  2. artha – economic development
  3. kama – sensual enjoyment
  4. moksha – liberation, the ultimate goal.
- Moksha is achieved through union with God (*yoga*).

Ultimate Goal

Within a broad spectrum of religious practices, Hinduism accommodates both material and spiritual needs. However, as material benefits are temporary, most traditions consider eternal moksha the ultimate goal.

Hindu texts detail four sequential aims – *dharma, artha, kama* and *moksha*. *Dharma* recommends righteous and regulated living, so that one is able one to acquire wealth, *artha*. With prosperity one can then enjoy *kama*, sensual pleasure. When one realises the futility of temporary gratification, one eventually seeks *moksha* (liberation). Some traditions, particularly of the *bhakti* school, accept *moksha*, but point out the selfishness in even desiring liberation. They mention a fifth goal called *prema* (love of God) or *nitya-lila* (eternal loving service).

Spiritual emancipation is therefore considered the main goal of life, and other goals are necessary stepping stones towards it. Hinduism thus recommends a balanced life with an ultimate spiritual goal. Liberation usually entails union with God, conceived of in various ways by different traditions. The word for this process is yoga, from which we can derive the English word yoke, meaning to join.

Scriptural Passages

"All performance of dharma is meant for ultimate liberation (moksha). It should not be performed for material gain. Furthermore, one who is engaged in the ultimate occupational service (dharma) should not use material gain (artha) simply for sense gratification (karma)."

Bhagavat Purana 1.2.9

Related Values/Issues

- Personal fulfilment
- Goal setting
- Planning our lives

Personal Reflection

- How important is it for us to have goals in life? What are the results of having clear goals?
- What are the consequences of having lofty long-term aims but no short-term objectives?

Related Practices:

Following the **system of four ashrams**, where material desires are met in a regulated way through the four stages of life with emphasis on renunciation towards the end of life. Only the second ashram, initiated at the wedding ceremony *(see left)*, allows for intimate contact between men and women, and the fulfilment of sexual desires.

Different Paths

There are various types of *yoga*, also called different *margs*, (paths). There are three main ones: *karma-yoga,* the yoga of selfless action; *jnana-yoga,* the yoga of spiritual knowledge; and *bhakti-yoga,* the yoga of loving devotion. Some add a fourth path called *raja yoga* or *Astanga-yoga,* the eight-step path, which includes physical exercises and culminates in meditation on God within the heart (*for more information on these four paths, see pages 44-45*).

There are different opinions as to the merits of each. Some say that all are equally valid, like parallel paths. Others favour a particular process claiming that the various yogas are successive steps on the same path. Practically all Hindus agree that whichever process one chooses it must be followed according to scriptural injunction rather than whimsically.

Useful Analogy 1:

Paths up a Mountain - the paths are many but the peak is one.

- This analogy is favoured by the advaita schools
- All paths are considered equal and chosen according to personal inclination

Useful Analogy 2:

The Yoga Ladder

– *the complete path of yoga is a ladder with progressive steps*
- This metaphor is used by the personalistic bhakti schools which claim that love of God is the ultimate goal.
- The bottom of the ladder is the beginning of spiritual life (selfless actions through karma yoga).
- The top of the ladder represents loving union with God (bhakti).
- At a particular stage (on one step) one may be known by that name (e.g. hatha-yogi) but if she progresses she will ultimately come to the topmost platform. Anyone who is making progress should not be criticised even if practicing on a relatively low level.

Common Misunderstandings

"Bhakti is for those who are less intelligent and predominantly on the emotional level."
Actually, many bhakti schools place great emphasis on knowledge but do hold that there is no wisdom (realised knowledge) without surrender to God.

Key Points:
- There are four main paths/steps to achieve yoga (union with God) –
1. **karma yoga** – selfless action
2. **jnana yoga** – spiritual knowledge
3. **raja** (astanga) **yoga** – meditation
4. **bhakti yoga** – (devotional service)

Bhakti-yoga

Raja-yoga

Jnana-yoga

Karma-yoga

29

Key Points:

- Shastra is the principle source of authority for most Hindus.
- Vedic knowledge was passed down orally until about 3,000 BCE, when *Kali-yuga* began and the written form became necessary.
- Personal and spiritual discipline is required to understand and realise scriptural knowledge.

Scriptural Passages

"One should know what is duty and what is not duty by the regulations of the scriptures."

Bhagavad Gita 16.24

Above: *Vyasa is said to have compiled the most important Vedic texts some 5000 years ago.*

Shastra (scripture)

Hindu scripture is sometimes called *shastra*. Since the Vedic wisdom was first transmitted orally it is also called *shabda-brahman*, spiritual sound. According to tradition, it was written down only when human memory began to deteriorate at the start of Kali-yuga (some 5,000 years ago).

Shabda-brahman is considered the most reliable form of authority for spiritual and related matters. However, Hinduism is not simply an authoritarian system of belief, and tends to synthesise religious commitment with open philosophical inquiry. It acknowledges the need for exploration and realisation of knowledge. Without appropriate conduct and values, informational and experiential knowledge will be inevitably misconstrued.

Many Hindu schools claim orthodoxy based on their adherence to shastra. Thus it remains a powerful source of authority and cohesion for the tradition.

A Useful Analogy:

The mother (who will know the identity of her child's father)

- As young children, we have no alternative but to depend on our mother to educate us: "this is a spoon," "this is a knife" and so on.
- If we wish to know the identity of our father, then the natural authority is our mother. In the same way the Vedas are considered our mother, who can reveal the identity of our father, God.
- In Hindu theology the love between mother and child is considered most pure. A mother will not let us down or intentionally mislead us.

Related Practices:

Pravachan (lectures on scripture).

Traditional practices of discussion, and debate, and submission to more learned teachers.

Common Misunderstandings

"Hinduism lets you do whatever you want and has no strict rules."
It is not quite so simple! Although flexibility in thought is encouraged, Hinduism puts great emphasis on orthopraxy, or adherence to certain practices. Even within the realm of philosophy, Hinduism has refuted certain doctrines, such as Buddhism and Jainism. This is not so much for their philosophical position but because they reject the Hindu scriptures. They are therefore called *nastika*. *(see page 118)*

Guru

The guru plays a central role in Hinduism, often acting as the intermediary between the soul and the Supreme. Many schools claim that God-realisation without spiritual mentorship is impossible, for one will inevitably be waylaid by *maya* (illusion). The guru is required in order to properly understand scripture. Many schools also claim that the blessings of God come through the genuine spiritual teacher, and that the teacher speaks and acts on behalf of God. The guru may also accept veneration on behalf of the Lord. Many Hindus accept *diksha*, initiation from a spiritual teacher, thus becoming a formal disciple. The principle of disciplic succession (*sampradaya*) is central to the transmission of spiritual knowledge.

Some traditions, such as the *advaita* schools equate guru with God. Others, such as most *bhakti* schools, insist that the spiritual teacher is God's representative and can never become God himself.

A Useful Analogy :

**The child of a wealthy man
– to please a multi-millionaire, give sweets to his child**

- Winning the favour of a wealthy man – say, through offering gifts – is difficult, but easy if we shower sincere affection on his child. By offering genuine respect to the guru and other saintly people, one pleases God.
- One cannot demand to see an important person, such as the Queen. However, if she becomes pleased with our service, then she will ask to see us.

Personal Reflection

- How important is a teacher? Can one learn from books alone?
- How does the concept of an intermediary compare with other religions?
- What is the stereotype of a guru? How can this be misleading?
- What problems might a Western teacher have with the concept of guru and the veneration shown him?

Related Values/Issues

- Respect for teachers/elders.
- Qualities of a teacher/authority figure.

Common Misunderstandings

"The guru is accepted and followed blindly."
The Bhagavad Gita (4.34) recommends faith based on rational inquiry.
See also "The Vet's Apprentice" (STO-117)

Key Points:

- Most Hindus consider a guru essential for spiritual life.
- The guru speaks on the basis of scripture and helps the disciple understand scriptural knowledge.
- Spiritual knowledge is often preserved and transmitted by *sampradaya* (disciplic succession).
- The guru is often seen as equal to God, either (a) quite literally, or (b) as God's representative.

Scriptural Passages

"Only unto to those great souls who have unflinching faith in both the Lord and the spiritual teacher are all the imports of Vedic knowledge automatically revealed"

Svetashvatara Upanishad 6.38

"This knowledge was thus passed down by disciplic succession, and the saintly kings understood it in this way."

Bhagavad Gita 4.2

ⓘ **For more information see:
Pages 47, 138, 43-146**

Key Points:

- The Hindu concept of time is cyclical (and eternal and degenerative).
- The Western notion of time is linear (and limited and progressive).
- There are four ages (yugas) that successively become more degenerated:
  (1) Satya (Krita)
  (2) Dvapara
  (3) Treta
  (4) Kali
- We are now 5,000 years into Kali-yuga (the iron age, or the age of quarrel and hypocrisy.

The concept of eternal and cyclical time lies at the heart of the Hindu world view and is closely related to the concept of atman. (Hindu sages claim that the individual's self-understanding determines his or her perception of the world.) Hindus consider the real self to be ever-existing, not only in the future but also from the past. This notion of two-way eternity, however, is not reserved solely for the realm of spirit (Brahman) but extends to this temporal world. Within Hinduism we find no 'year dot,' nor a final cataclysm. The closing of one door implies the opening of another. Destruction of the cosmos only portends its re-creation. The entire material world is thus subject to everlasting cycles of creation, sustenance and destruction.

This universe is said to exist for a lifetime of Brahma, the creator. His one day is 1,000 maha-yugas (great ages). Each *maha-yuga* consists of *four yugas* (ages), each progressively shorter and more degraded. They are the golden, silver, copper and iron ages, (*see below-left*). According to tradition, we have had just over 5,000 years of *Kali-yuga* and there remain 427,000 years. At the end, the final incarnation of Vishnu, Kalki, is scheduled to appear, heralding the dawn of yet another golden age.

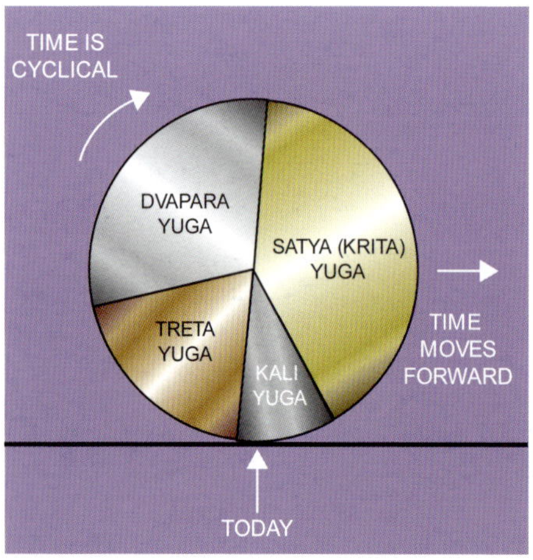

TIME IS CYCLICAL

DVAPARA YUGA

SATYA (KRITA) YUGA

TRETA YUGA

KALI YUGA

TIME MOVES FORWARD

TODAY

The diagram above represents the entire cycle of four ages. As the wheel of time roles along, the ages progress in an anti-clock wise direction. The diagram shows how we have just started Kali-yuga, and are moving towards the next Satya-yuga.

Satya yuga –	1,728,000 years
Dvarapa yuga –	1,296,000 years
Treta yuga –	864, 000 years
Kali yuga –	432,000 years
Total cycle (mahayuga) –	4,320,000 years

Useful Examples:

The day, week, month, year and greater cycles (e.g. ice ages)

These may be useful in considering how time might be cyclical.

- The day is naturally cyclical, based on the Earth's rotation.
- The Hindu week is seven days, and based on the same seven planets (Sun, Moon, Mars, Mercury, Jupiter, Venus and Saturn) as in the West.
- The Hindu calendar is based on real months (phases of the moon), as is Easter in the Christian calendar.
- The year is based on the cycles of the Earth round the Sun.
- Hindu texts mention greater natural cycles of 12 years, 60 years, etc. up to many millions of years. This may be compared to the familiar concept of recurring ice ages.

Related Stories

"The Oldest Man in the World" (STO-115)
   -*Aeons are nothing compared to eternity.*

"Creation - adapted from the Bhagavat Purana" (STO-116)
   -*One of the best books on the subject of creation.*

"The Beggar Meets God" (STO-117)
   -*A humorous way into the subject.*

Related Values/Issues

The largely accepted linear approach to time, impacts on a wide range of issues:

- material evolution theory.
- scientific creation myths (e.g. Big Bang).
- attitudes towards material progress.
- sustainable economic growth (is it possible?).

Personal Reflection

- What are our thoughts on eternity?
- If the world began on a certain date, what happened before that?
- Why does time seem to go quicker as we get older? And when we are happier?
- "We never get any younger, you know!" Why not?

Scriptural Passages

"By human calculation, a thousand ages taken together form the duration of Brahma's one day. and such also is the duration of his night."
   Bhagavad Gita 8.17

"Brahma lives . . . 311 trillion and 40 billion earth years"
   Bhagavad Gita 8.17 purport

"Time I am, destroyer of the worlds, and I have come to engage all men."
   Krishna in Bhagavad Gita 11.32

Meaning and Purpose

What is time? Why do we fear it so much? What is its real nature? How does it benefit us?

ⓘ **For more information see:**
Pages 68-69, 112, 116-117

Key Points:

- The material world is endlessly created, sustained and destroyed through the agency of the Trimurti *(page 48).*

- It rests in Brahman, from whom it is generated, by whom it is sustained, and into whom it merges upon annihilation.

- There are many enclosed material universes.

- There are three main material worlds – lower, middle and upper.

Above Top: The innumerable universes emanating from Vishnu.

Above: Brahma creates the material world, which is often called the 'one-quarter creation', expressing how it is far it is smaller than the spiritual world (the 'three-quarters portion'). Most souls are liberated, just as in the state most people are free citizens rather than imprisoned.

Far right: Lord Shiva is called the destroyer and, through his dancing, brings about universal destruction. He is also the male creative principle in the world, injecting the souls into the womb of material nature (Shakti).

With its cyclical notion of time, Hinduism teaches that the material world is created not once but repeatedly, time and time again. Additionally, this universe is considered to be one of many, all enclosed 'like innumerable bubbles floating in space.' Within this universe, there are three main regions: the heavenly planets, the earthly realm and the lower worlds. Scripture goes into some detail as to the nature of these regions and their respective inhabitants.

Hinduism is therefore not predominantly earth-centred, and puts much emphasis on other 'planes of existence' – various material abodes and the spiritual realm itself. This is reflected in Hindu stories and specifically through the concept of lila (divine pastime). These *lila* take place in the spiritual world and are replicated at sacred locations on earth.

There is no one simple account of creation, and there are many detailed and inter-related stories. Central is the narration of the sacrifice of the primal being (*purusha*), found in the Rig Veda. On the metaphysical level, the universe is created from sound (Vak). Sound corresponds to ether, the subtlest of the five material elements. According to such *sankhya* philosophy, the elements develop progressively from subtle to gross.

The *atman*, more subtle than any matter, generates his own successive material bodies. This world and its creatures are here to facilitate the soul's self-centred desires, and ultimately to enable his return to the spiritual world.

A Useful Analogy:

The prison house

The material world is but a small portion of God's kingdom and a place for those who wish to become the centre of enjoyment.

- The material world and its suffering is not really God's desire, just as a government would prefer that there were no prisons.

- Though the government provides and organises the prison service, the criminal is responsible for his or her situation. Similarly, though God creates this world, the soul creates his own happiness and distress.

- The world is a place where fallen souls attempt to enjoy existence separately from God.

- The ultimate purpose of the world is reformation of character and attitude, by which the soul can attain liberation. The souls suffers not so much through his location but through his rebellious attitude.

Related Stories

"Creation – adapted from the Bhagavat Purana" (STO-116)
    -One of the best books on the subject of creation.

"The Sacrifice of the Purusha" (STO-118)
    -A well known story from the Rig-Veda.

"The Brahmin and the Cobbler" (STO-113)
    -How God's creative powers are exhibited in nature.

One Account of Creation

Vishnu, as soul of the entire cosmos, produces countless universes from his breathing and the pores of his skin. He enters each universe, as the universal soul. From his navel springs a lotus flower, upon which is born Brahma. Brahma performs austerity and creates the world from sound, beginning with the Gayatri mantra.

Before he commenced creation, Brahma wanted to perform *yajna* (sacrifice) since the universe is created and maintained only through sacrifice. As yet, he had no ingredients. Therefore, the Supreme Lord agreed to become the necessary ingredients. Through that *yajna*, all species were created, as well as human society, with its places of residence, its languages, and so on. Brahma also created the various occupations and the corresponding system of four *varnas*. Thus the brahmins represent the head of the Supreme Lord; the *kshatriyas* are his arms, the *vaishyas* his thighs and the *shudras* his legs *(see page 26)*.

Related Values/Issues

- Life on other planets.
- Our role in this world.
- Environmental issues.
- Evolutionary theory.
- Scientific creation theories (e.g. Big Bang).

Scriptural Passage

"After one day of Brahma (the Creator), a partial annihilation occurs and the three planetary systems are destroyed. The universe is therefore not manifest during Brahma's night, which is of the same duration as his day."

Bhagavat Purana 12.4.4

Personal Reflection

- How do Hindu ideas of creation compare with others, both religious or secular?
- Do we consider the earth or our own country the centre of the universe? And *(connected to the previous spread)*, is the current moment in history the most important? Why do we sometimes think like this?

Meaning and Purpose

What is the purpose of creation? Why are there many species of life? Why is there so much suffering in this world? What is the role of humankind in relation to creation?

Common Misunderstandings

"The story of the primeval man is a 'naïve and pictorial way' of trying to explain creation."

Many Hindus do not believe that mythology is simply a poor precursor to the scientific age. Although the word myth can mean 'something untrue', it also refers to an alternative way of mapping reality, with reference to higher planes of existence. Traditional Hinduism does not root its own heritage in a tribal, Darwinian past.

"Hindus believe that living beings are all created . . ."

For Hindus, the creation of this world does not include the creation of the spiritual beings (souls), which are eternal. The soul is never created in the real sense, though the word is sometimes used to express how it is dependent on the Supreme. Creation entails the injection of the souls into the material energy.

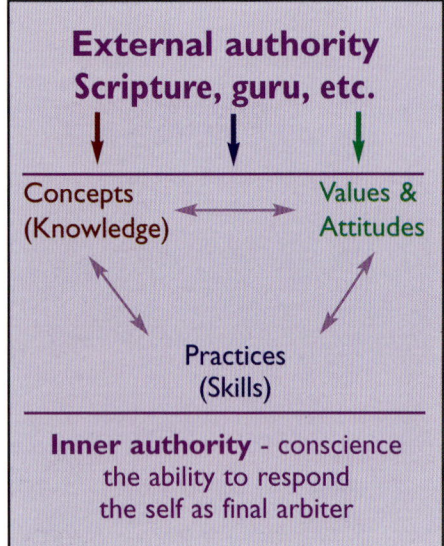

External authority
Scripture, guru, etc.

Concepts (Knowledge) ←→ Values & Attitudes

Practices (Skills)

Inner authority - conscience
the ability to respond
the self as final arbiter

Above: The relationship between concepts, values and practices, all informed by authority.
Below: two important authorities – spiritual (the brahmin) and social (the kshatriya) - who should work co-operatively.
Bottom: a quote endorsing the benefits of allocating different standards to different people.

Scriptural Passages

"Four types of people quickly perish - the shy courtesan, the immodest housewife, the contented kshatriya (warrior) and the discontented brahmin."

Chanakya Shloka

Within most books on Hinduism, little is written explicitly on Hindu values and attitudes. Since values are subtle, and exhibited largely through behaviour, most texts explore them thematically, through topical issues. *(We have also similarly categorised material in this way in the auxiliary booklet, "Moral Issues in Hinduism".)* However, it is useful to study Hindu values systematically, and it is particularly rewarding to examine how they inter-relate with concepts and practices *(as shown to the left).* According to Hindu thought, the dynamics between these three items include the following;

1. **Concepts** significantly inform **values** *(see page 38).*
2. **Values** are demonstrated through **practices** *(see page 39).*
3. Nurturing suitable **values**, through **practice** of morality and spiritual discipline, is necessary to assimilate **knowledge**.

With this emphasis on realisation of knowledge, the tradition considers the religious life as a system of education. Important to this process is the role of authority, in the form of texts and teachers *(see pages 30-31).* As scripture clearly discusses all three items – concepts, values and practices *(see page 122).* The guru is considered indispensable in explaining scripture, modelling exemplary behaviour, and providing hands-on guidance. Crucial to the whole process, to appropriately respond to life, is the role of conscience, the guru within *(see pages 20-21).*

Although Hinduism is an accommodating tradition, its values are not entirely fluid. They may not be constrained by a single or static set of beliefs, but they are guided by the need to comply with universal principles, and the desire to discern truth from illusion *(maya).* In exploring this topic, therefore, it is useful to recognise that Hinduism has its own distinctive perspectives, as we list below:

■ Values are closely connected to the execution of dharma in terms of specified duties, both spiritual and socio-religious.

■ *Sanatana-dharma* supports the ideal of shared values, the spiritual virtues that are recognised by all authoritative religious traditions. These characteristics are considered to be inherent within the heart of all beings, and to be invoked from within rather than imposed from outside.

■ *Varnashrama-dharma* allocates different specific values to the respective *varnas* and *ashramas*, often as stepping-stones towards ideal character *(represented by brahmins and sannyasis).*

■ Values are often transmitted through story, illustrating the dynamics between knowledge, character, and the ability to execute dharma and respond to situations.

■ Hindu values may differ from those currently prevalent in the UK. They often challenge 'political correctness', and may even differ from those taught within schools. Notions of authority are considered important to ensure that values aren't unduly swayed by popular sentiment.

Important Virtues

The following are twelve of the most important qualities listed in scripture. Naturally this list, and the priority given to each virtue, will vary from one tradition to another.

Important Hindu Virtues

Ahimsa (non-violence) – based on the concepts of *atman* and reincarnation.

Mind and sense control – considered essential for any form of morality.

Tolerance - necessary in order to deal with inconveniences in the performance of one's dharma.

Hospitality – demonstrating magnanimity, and the value of service (*seva*).

Compassion – based on notions of *atman*, and the ability to feel for others as we feel for ourselves.

Protection - an essential duty is to give shelter to others, especially those less fortunate.

Respect – for all living beings and for the sanctity of all life.

Wisdom – knowledge is contrasted with ignorance, the Hindu equivalent of the 'good-evil' paradigm.

Austerity – essential to gain wisdom in addition to mere theoretical knowledge.

Celibacy – important for spiritual life. Only one of the four ashrams is permitted sexual gratification.

Honesty - essential to build legitimate trust within relationships and to avoid self-deception.

Cleanliness – includes external hygiene and inner purity; essential for brahmins.

Personal Reflection

■ What do we value in life? How much are our values determined by our own likes and dislikes – or even prejudices? Do we inordinately try to rationalise and justify our opinions, in order to defend them? Can we stand up for our values, but at the same time be prepared to re-evaluate them?

■ How do we know what are worthy values? What are the criteria? Who do we think should determine them?

Related Practices

Most important for developing both knowledge and character are various moral restraints, such as sexual chastity and restraint from meat-eating, gambling and intoxication. Such apparent needs are either given up completely or, especially in the lower *varna*s, met in a regulated way.

Related Stories

Many, but especially from:

■ The Mahabharata
■ The Ramayana
■ The Puranas
■ The Panchatantra and Hitopadesh

Common Misunderstandings

"The only Hindu value of note is 'ahimsa' and all moral issues can be effectively explored though it."

There are hundreds of values and virtues listed in sacred texts. Many should be considered if we are to understand Hindu responses to a wide range of issues.

Scriptural Passages

"Peacefulness, self-control, austerity, purity, tolerance, honesty, knowledge, wisdom and religiousness – these are the natural qualities by which the brahmanas work."

"Heroism, power, determination, resourcefulness, courage in battle, generosity and leadership are the natural qualities of work for the kshatriyas."

Bhagavad Gita 18.42-43

See also:
Bhagavad Gita 13.8-12, 16.1-3.

Quote

"Allocating different standards to different people does not contradict the notion of common virtues, but is a means of ensuring that they are obtainable by everyone. Additionally, individuals may express the same values, such as selfless service, in quite different ways."

Indriyesha Das

Values and Concepts

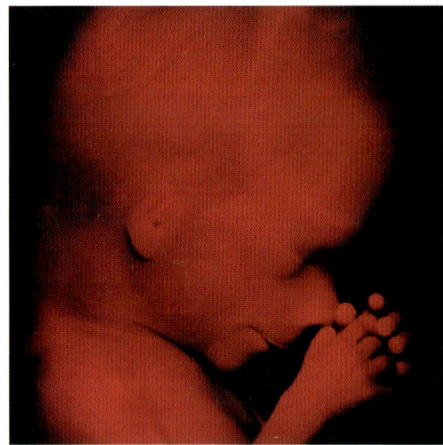

There is naturally a close connection between the values of any tradition and its underlying beliefs or concepts. For example, belief in reincarnation significantly influences Hindu attitudes towards animals, and issues on the sanctity of life, such as abortion. According to Hindu theology, the highest values are related to *sattva*, the quality of goodness, represented by the brahmins. Such values should be based on knowledge and a clear and objective perception of reality. The values inherent within the other three *varnas*, although desirable for members of that *varna*, are influenced by political, economic and sensual expediency respectively, and cannot be the leading values in society.

Top: an example of how concepts help to clarify stances on specific issues. Abortion is unacceptable to those Hindus who believe that the soul enters the womb (again) at the time of conception and is clearly an autonomous living being, even though it is physically connected to the mother. Not all issues are so easily resolved, however, and tradition points to the need for developing great discretion.
Left: The traditional school (Gurukula), essential for training discerning brahmins who possess vision and values based on a clear perception of reality.
Bottom: A table correlating the twelve main concepts to values and issues.

Common Misunderstandings
"Hindus are fatalistic because they believe in karma and reincarnation."

No, most are not. Many might interpret karma as a means to become responsible for our actions. (We should avoid judging another's concepts in terms of our own world-view and values).

Concepts	Related Issues or Values
Atman	The sanctity of life. Issues regarding one's true identity. Prejudice and negative discrimination.
Reincarnation & Samsara	Compassion for others; the nature of suffering; attitudes towards wildlife. Abortion. The sanctity of life.
Karma	Personal responsibility and accountability; foreseeing the consequences.
Prakriti and Guna	Model for analysing/categorising behaviour; goodness considered basis of ideal character; sustainability relates to ecological/economic issues.
Maya	Self-deception and mistaken notions; honesty with oneself and others.
Liberation	Purpose of life; without mind and sense control, no real morality.
God	Service. Attitudes towards God, authority figures. Proprietorship.
Dharma	Rights and responsibilities; common values and the notion of different values. Family issues. Equality and diversity. Material sense of identity and belonging. Sexual morality. Protection of dependants.
One goal/many paths	Inclusion; acknowledging people for what they are, not what they should be; unity in diversity.
Guru and Scripture	Sources of knowledge; authority (especially notions of natural, well-wishing 'elders'); appropriate respect for authority; discernment.
Time	The predominant Hindu world view. Transience. Material scientific progress.
Creation	The nature and purpose of the world. Environmental issues.

Values in Practice

Values are meant to be practiced, and specifically through dharma. This refers to both socio-religious practices according to *Varnashrama-dharma* and specific spiritual practices, such as *puja*. Many Hindu stories are about the difficulties encountered in performing one's dharma and the difficulties in distinguishing between right and wrong in trying or unusual circumstances.

Left: By performing worship in accordance with Sanatana-dharma, Hindus practice certain values. Offering our respects to the deity invokes an innate sense of loving service.

Right: Arjuna on the battlefield, bewildered about performing his duty. Dharma is not to be performed blindly, and there are many problems faced in its proper execution. Arjuna's situation is a template for problems, and illustrates the importance of knowledge in qualifying sentiment and in redressing inappropriate values (in this case misplaced compassion).

Left: Culture is an important means of transmitting values. Also essential is the role of parents in establishing the suitable domestic ethos and in performing the rites of passage that purify the soul.

Right: A rural setting, considered to be influenced by the of quality of goodness, is considered important in developing the appropriate values and attitudes.

Common Misunderstandings

"Hindus don't eat meat because they believe they may come back as an animal."
(See also Common Misunderstandings, page 11).
We should be careful about how we relate the moral practices of others to their concepts, and check that our ideas are backed up by members of that tradition.

"For Hindus, moral decisions are determined by dharma."
This is largely true, but could wrongly imply a thoughtless pursuit of duty. Hindu texts encourage consideration of time, place and circumstance, and particularly the results of executing dharma. If the consequences contradict the principles underpinning such duty, it should be abandoned. Dharma should not be followed blindly.

Quotes

"The still small voice within you must always be the final arbiter when there is a conflict of duty."
Mahatma Gandhi

"Even there is duty, we have to see what will be the effect of that duty. Nothing should be done blindly"
A.C. Bhaktivedanta Swami

Values and Story

Within Hindu tradition, story remains an essential means of transmitting values. Heroes and heroines embody ideal virtues, which they exhibit through exemplary behaviour. Many of the stories focus on the *kshatriyas* and *brahmins*, the two classes most responsible for maintaining social and spiritual culture and corresponding norms of behaviour. Stories can be explored repeatedly, with the reader or listener gaining progressively deeper insight.

The tales of Krishna, particularly those discussing his childhood and youth, are perhaps the most famous. They are readily accessible even to young children, and yet illustrate profound truths about God and Hindu attitudes towards him. Many texts compare the soul's relationship with the Supreme to relationships found in this world. These familial exchanges are sweet, loving and saturated with pleasure, devoid of fear, guilt, and other debilitating traits. God is replete with unlimited attractive features, and the soul delights tirelessly in his company. Krishna's *lila* (spiritual pastime) as the butter thief *(left)* shows how God is the source of all human tendencies, even mischief. Krishna's stealing, however, is bereft of greed and envy, and serves only to enhance the love of his devotees. For centuries, such stories have captured the hearts of millions of Hindu people.

Stories often illustrate key values. The tale of Mrigari the hunter *(left)* examines non-violence *(ahimsa)* and its relationship to key concepts such as karma and reincarnation. It reflects the Hindu tendency to see life not merely through its physical symptoms but through the eyes of the consciousness inherent in all species. This story is relevant to issues of diet, hunting, empathy, violence, compassion and animal welfare. It also illustrates the role of the guru in transforming the lives of others. Many narratives explore the qualities of such spiritual leaders, and their abilities to instill wisdom and character in others. Before meeting his spiritual teacher, Mrigari used to enjoy half-killing his victims. Afterwards, he avoided all violence, even going out of his way to avoid stepping on ants.

Scriptural Passages

It is said that great personalities almost always accept voluntary suffering because of the suffering of people in general. This is considered the highest method of worshiping the Supreme Lord, who is present in everyone's heart.

Bhagavat Purana 8.7.44

The *kshatriya* class carried responsibility for protecting its citizens – and not just in human society. A pigeon, about to be devoured by a hawk, took shelter of King Shibi *(left)*. The hawk subsequently insisted that he also had a right to protection and that the king must provide eatables for all dependants, including carnivores. Maharaja Shibi resolved the problem by cutting and donating flesh from his own body, equal in weight to that of the pigeon. Once on the scales, the pigeon miraculously became heavier and heavier and the king was about to sacrifice his entire body. Two demigods then revealed that they had decided to test the king by taking the forms of the two contesting birds. Many Hindu stories focus on the grave responsibilities of public leaders.

Some stories illustrate how traditional values can clash with contemporary ideals. Draupadi, one of the heroines of the Mahabharata, accepted the role of a faithful wife and yet was an influential, assertive and discerning woman. Although Hinduism assigns specific roles to women, it in no way condones their exploitation. On the contrary, Draupadi's tale teaches that those who offend women lose all good fortune. As a result of offending Draupadi, millions of nobles had to lay down their lives on the plains of Kurukshetra. Draupadi's character may appear somewhat ambiguous. Though she demonstrated the fiery self-esteem often associated with royalty, she also exhibited remarkable compassion by forgiving the murderer of her five adolescent sons. In India today, there are traditions which focus on the veneration of Draupadi.

Contemporary, everyday people also play an important role in nurturing moral conduct, with their daily struggles to follow the lofty examples set by their role-models. For them, the tradition places more emphasis on moral behavior than on conformity to a particular belief or doctrine. Morality is largely realised through the respective duties allocated to the different sectors of society. The prime responsibility for values rested on brahmins (teachers and priests), *kshatriyas* (administrators) and parents, reflecting the need for an appropriate ethos in the school, temple, home and state. Thus values were nurtured through an appropriate social system as well as through the example of individuals. Also important was etiquette. Customarily, juniors offered respect to elders by bowing and touching their feet, and seniors in turn bestowed their blessings. Elders were considered sources of wisdom and good counsel. Today, as values change within the Hindu community, still conspicuous is the respect and veneration offered to holy people and family elders. Story remains a principal means of preserving such culture and etiquette.

Above: Shravana Kumar, who exemplifies the Hindu ideal of service to elders, in this case his parents. Shravana was accidentally killed by King Dasharatha, Rama's father, for which the king later died as a result of separation from his own son. Respect for elders does not automatically imply contempt for those of lesser status — well illustrated by the story of King Rantideva.

Common Misunderstandings

"Hindu stories are symbolic, so we can derive whatever meaning we like from them; we can also change them to promote values we consider suitable to students."

Many Hindus do not consider their stories and 'myths' to be entirely metaphorical (in the same way as, say, fairy tales). Out of respect for the tradition, it is better not to change stories or to use them to illustrate values other than those originally intended.

(i) **For more information see:**
Pages 91, 126-127, 129, 130
'Stories' on the CD-ROM

Above: Chanakya Pandit, the minister of King Chandra Gupta. Chanakya compiled the popular Niti Shastra (also called the Chanakya Shloka).
Below: a comic book narrating some of the legendary stories of Birbal.

Proverbs, like stories, are a popular way of transmitting values and wisdom. Much moral instruction is present in the Niti Shastra texts, such as those compiled by Chanakya Pandit *(see also page 131)*.

Also popular are the legends that have grown up around various people such as Birbal, the chief minister of emperor Akbar. Such stories are available to children through comics such as those published by "Amar Chitra Katha" They also publish comic versions of other tales, such as those from the epics and Puranas, as well as the popular animal stories told in the Panchatantra *(see pages 91, 131)*.

Proverbs

- To eat or not to eat? Better not to eat – unless it's the middle of winter (for then the digestion will be strong). To go or not to go? Best to stay put – unless you have a call of nature, and then you must go!
- Better to have an intelligent enemy than a foolish friend.
- One should entertain neither enmity nor friendship towards an evil person; a piece of coal, when hot, burns the hand, when cold, blackens it.
- When an elephant is in trouble, even a frog will kick him.
- One who cannot dance blames the floor
- These six should never be given up: truthfulness, generosity, good humour, friendliness, forgiveness and contentment.
- Do not be despondent because of ill fate: there cannot be sesame oil without the crushing of sesame seeds.
- Do not entertain thoughts of revenge unless you are capable of action – the chick pea hopping up and down will not break the pan it is fried in.
- Self-praise is no praise.
- One who speaks of others' faults in an assembly proclaims his own defects.
- Don't listen to others secrets.
- Worship of elders is the root of humility.
- One should not argue with the intelligent, the foolish, friends, teachers or the beloved.
- The wealth of learning cannot be stolen by thieves.

Personal Reflection

- Which Hindu proverbs have equivalents in our culture? What relevance does this idea of common truths and values have to notions of *Sanatana-Dharma*?

Part 2 - Central Practices

 **Chapter 3 – Worship** (focuses, practices and places)

 **Chapter 4 – Festivals**

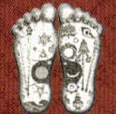 **Chapter 5 – Pilgrimage**

 **Chapter 6 – Rites of Passage**

 **Chapter 7 – Dharma**

Hinduism is often called 'a culture' or 'a way of life', illustrating how spirituality and daily activities are practically inseparable. Consequently, 'Hindu practice' - as we explore in these next two parts - is an extensive topic. Here in Part Two, we purposely focus on those activities that directly nurture the individual's spirituality. Each of the five chapters examines one of the nitya-karmas – the five activities considered essential for any practicing Hindu. The brief introduction deals with 'the four main paths', which incorporate these spiritual practices.

In order to understand the spiritual practices outlined in Part Two, it is useful to have an overview of the main processes or 'paths' *(see page 29)*. Some authorities list three, others add a fourth. Many thinkers claim that all paths are equally valid and effective and that the choice depends on individual inclination. Others suggest that all four paths are stepping stones along one spiritual path, each building progressively on the previous, more elementary disciplines. Either way, it is not that the different paths are tightly compartmentalised – each may contain elements of the others. Additionally, there may be higher and lower understandings of each path, as we explore below.

Karma yoga (the yoga of selfless action)

Karma yoga begins with the understanding that selfish action binds the soul. By giving up the fruits of action, one is relieved from the reactions to self-centred activities. This does not mean giving up the activity itself, for karma yoga, on a lower level, recommends that all activities be linked to a greater cause. Karma yoga specifically refers to sacrifices offered to various deities to attain material necessities in this life and the next, without accruing any reaction. On the highest level, karma yoga means the unreserved dedication of all activities to serve the Supreme Lord. Karma–yogis tend to have a materially progressive attitude towards the world and their aim is often the heavenly planets.

Jnana yoga (philosophical research and wisdom)

Whereas karma yoga usually involves *bhukti*, enjoying worldly pleasure, *jnana* yoga promotes knowledge through reclusion, study and sense abnegation. Activities and the necessities of life are minimised. Since the pursuit of wisdom and realisation is not simply an academic exercise, much emphasis is placed on becoming free from the sensual desires that delude the soul. *Jnana* is sometimes considered the antithesis of karma. *Jnana*-yogis negate the world and usually aim at liberation (*mukti* or *moksha*).

Astanga/Raja Yoga (physical exercises and meditation)

Asta means 'eight' and *anga* means 'part.' *Astanga* yoga is a process divided into eight distinct and essential stages, based on the Yoga Sutras of the sage, Patanjali. It is explored succinctly in the *Bhagavad-gita*. Many modern practices of yoga are related. However, Patanjali's system requires the observation of standards difficult for most contemporary practitioners. The *sutras* discuss superstates of consciousness and the obtainment of eight main types of mystic power, such as the ability to become 'smaller than the smallest.' India is replete with tales of such feats, which are largely accepted as feasible. Nonetheless, Patanjali warns the yogi not to become enamoured of such mystic powers but to keep the mind fixed on leaving the material realm. The highest perfection is to focus on God within.

Bhakti Yoga (the path of devotional service)

Bhakti appears to be the path most recommended in the Gita. Krishna says that at the beginning, *bhakti* yoga appears simple, but as it is perfected and as the practitioner matures, it combines all types of yoga. Within modern Hinduism, *bhakti* yoga remains the predominant path towards spiritual fulfilment. It includes the external and symbolic worship of the *murti*, other practices such as pilgrimage and the sophisticated processes of inner development. It has often been condescendingly presented as suitable to those with emotional rather than intellectual dispositions, but thinkers such as Ramanuja, Madhva and Vallabha have refuted such claims. Their theologies emphasise the importance of developing *bhakti* based on knowledge. They also stress the importance of grace in achieving such spiritual knowledge, often received via the guru, the mediator of God's mercy. Though *bhakti* may involve approaching God for material benefit or liberation these are technically karma yoga and jnana yoga respectively. *bhakti* yoga is sometimes considered the synthesis and ultimate goal of karma and *jnana*. The goals of many *bhakti* schools transcend both bhukti (enjoyment) and *mukti* (liberation) and aim at pure, selfless service to a personal God.

Left: The popular path of bhakti is considered by many to be only a stepping-stone to what they consider the more difficult process of knowledge. Other groups consider bhakti to be higher than jnana, considering that "the heart rules the head". Some consider all paths to be equal. Here as an act of devotion, a priest offers arti (page 57) to the temple deities.

Personal Reflection

■ Are these paths confined to Hinduism or are they also found in other religions? If so, in what ways?

■ Ask yourself: " What do I know about yoga as practiced in the West?" "What have I learned or how have my ideas changed?"

Scriptural Quotes

on karma yoga

"Therefore, without being attached to the fruits of activities, one should act as a matter of duty, for by working without attachment one attains the Supreme."

on jnana yoga

"In this world, there is nothing so sublime and pure as spiritual knowledge, which is the mature fruit of all mysticism. One who has become accomplished in the practice of yoga enjoys this knowledge within himself in due course of time."

on raja yoga

"To practice astanga-yoga, one should go to a secluded place and should lay kusha grass on the ground and then cover it with a deerskin and a soft cloth. The seat should be neither too high nor too low and should be situated in a sacred place. The yogi should then sit on it very firmly and practice yoga to purify the heart by controlling his mind, senses and activities and fixing the mind on one point."

on bhakti yoga

"If one offers Me with love and devotion a leaf, a flower, fruit or water, I will accept it."

Bhagavad Gita 3.19, 4.38,
6.11-12, 9.23

Glossary Terms

bhukti - *worldly pleasure*
mukti - *another word for liberation*

ⓘ **For more information:**
Pages 28-29

Chapter 3
Worship

Glossary Terms for Worship

- **Puja** - *usually refers to ritual worship of the murti.*
- **Bhajan** - *adoration; indicates worship with love. Often refers to devotional singing or the hymns themselves.*
- **Seva** - *indicates service (and the appropriate mood of worship).*
- **Yajna** - *sacrifice (an important aspect of worship).*

Hindu worship encompasses a broad range of activities, including even dance and drama. In this book we include such practices under "Expressions of Faith" *(see Chapter 5)*. In this chapter we focus on practices which to the Western mind seem more clearly 'acts of worship.'

Hindu worship displays a number of distinct features:

1. The presence of the Divine is perceived in diverse ways and tends to be inclusive. Thus, there is a complex array of focuses of worship *(see next page)*.

2. Much worship is performed individually, though in some traditions, like many in the UK, communal worship plays a central role.

3. Hindu worship often takes place outside the temple, especially in the home.

4. There are no specific days of worship, though days of the week are associated with particular deities (e.g. Shiva is honoured on Monday and Hanuman on Tuesday). In the UK, Sunday has become most important, as most Hindus are working during the week.

5. The time of day is important. The hours on either side of dawn are considered most auspicious for worship, for they are influenced by the quality of goodness *(see pages 14-15)*. In India many temples begin their first public ceremony between four and six in the morning. Other ceremonies take place during the day; evening worship is particularly popular.

6. Worship is often more spontaneous and less tightly regulated than in much Western religion, and individuals are usually quite free to join and leave ceremonies.

7. Hindu worship often appears to lack the solemnity we sometimes associate with religion. God can be worshipped with awe and reverence but also with warmth, joy and affection, as if He is a close friend or a loved one.

The early morning hours are the most peaceful and conducive to worship, prayer and meditation. In India, people tend to get up much earlier than in Britain.

Quote

"For me, the highlight of the day is the morning worship. It is such a sweet and peaceful experience, and one I hope that I will never lose."

Avadhuta Priya Dasi

In this chapter we will look at:

Focuses of Worship

Unity and Diversity

Hinduism is an extremely diverse tradition and can seem daunting when one is trying to understand the numerous deities and other objects of worship. It is too simplistic to explain these complexities by resorting to claims of pantheism or polytheism *(see pages 22-23)*. The following two notions may help us understand the many focuses of worship.

(1) Ultimately, the Vedas recommend selfless worship of the One Supreme, however one conceives of Him. Simultaneously they recognise various stages on the path to God-realisation and accommodate worship of other deities for material gain and gradual elevation.

(2) God may be worshipped through his many representatives, which are natural and benign authorities. Hindu thought tends to regard them as inclusive of God rather than exclusive.

The following list indicates some of the diverse focuses of worship:

1. The Supreme (God).
2. The variety of gods (devas) and goddesses (devis) and minor deities (devatas).
3. The spiritual preceptor (*acharya* or guru).
4. The teacher (also called guru).
5. The qualified brahmin.
6. The monarch (as the representative of God).
7. Family elders (like the mother and father).
8. The cow (as mother) and bull (as father).
9. Sacred plants (such as the Tulasi and Bilva).
10. Sacred rivers (such as the Ganga).
11. The land (considered one of the natural mothers), and those places where God and holy people have appeared.
12. All living beings (as parts of God).

Key Points

- Hinduism tends to accommodate all people with different concepts of the Supreme so that all can gradually progress towards ultimate self-and God-realisation.

- God is worshipped directly and also through his natural representatives (benign authorities). Hindus consider that venerating items connected with God further glorifies Him rather than detracting from His greatness.

Above: *Tulasi plants, venerated by the followers of Vishnu. The Bilva tree is similarly sacred to devotees of Shiva. Other important trees are the neem, banyan, mango, banana and coconut.*

Common Misunderstandings

"Hinduism is entirely inclusive. Hindus believe that they can worship anyone and achieve the same result."

The quote below challenges this rather simplistic understanding:

"Those who worship the demigods (devas) will take birth amongst the demigods; those who worship the ancestors will go to the ancestors; those who worship ghosts and spirits will take birth among such beings; and those who worship Me will live with Me."

Bhagavad Gita. 9.25

Scriptural Passages

"Of all types of worship, worship of Vishnu is supreme. But even higher than that is the worship of those things related to Vishnu."

Lord Shiva in the Padma Purana

The Trimurti

Brahma - the creator *(in charge of raja-guna - the quality of passion).*

Vishnu - the maintainer *(in charge of sattva-guna - the quality of goodness).*

Shiva - the destroyer *(in charge of tama-guna - the quality of ignorance).*

In the material world there are three principal deities called the trimurti (literally 'three deities'). They correspond to God's functions of creation, sustenance and destruction *(see also prakriti - page 14).*

God also exists beyond this world, as an impersonal force and/or as the Supreme Person. Most commonly that transcendent Supreme is identified with Vishnu, or one of his forms (i.e. Krishna, Rama or Narayana).

2. Vishnu

3. Shiva

Above: **Vishnu,** *all-pervading yet also a person. He is most often worshipped in his forms as Krishna and Rama (see Page 50).*
Above right: **Shiva,** *with his carrier, Nandi the bull. Shiva is in charge of universal destruction, though he also has a role in creation. He represents the male principle within this world, while his female counterpart, Shakti, is his consort and the personification of material energy (Mother Nature).*
Right: **Brahma,** *the creator (or secondary creator, since he is born of Vishnu, the original creator). Direct worship of Brahma is rare, and in India there is only one major temple dedicated to him in Pushkar, Rajasthan. Some consider him to be worshipped indirectly through the chanting of the Gayatri mantra, since Gayatri is one of his consorts.*

Common Misunderstandings

"The trimurti, the Hindu Trinity,..."

The implied comparison here with Christianity is potentially misleading, and hence the term 'Hindu Trinity' is best avoided.

1. Brahma

The Three Main Focuses of Worship

There is another group of three deities – the three main focuses of worship. They again include Vishnu and Shiva, but Shakti replaces Brahma. They correspond to the three main denominations, as shown to the right. *(Sometimes a fourth denomination, worshipping many deities, is included – see page 132)*

(Sometimes a fourth denomination, worshipping many deities, is included – see page 132)

The three main types of worshipper in order of prominence

Vaishnavas - worshippers of *Vishnu*
Shaivites - worshippers of *Shiva*
Shaktas - worshippers of *Shakti*

4. Shakti

Above: Shakti is the consort of Shiva and is considered the personification of material energy (Mother Nature or Prakriti). Like nature she can be nurturing and bountiful but also cruel and dangerous, As Parvati she is kind, but as Kali appears cruel and frightening. Durga, in a warlike form, is equipped for battle to protect her devotees. The picture above shows her in her form as Durga. Shakti is often addressed as Devi (goddess) or Mataji (respected mother). This term is also used to address the other goddesses, who are the 'Shaktis' of their respective spouses. Therefore, the worship of Shakti sometimes includes the veneration of both Lakshmi and Sarasvati (see right), as in the festival of Navaratri. Shakti literally means 'energy'.

Four Main Deities

This double page spread shows the four main deities. All other deities fall in one of four corresponding categories:
(1) as a form of Vishnu (2) as a form of Shiva
(3) as a goddess (Shakti) (4) as a powerful soul, who has taken on a very elevated body (such as that of Brahma).

Divine Couples

Two of the three main focuses of worship, namely Shiva and Shakti, are husband and wife. They are shown below as Shiva and Parvati, together with Ganesh, one of their two sons.

Similarly, the other two members of the *trimurti* have their consorts. There are thus three main goddesses, the respective partners of the *trimurti*, as shown below:

Vishnu	**+**	**Lakshmi**
Shiva	**+**	**Shakti**
Brahma	**+**	**Sarasvati**

Krishna and Rama (as Vishnu forms) have their respective consorts, Radha and Sita *(see page 50)*, who are forms of Lakshmi.

(see page 50)

Animal Carriers

On this spread, Shiva is shown with his mount, the bull called Nandi. The four main deities shown here have their respective mounts, as shown below:

Vishnu – Garuda, the giant eagle

Shiva – Nandi the bull

Brahma – the swan

Shakti – the lion or tiger

Twelve Principal Deities

In addition to the four most important deities, we have added a further eight . Only brief information is given on each here, as further details are included on each of the twelve, A4 photo-cards and on the CD-Rom. (Included in the "Heart of Hinduism" Teaching Pack).

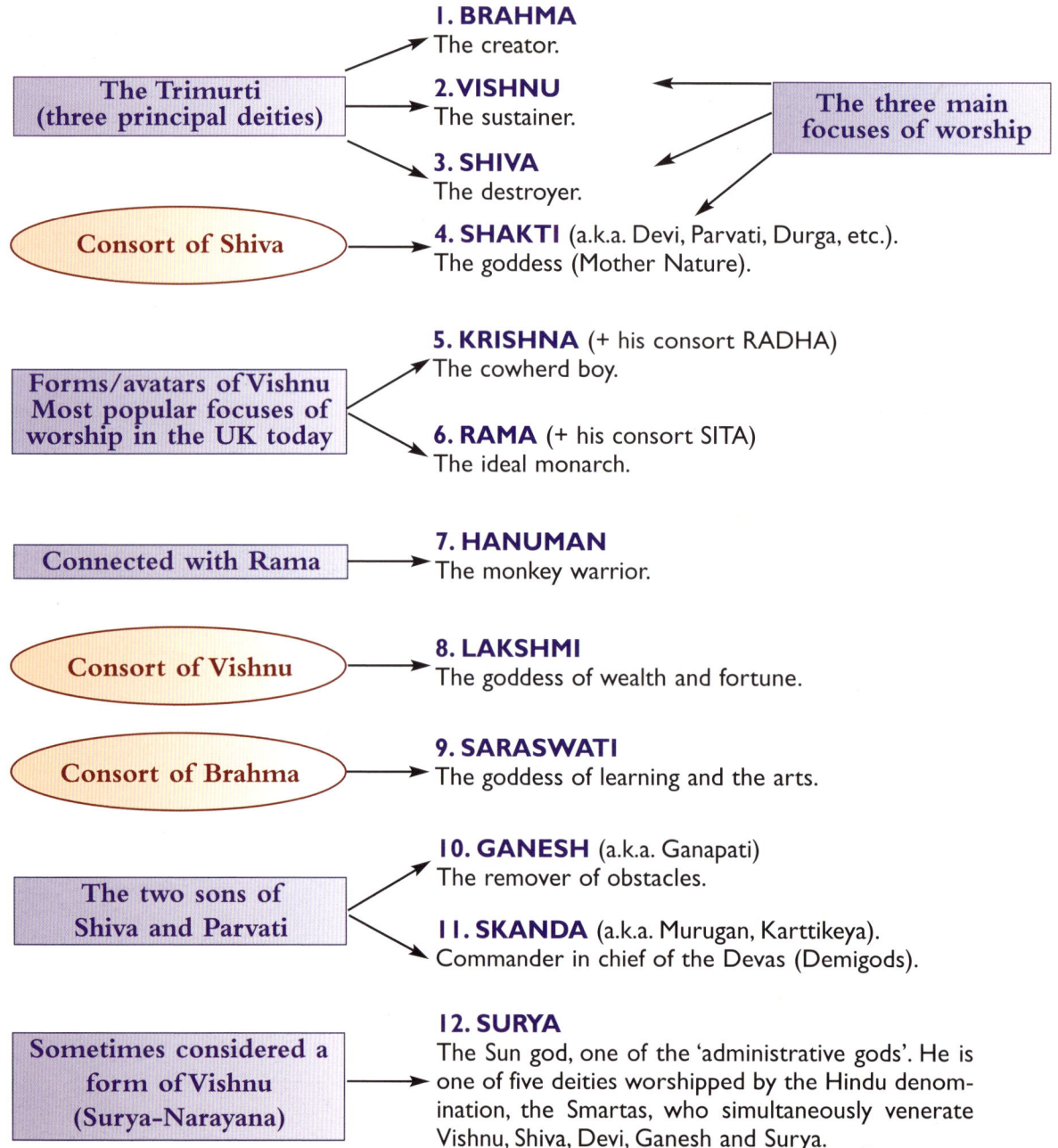

The Trimurti (three principal deities)

1. BRAHMA
The creator.

2. VISHNU
The sustainer.

3. SHIVA
The destroyer.

The three main focuses of worship

Consort of Shiva

4. SHAKTI (a.k.a. Devi, Parvati, Durga, etc.).
The goddess (Mother Nature).

Forms/avatars of Vishnu Most popular focuses of worship in the UK today

5. KRISHNA (+ his consort RADHA)
The cowherd boy.

6. RAMA (+ his consort SITA)
The ideal monarch.

Connected with Rama

7. HANUMAN
The monkey warrior.

Consort of Vishnu

8. LAKSHMI
The goddess of wealth and fortune.

Consort of Brahma

9. SARASWATI
The goddess of learning and the arts.

The two sons of Shiva and Parvati

10. GANESH (a.k.a. Ganapati)
The remover of obstacles.

11. SKANDA (a.k.a. Murugan, Karttikeya).
Commander in chief of the Devas (Demigods).

Sometimes considered a form of Vishnu (Surya-Narayana)

12. SURYA
The Sun god, one of the 'administrative gods'. He is one of five deities worshipped by the Hindu denomination, the Smartas, who simultaneously venerate Vishnu, Shiva, Devi, Ganesh and Surya.

Note 1: Sometimes Krishna – and less often Rama – is considered the original Godhead, rather than an avatar of Vishnu (as is stated above.) The terms 'Vishnu' and 'Krishna' are almost synonymous, despite some debate about their respective positions.

Note 2: Radha and Sita are not included in the list of twelve principal deities since they are rarely, if ever, worshipped separately form their respective husbands.

5. Krishna & Radha

6. Rama & Sita

7. Hanuman

12. Surya

These pictures show eight of the twelve main Hindu deities outlined in the previous page. Photos of the other four main deities are shown in the previous spread.

The complete set of twelve pictures is also available on A4 photo-cards. Further details, along with a complete list of the Ten Incarnations of Vishnu, are found on these cards and on the CD-Rom.

8. Lakshmi

11. Skanda

10. Ganesh

9. Saraswati

Avatars, Expansions and Epithets

Avatars and Expansions

An important concept within Hinduism is that of avatar – meaning literally, "one who descends." The closest English word is "incarnation." This is technically incorrect since many Hindu sects (especially Vaishnavas) believe that God does not adopt a material (carnal) body, but appears in spiritual form.

Another important notion is that God, or a specific deity, can expand and multiply him or herself into unlimited divine forms. In other words there may be different forms of a deity even if they are not avatars.

Vishnu is most famous for his many avatars of which ten, the Dashavatara, are principal. Of these, Krishna and Rama are the two most popular focuses in the UK today. Avatars feature less prominently in Shaivism. Nonetheless, Shiva has several important forms, such as 'Nataraj', the Lord of Dance, and the Rudras, representing his angry and frightful aspects.

Shakti, the consort of Shiva, has many forms and incarnations: some are kind and loving, such as Parvati, and others warlike and fearful, such as Durga and Kali.

Epithets

The different deities have various names. As we mentioned above, each one may refer to

- a particular form or expansion.
- a specific incarnation.

In other cases they are simply alternative names or epithets and often refer to

- a particular activity performed by that deity.
- a quality or feature of that deity.

Examples

Vishnu – *Narayana* – *Krishna* – *Rama* - *Govinda*
Shiva – *Nataraja* – *Rudra* – *Mahadeva* – *Mahesh*
Shakti – *Devi* – *Mataji* – *Parvati* – *Durga* – *Kali*

In the chart *(above)*, **Narayana** is a form of **Vishnu** in the spiritual realm. **Krishna** and **Rama** are also Vishnu forms, often considered his avatars *(see page 50, note 1)*. **Govinda** *(see top left)* is a name of Krishna meaning "one who gives pleasure to the cows".

Mahadeva and **Mahesh** are epithets of **Shiva**. **Rudra** is a particularly angry form (or expansion). **Nataraja** (the King of Dancers) is a name of Shiva *(see left middle)*.

Shakti is quite a technical name for 'the Goddess.' She is most often called **Devi** and affectionately called '**Mataji**' (respected mother). **Parvati**, **Durga** and **Kali** *(see left)* are distinct forms of Shakti.

Minor Deities

Administrative gods

In addition to the 12 main deities listed on page 50 there are also a number of minor deities (keeping in mind that certain Hindus may consider them more exalted or even Supreme!). They are generally considered to have specific roles within this universe. The main ones are also considered to have charge over the eight directions, beginning with the East and moving clockwise (i.e. Indra is in charge of the East, Agni the South East, Yama the South, etc.).

Indra	King of Heaven/ god of **rain**
Agni	deity in charge of **fire**
Yama	deity presiding over **death**
Surya	presiding deity of the **sun**
Varuna	presiding deity of **water**
Vayu	presiding deity of the **wind** (air)
Kuvera	treasurer of the demigods (god of **wealth**)
Soma (Chandra)	presiding deity of the **moon**

These deities are usually associated with earlier, 'Vedic' Hinduism, and are rarely worshipped today, except perhaps Surya. Still prominent, especially in South Indian temples, is the worship of the 'nine planets' *(see page 100)*.

Minor Deities

Deva or devata means demigod. Sthala devata specifically refers to a minor deity who has jurisdiction over a particular place – a river, forest or village. They are often worshipped in village shrines. A popular deity is Sitala *(below)*, the goddess of small-pox, who is worshipped in the hope of avoiding the disease.

Above: Indra, 'the King of Heaven,' was apparently very popular in early Vedic Hinduism and is considered to be in charge of the administrative demigods. Here he is offering his obeisances to Lord Krishna in connection with the pastime, "The Lifting of Govardhan Hill."

Other 'higher beings'

There are many other lesser deities and higher beings, who often appear in the various stories. These include:

The **Asuras** *(demons) who always fight.*

The **Devas** *(the gods or demigods).*

The **Apsaras** *(celestial nymphs).*

The **Nagas** *(celestial serpents).*

The **Gandharvas** *(heavenly singers).*

The **Rakshasas** *(a race of man-eaters).*

The **Prajapatis** *(progenitors of mankind).*

'Modern' Dieties

Some deities have risen to prominence more recently. They include:

Santoshi Ma *— the goddess of content-ment, worshipped mainly by ladies*

Ayyappan *— popular in Kerala, he is con-sidered the son of Shiva and Mohini (the female incarnation of Vishnu)*

Types of Worship

Scriptural Passages

"If one offers me with love a leaf, fruit, flower, or water, I will accept it."

Bhagavad Gita 9.26

Within Hinduism, worship can include a wide range of practices and the boundaries between worship, service, glorification, etc. are not distinct. We have included some features of worship, such as drama and dance, under Chapter Five. Below we list ten principal acts of worship. Of these, the first two are most important. Keep in mind, though, that some traditions will differ. The Arya Samaj *(see page 140),* for example, places *havan* at the top of their list).

Some of these practices are performed individually and some congregationally – and many can be both. Additionally, all of them can be performed at home as well as in the temple.

Ten Types of Worship

1. **Puja** – ritual worship, especially of the deity.
2. **Arti** – the greeting ceremony with lamps, etc.
3. **Bhajan or Kirtan** – hymns and chants (often during arti).
4. **Darshan** – taking audience of a deity or holy person.
5. **Prasad** – offering and eating sacred food.
6. **Pravachan** – talk or lecture on the scriptures.
7. **Havan** – the sacred fire ceremony.
8. **Japa/Meditation/Prayer** – internal practices of worship.
9. **Parikram/Pradakshina** – circumambulation.
10. **Seva** – active service, to the deity, holy people, etc.

Above: Visitors at Bhaktivedanta Manor, one of the most popular temples in the UK. It is renowned for its high standard of puja (deity worship).

Visiting the temple:

"At about six in the morning, I do my own *puja* at home. Later, on my way to work, I briefly visit the temple for *darshan*. I ring the bell as I enter the temple room and pay my obeisance to the murtis. I say some prayers for God's protection and put a few coins in the donation box. I then sip some charanamrita (holy water) and one of the priests gives me some *prasada* [sanctified food]."

"On Sundays we sometimes go for the early morning *arti* at 4.30 a.m. After that we worship Tulsi by circumambulating her and having *kirtan*. Then I join the other devotees for japa meditation on our beads. Later, after the priests have dressed the deities in their day outfits, the curtains open and we greet them with a short *arti*. After this comes *guru-puja*, in which we offer flowers to the spiritual master. Then one of the priests sings a short *bhajan* and gives a lecture. Sometimes at the end I ask questions about spiritual life. After breakfast I do some service, often by helping set up for a wedding. During the wedding there is a sacred-fire ceremony."

The Murti

Worship of the murti, the sacred image, is central to Hinduism. Many of the nineteenth century reform movements rejected the practice as outdated and superstitious. Nonetheless, sacred-image worship remains central today in helping many Hindus develop and express their relationship with God.

Useful Analogy 1:

The post box

The murti is compared to a post box that is authorised to accept mail on behalf of the central post office.

- As most people live far from a central sorting office, the post office installs local boxes. Similarly, though most people cannot approach God in his abode, he appears as the murti before those who sincerely desire to serve him.

- We cannot put mail in any box; it must be authorised. Each box is made and installed under the authority of the post office. Similarly, sacred images should be made and worshipped only under scriptural guidance.

Useful Analogy 2:

The expert electrician

- Though the murti is perceivable to our senses, Hindus consider it Brahman (spirit). Hindu thinkers differentiate between matter and spirit, but on a higher level consider both to be Brahman. God can change matter into spirit and spirit into matter. He is compared to an expert electrician who can use electricity to refrigerate and to heat. Though people in ignorance cannot perceive spirit (and hence God), the Lord may agree to appear before them in a visible form so that they can develop their relationship with him. The murti, though appearing to be matter, may function as spirit.

Personal Reflection

- What experience do we have of practices that resemble deity worship? Why do we build statues of famous people or keep pictures of the deceased (whose graves we may venerate).

Common Misunderstandings

"The images are merely meditational aids, and represent the different aspects of God who is invisible; Hindus don't actually worship their murtis."

Many branches of Hinduism do not agree. Both practically and theologically, the murti may be considered to be God or the specific deity it represents. Some Hindu groups consider the murti a form of avatar.

Sensitive Issues – Idolatry

The question of idolatry naturally arises for many non-Hindus encountering image-worship. It is especially relevant in schools where teachers and pupils are predominantly Christian or of other religions that have reservations about idol-worship, or practices that resemble it. The more developed strands of Hinduism have sophisticated theologies which differentiate between (what they consider) genuine deity worship and that which is unacceptable (or on a lower level of understanding). Naturally, they reject apparently similar practices focussing on demonic forces and which are influenced by the quality of ignorance (tamas). Deity worship should be performed in goodness, and there are strict rules regarding its scientific execution and the character and conduct of those performing it..

Puja (ritual worship)

Puja refers to worship, particularly of the sacred image. Each *sampradaya* (denomination) has elaborate rules for its performance, and the practical details vary considerably. *Puja* usually involves bathing and dressing the deity and offering various auspicious items, such as water, perfume and flowers. It often culminates in the offering of food, and is immediately followed by the *arti* ceremony. *Puja* generally includes a minimum of 16 devotional acts.

Worship offered at home is usually a scaled-down version of the grand temple services. It may be offered a day or just once a week, whereas scheduled temple worship must continue daily from early morning to late evening. *Puja* is usually considered an act of devotional service to God or the chosen deity.

Above: Temple priests bathe the murti early in the morning.
Below: A lady sews a new costume for the temple deities, who are dressed daily after bathing. The new outfit will be offered on a festival day.
Right: Flower garlands are an important feature of the deity's costume. This man sells them to worshippers outside a temple in India.
Below right: Food offered on the shrine just before the arti ceremony. After the arti, morsels of the prasad are received by worshippers.

The Arti Ceremony

A*rti* is the most popular ceremony within Hinduism, often performed in temples six or seven times per day. It is a greeting ceremony offered to the *murti* and also gurus, holy people and other representations of the divine. *Arti* is often called 'the ceremony of lights' but usually involves offering more than just a lamp. The priest or worshipper offers various auspicious articles by moving them in clockwise circles before the deity. At the same time he or she rings a small hand bell, while meditating on the forms of the deity. During the entire ceremony, which normally lasts from five to thirty minutes, the worshipper offers incense, a flower, water, a five-wick lamp, a lamp with camphor and other items. The ceremony is often announced and concluded by the blowing of a conch-shell. During the ceremony the offered lamp is passed around the congregation; members pass their fingers over the flame and reverently touch them to their foreheads. The offered flowers are also passed around worshippers and the water is sprinkled over their heads.

Arti is usually accompanied by singing *(bhajan/kirtan)* and out of respect worshippers usually stand for the entire ceremony.

Above: A priest (pujari) offers the midday arti. Each article, such as the lamp shown here, is offered using the right hand.
Left: The flame is passed around the congregation. Some place coins on the plate which is returned to the altar.
Below Left: The arti tray, after the ceremony.
Below: A temple sign listing the six arti ceremonies. The times on the right show when the shrine is open for taking darshan (audience).

DEITY SCHEDULE			
AT BHAKTIVEDANTA MANOR			
ARATI TIMES		DARSHAN TIMES	
4 30	4 55 AM	4 30	5 00 AM
7 00	7 10	7 00	11 45
12 30	12 55 PM	12 30	1 00 PM
4 20	4 30	4 20	6 25
7 00	7 25	7 00	7 30
9 00	9 10	9 00	9 30

Besides *puja* and *arti*, there are eight other major forms of worship.

Bhajan / kirtan

Bhajan means adoration and refers to devotional hymns, usually sung in small groups or by the entire congregation. *Kirtan* means glorification and more specifically indicates the repetition of mantra to the accompaniment of musical instruments. *Bhajan* and *kirtan* are particularly central to *bhakti* (devotional) movements and are often performed during the *arti* ceremony. Common instruments are drums, (such as tablas and mridangas), hand-cymbals and the harmonium *(see also page 93)*.

Darshan

Darshan literally means "seeing," though it is better translated as "audience." Devout Hindus generally present themselves before the deity in a temple or before a holy person to receive their blessings. They pay respects through *pranam*, bowing the head and folding the hands (though some may make obeisance by prostrating themselves). Traditionally they bear an offering, in money or kind (fruits, flowers, grains, etc.), and may offer prayers. Many Hindus will visit a temple each morning to "take *darshan*". Afterwards they will sip some charanamrita (holy water collected after bathing the *murtis*) or accept some *prasada* (sanctified food). Many visitors will not only take *darshan* but also stay for one of the *arti* ceremonies.

Prasad

Regularly offering food to the deities is technically an integral part of *puja*, but deserves special mention. Visitors to the temple conclude their *darshan* by accepting morsels of prasada (sacred food) offered to the deity. In larger temples, meals (normally vegetarian) are offered several times per day and the 'remnants' are considered to purify body, mind and soul and to bestow spiritual merit. Some devotees will eat nothing but *prasada* and will offer all their meals to the household deity before eating it themselves *(see also pages 65, 98)*.

Pravachan

Pravachan refers to a philosophical lecture based on a verse, or verses, from one of the Vedic texts such as the Bhagavad Gita. This is delivered by a priest or guru and often followed by questions and answers or a general discussion. The speaker may sit on an elevated seat out of respect for the authority of scripture. Hearing about spiritual topics is said to divert the mind from the mundane, strengthen one's powers of discernment and purify the heart.

Personal study of sacred books *(see page 122)* is also an important spiritual practice.

Havan

Havan is translated as 'fire sacrifice' or 'sacrificial fire.' It is also called '*homa*' or '*agnihotra*.' This procedure is undertaken particularly on festive occasions and for rituals such as initiation and marriage. Some Hindus practice it daily as part of their regular worship. Grains and ghee are offered to through the fire, and with the chanting of various mantras. Particularly notable is the ancient chant '*Svaha*', recited as the grains are tossed into the flames. For some groups, such as the Arya-Samaj, this ancient practice, is central to their worship.

Japa and meditation

Japa refers to the quiet or silent recitation of a mantra (such as "Om Namo Shivaya" or the well-known Hare Krishna mantra). This is generally performed on a mala, a string of 108 beads. The beads are usually made of Tulsi wood (for Vaishnavas) or Rudraksha beads (for Shaivas). Another popular form of meditation is the recitation of the Gayatri mantra, *traditionally* observed by brahmins at dawn, noon and dusk. Japa and other forms of meditation are considered to purify the heart of selfish desires and to invoke love of God.

Prayer is also an important part of worship, and Hindus may either recite standard prayers, or simply express their heartfelt devotions. It is customary to offer words of glorification before asking for some boon or blessing.

Circumambulation

Circumambulation is another form of offering respect and worship and is generally performed in a clockwise direction. In or around many temples there is a walkway for circumambulation of the deity, sometimes performed whilst chanting on japa beads *(see above)* or singing. Pilgrims circumambulate holy spots, entire sacred towns or even the whole of India - often barefooted out of respect for sacred ground.

Seva

Active service to the deity is considered a form of worship, and in many temples the priests are constantly engaged not only in puja but many secondary functions. Lay members also offer their services by helping in cleaning, cutting vegetables, etc. Many traditions consider service to holy people, even in apparently mundane matters, a means of winning the Lord's blessings. Service to holy places, through sweeping the *land* or serving pilgrims, is also considered meritorious.

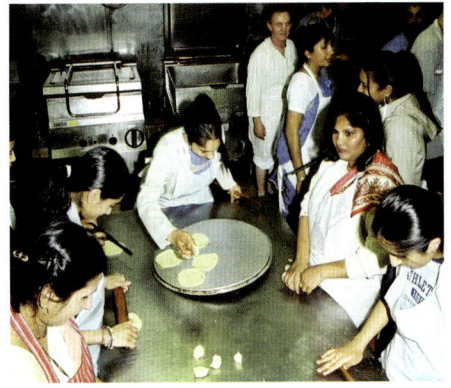

The Temple (Mandir)

Top: Krishna & Radha at a temple in Britain. The deities, installed on the shrine, are considered the proprietors of the temple and all activities revolve around their service.
Below: A roadside shrine dedicated to a goddess.
Below right: The temple of Balaji in Tirupati, which on an average day receives over 25,000 visitors.

Indian tradition holds that a town or village without a temple is uninhabitable. The Mandir is not primarily considered a place for communal worship but the home of God, or the particular Deity. Temple activities thus revolve around the sacred image(s) installed upon the altar. An appointed priest, or team of priests, normally performs the *Puja*. One of the main functions of the temple is to create an atmosphere surcharged with spirituality and hence temples are often built on holy sites. During quieter periods the temple provides opportunity for peaceful reflection. At other times, it is a bustle of noise and activity.

Temples vary considerably in size, beginning with tiny outdoor shrines and humble village *mandirs*. The larger temples are elaborate and often the centre of an ashram (place of spiritual culture) with a large number of brahmin priests living within or nearby. The temple of Balaji in Tirupati (South India) is reckoned to be the largest, with a total staff of over 6,000.

There are a number of architectural styles, but the chief ones are the North Indian (Nagara) and the South Indian (Dravida). Details for temple construction are laid out in certain scriptures such as the Vastu-shastra and the Shilpa-shastra *(see page 124)*. To help build a temple (e.g. through offering financial support) is still considered an act of piety.

In the UK, the first temples tended to be converted public buildings, such as school halls and churches. They often have an orange flag flying from the roof. Now there are an increasing number of purpose-built mandirs, in both modern and traditional styles (or a combination of both.) Temples in Britain, unlike those in India, often double up as community centres, where Hindus can meet and organise social, cultural and charitable events. Throughout the UK, there are now about 150 temples featuring regular worship.

Temples vary considerably, but the diagrammatic plans below show some of the important features of traditional buildings in North India. Buildings in the South or outside of India are often quite different.

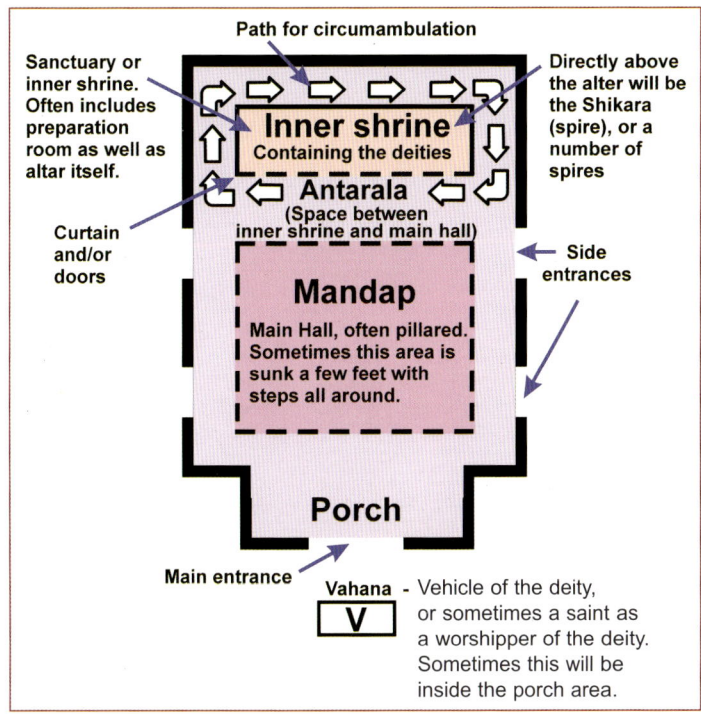

Path for circumambulation

Sanctuary or inner shrine. Often includes preparation room as well as altar itself.

Directly above the alter will be the Shikara (spire), or a number of spires

Inner shrine
Containing the deities

Antarala
(Space between inner shrine and main hall)

Curtain and/or doors

Side entrances

Mandap
Main Hall, often pillared. Sometimes this area is sunk a few feet with steps all around.

Porch

Main entrance

Vahana - Vehicle of the deity, or sometimes a saint as a worshipper of the deity. Sometimes this will be inside the porch area.

V

Above: The Shakti mandir in Leicester founded in the 1970's is a good example of an early temple. One can see the Christian cross and the trident, a Hindu emblem.
Left: Opened in 1996, the Swami Narayana Mandir in North London is a traditional North Indian temple.
Below Left: The plan of a typical North Indian temple. South Indian temples are more complex, and are usually surrounded by a number of concentric walls each with a number of elaborate gateways (gopurams).

Main external features of the mandir

- An orange flag
- Spires above the shrine (mainly in the north)
- Gopurams - tall gateways (in the south)
- Intricate carvings, usually of various deities
- Tanks for bathing (especially in the south)

Inside the Mandir

A *mandir* has many internal features, which one can fully appreciate only by visiting. Below we list what we might experience on entering a temple. Some *mandirs* have fewer facilities, and others far more. The more elaborate are often part of an entire complex that includes residential quarters, guest rooms and educational facilities.

Above: The main hall in the Sanatan Mandir, Leicester.
Right (Clockwise from Bottom–left):
- Worshippers taking off their shoes upon entering the temple.
- Ringing the bell on entering the temple room.
- Two girls taking Charanamrita (holy water) after taking darshan.
- Placing money in the donation box after the arati ceremony.

• Racks for shoes (sometimes manned in larger temples)	*see above*
• The fragrance of incense	*see page 97*
• Main hall (temple room)	*see above*
• Bell to ring upon entry – to announce one's arrival to the deity	*see above*
• Pictures/posters of saints, deities, and associated stories	*see pages 94*
• Hindu symbols	*see page 95*
• Musical instruments – including drums, cymbals, harmonium	*see page 93*
• Sacred books – for reading and giving lectures	*see page 122*
• Main shrine (at the front); often many smaller shrines, usually to the sides	*see above*
• Donation box before the shrine	*see above*
• Murtis within the shrine areas	*see pages 55, 60*
• Charanamrita (holy water in a bowl near the altar)	*see above*
• Prasada, sacred food, handed to worshippers at the altar, or as they leave	*see page 98*
• Priest or priests	*see page 64*
• Kitchen and dining area	*see page 98*
• Auditorium for music, drama, dance, and other cultural performances	*see pages 92-93*
• Shop selling religious artifacts, books, and other religious souvenirs.	
• The temple administrative office	

The Shrine

The shrine is the sacred centre of the *mandir*. It houses the temple deities and is usually situated at one end of the main hall. To the side or close by is a room in which the priests prepare for worship according to a fixed daily schedule. Often only the priests, freshly bathed and wearing clean clothes, are allowed to enter these sacred areas.

Glossary Terms

Garba griha *–the inner sanctum of the temple (Garba literally means 'womb', and griha means 'house')*

Left: one of the two shrines at Bhaktivedanta Manor Temple in Hertfordshire. It is dedicated to Sita and Rama, who are accompanied by Rama's favourite brother, Lakshman, and by the monkey warrior, Hanuman.
Many temples not only have a main altar, but feature many smaller, adjacent shrines dedicated to other deities and saints. It is common to have a shrine of Ganesh who is worshipped first to remove any impediments before approaching the main deity or deities.
Puja itself is an intricate and sophisticated art form. The backdrop in this picture was sewn by craftsmen in the ancient town of Vrindavana. This temple grows its own flowers for the vases and for the garlands which are made and offered each day with a change of costume. In some temples the colour of the daily costume will correspond to the ruling planet of day of the week (e.g. gold on Sunday, silver or white on Monday, red on Tuesday, etc.)
In this temple, the deities (murtis) wear two outfits each day – one for the day and one at night.

Many Hindus live in villages, where the mode of worship is quite different from that in the sophisticated temples we find in Indian towns, or outside of India. Worship takes place outside, often without an elaborate *murti* or an aesthetically decorated shrine. Worship may be at a particular tree (such as the Pippal), a group of stones or a symbol, such as a trident. In some places, the procedures are related to one of the major denominations but in others have little obvious connection. It is most often linked with Shaktism, and worship of various goddesses. Each village has a shrine to its own *gramyadevata* - guardian deity - whom the villagers approach for material benefits such as good crops and protection of children.

Most Hindu homes contain a shrine, often simplified versions of those found in temples. Usually the large temple deities will be replaced with smaller *murtis*, or with framed pictures.

***Above:** a simple village shrine.*

The Temple Priests

Key points:

- The temple priest is called the *pujari* ('one who performs puja')
- They are often called or named *purohit*
- They are often addressed as pandit (or pandit-ji), out of respect for their learning
- They are usually brahmins (by birth and/or qualities)
- Priests are expected to follow strict rules regarding inner and outer purity in order to retain the sanctity of the temple
- Most are men but some groups accept women as priests

Each temple will have its priest or even a whole team. They often come from the brahmin community. As well as performing the regular worship, (puja, the arti ceremony, etc.) they may conduct special ceremonies such as various rites of passage, both in the temple and at people's homes. Traditionally only men are allowed into the priesthood, though certain movements such as ISKCON also welcome women.

Within the UK trained priests were originally brought in from India, but certain organisations and *sampradayas* now train their priests locally. They are expected to follow certain rules and regulations such as following a vegetarian diet, and abstaining from intoxication and gambling. Traditionally many priests were learned and hence called 'pandit.' They were expected to be knowledgeable in scripture and Sanskrit.

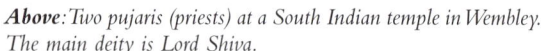

Above: Two pujaris (priests) at a South Indian temple in Wembley. The main deity is Lord Shiva.

Above left: Some traditions allow women to enter the priesthood. Here an Indian lady at Bhaktivedanta Manor temple performs ritual bathing.

Right: Most priests are brahmins, whose other main function is education. Brahmins are often called pandit, meaning 'learned scholar'. Here a western-born brahmin tells the story of Rama & Sita to schoolchildren.

Worship in the Home

Hinduism is notable for its emphasis on home worship. Most Hindus have a shrine at home. For some this will be a few pictures on a shelf in the living room or kitchen. Others, particularly the more wealthy, will dedicate a whole room to worship and meditation.

The shrine will contain images of the family's chosen deity, either as a framed picture or in the form of a *murti*. Worship is often a scaled-down version of the elaborate *puja* performed in the *mandir* and performed by the ladies of the household, early in the mornings. Children may also be taught their tradition by actively involving them in such worship.

In some homes, all food is offered to the deities before eating. In order to keep the home pure and sanctified, Hindu people usually do not wear shoes inside. Some will also avoid other habits they consider unclean, such as smoking and drinking, eating meat and having dogs and cats inside the house. Most Hindus consider it essential to bathe at least once a day, especially before worship.

Above: a typical family shrine. The standards of worship are not usually as strict as in the temple. The sacred images are bathed and dressed each Sunday, whereas in most mandirs such worship is performed every morning.

Left: This family in North London conducts arti twice a day, morning and evening. They usually visit their local temple on weekends and for major festival days.

Below left: A young Hindi girl offers incense at the family shrine. Children assimilate many religious and social values within the home.

Quote

At home, all our food is offered to God. My Mum puts a little of each dish into stainless steel bowls on a tray. Then she puts it on the shrine and says some prayers while ringing the bell. Afterwards we all say a prayer before eating.

(Subhadra, aged 11)

Glossary terms

Kula-deva – *the traditional family deity*
Ishta-deva – *the specific deity a person chooses to worship*

Chapter 4
Festivals

Above: *Janmashtami celebrations at a temple in the UK.*
Below: *The Ratha-yatra, originally from Puri, and now celebrated annually in London and in other cities throughout the world.*

Hinduism almost certainly has a longer list of festivals than any other religious tradition, and there are considerable regional and denominational variations. Twelve of the more popular and widely celebrated events are listed on the next page.

Purposes of Festivals

Festivals are generally times for celebration and remembrance. Other purposes are:

- To create a special atmosphere, diverting the mind from worldly concerns and joyfully focusing on spiritual matters.
- To invoke the soul's natural qualities by creating an environment replete with auspiciousness and the abundant gifts of nature.
- To give people spiritual impetus and inspiration, which helps them perform their daily duties.
- To dovetail the natural tendency for celebration with spiritual goals.
- To forge a healthy sense of belonging by peacefully bringing together individuals, families and communities.

Main Practices during Festivals

- Fasting and feasting.
- Distribution of food (especially prasad).
- Giving in charity (to temples, saints, the poor, etc).
- Visiting the temple.
- Visiting relatives.
- Glorification of God (*kirtan*, *bhajan*, story recitals, dance, drama).
- Manufacture and worship of temporary deities.
- Taking temple deities in procession *(see left)*.
- Wearing new clothes.
- Decorating houses, streets and temples with fruits, flowers, leaves and banana leaves.

Types of festivals

There are three main types of festivals:

1. Celebrating a significant event in the life of a deity
   e.g. Janmashtami is Krishna's birthday.
2. Celebrating a significant event in the life of a holy person
   e.g. the birthday of a particular guru.
3. Seasonal festivities or customs, e.g. spring festivals like Holi.

Festivals in the first category have become more universal and widely celebrated; the most important ones are Indian public holidays. Festivals in the third category are often exclusively regional, or regional variations of broader festivals e.g. Pongal in Tamil Nadu, which marks Makara Sankranti. Others, such as Holi, are celebrated internationally. Special days within the second category are often relevant only to a particular group (*sampradaya*) for whom the particular saint has significant relevance.

The following is a list of twelve main festivals. Of these, the seven in bold are perhaps most important to Hindus in the UK. We have also listed the corresponding deities and any related stories.

Twelve Important Festivals

Name	Time of Year	Relevant Deity	Related Stories
1. Sarasvati Puja	January	Sarasvati	Saraswati curses Brahma
2. Maha Shiva Ratri	Feb/March	Shiva	Stories of Shiva
3. Holi	March	Vishnu (Narasimha)	Prahlad & Narasimha (& Holika)
4. Rama Navami	Mar/April	Rama	Ramayana, especially Rama's birth
5. Hanuman Jayanti	April	Hanuman	Ramayana, especially later episodes
6. Ratha Yatra	June/July	Jagannatha	The proud merchant
7. Raksha Bandhana	August	none specifically	Indra wears a rakhi
8. Janmashtami	Aug/Sept	Krishna	Krishna's birth and childhood
9. Ganesh Chaturthi	Aug/Sept	Ganesh	How Ganesh received his head
10. Navaratri/Durga Puja	Sept/Oct	Shakti, Parvati	Durga kills Mahisha, and others
11. Dussehra	October	Rama	Ramayana
12. Diwali	Oct/Nov	Lakshmi/Rama	Stories of Lakshmi/Ramayana

Note: Diwali usually spans five days and for many Hindus is the New Year. It includes a number of festivals, which some consider special days in their own right. These include (1) Govardhana Puja (worship of the sacred hill lifted by Krishna), (2) Annakuta (the offering of grains), (3) Go-puja (worship of the cow), and (4) Bratra-Dvitiya (sister's day).

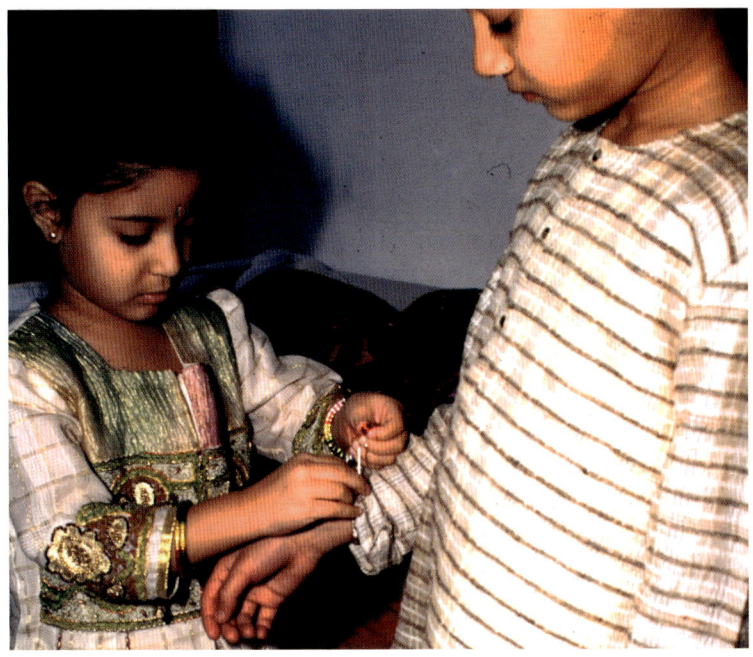

Scriptural Quote

"Utsava means 'pleasure.' Whenever some function takes place to express happiness, it is called utsava. Utsava, the expression of complete happiness, is always present in the Vaikunthalokas, the abode of the Lord."

Bhagavat Purana

Quotes

"My favourite festival is Janmashtami, because there are pizza tents with chips and because it's Lord Krishna's birthday."
Sachin Kumar (aged 11)

"I like Navaratri the best because of all the dancing. My second favourite is Raksha Bandhan, when I tie a rakhi on my brother's wrist."

Dipika Patel

The Year

The Hindu calendar is based on lunar months corresponding to the phases of the moon. In one year there are twelve months of 29.5 days, accounting for a total of 354 days. The shortfall means that the date of each festival moves back 11 days each year. To rectify this, an extra leap month is added about once every three years. The Hindu calendar is therefore luni-solar, with a precise month and an approximate year.

The year - starting with Makara Sankranti, the sun's entrance into Capricorn - is divided into two halves and six seasons. There are various ways of reckoning the New Year; most common is the day after the new moon in the month of Chaitra or, in Gujarat, the day after the Diwali new moon. Various eras are used for numbering the years; the most common are the Vikrami Era, beginning with the coronation of King Vikram aditya in 57BCE and the Shaka Era, counting from 78 CE. In rituals the priest often announces the dates according to Kali Yuga, *(see page 32)*. For these three systems, the year 2000 corresponds to 2057, 1922 and 5102 respectively, though the last figure is subject to some debate.

The Month

Within each month, there are two 'fortnights', each consisting of 15 'lunar days.' Although the solar and lunar days technically begin at different times, each solar day is ascribed one particular lunar day numbered from one to fifteen, either of the bright fortnight (waxing moon) or the dark fortnight (waning moon). Months average out to 29.5 days, so occasionally a day will be dropped. For example, in one month, the fourth day of the waxing moon may be followed by the sixth.

There are two main calendars. In North India, the month generally begins with the full moon, in South India with the new moon. Festival days will still fall on the same day, or very closely, but the name of the month may be different. For example, Krishna's Birthday falls on the 8th day of the dark moon; in the North this is in the month of Bhadra; in the South in Shravana. *(the months are shown on the diagram, next page)*

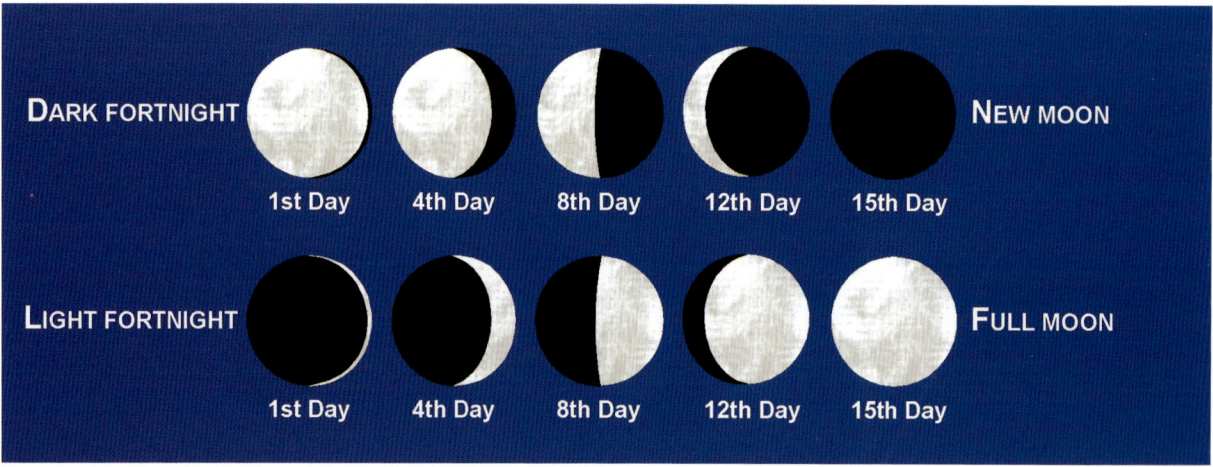

The Week

The week is divided into seven days, each corresponding to one of seven planets, exactly as in the West. No day is particularly special but each is related to a specific deity. For example, Monday is often associated with Shiva and Tuesday with Hanuman. Hindus may perform fasts and recite prayers to supplicate a particular deity on the corresponding day of the week.

The Day

The day usually begins at dawn, or just before, according to which astronomical and astrological systems are used. The day is divided into 15 muhurtas, each of about 48 minutes, and the night is similarly divided. Traditionally brahmins chant the Gayatri mantra at sunrise, noon and sunset because these are considered particularly important times of the day. The first two muhurtas (about 1 hour) of the morning before dawn are considered most auspicious, especially for spiritual practices.

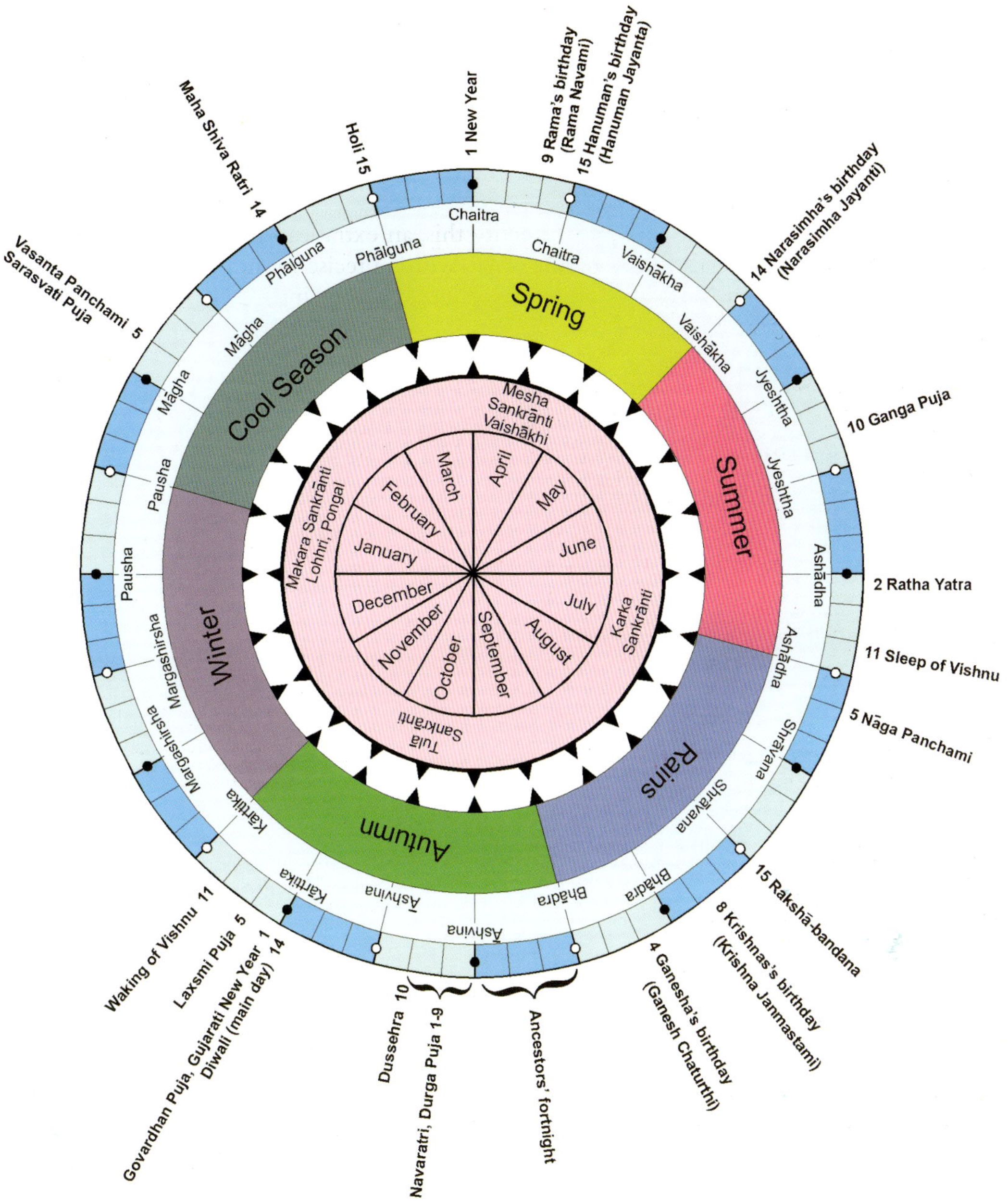

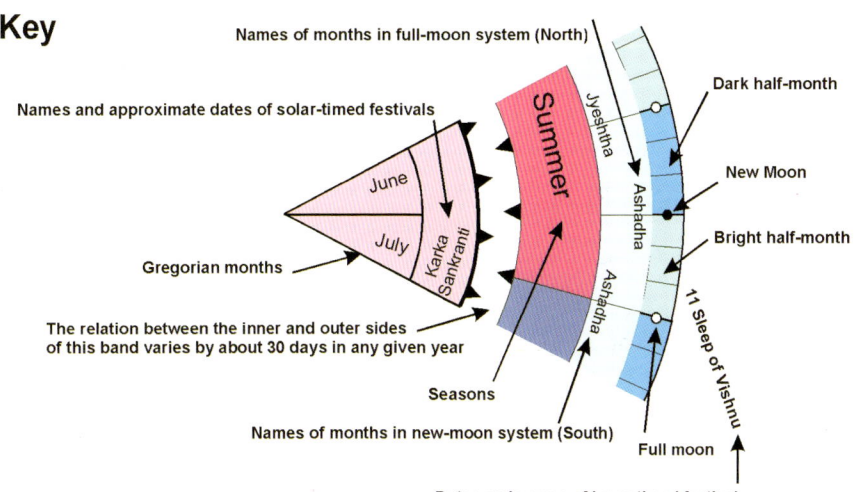

The diagram shows the Hindu year, with months and corresponding festivals, arranged as concentric circular bands:

- Maha Shiva Ratri 14
- Holi 15
- 1 New Year
- 9 Rama's birthday (Rama Navami)
- 15 Hanuman's birthday (Hanuman Jayanta)
- 14 Narasimha's birthday (Narasimha Jayanti)
- Vasanta Panchami 5 Sarasvati Puja
- 10 Ganga Puja
- 2 Ratha Yatra
- 11 Sleep of Vishnu
- 5 Nāga Panchami
- 15 Rakshā-bandana
- 8 Krishnas's birthday (Krishna Janmastami)
- 4 Ganesha's birthday (Ganesh Chaturthi)
- Ancestors' fortnight
- Navaratri, Durga Puja 1-9
- Dussehra 10
- Govardhan Puja, Gujarati New Year 1 Diwali (main day) 14
- Laxsmi Puja 5
- Waking of Vishnu 11

Months (outer ring): Chaitra, Vaishākha, Jyeshtha, Ashādha, Shrāvana, Bhādra, Āshvina, Kārttika, Margashirsha, Pausha, Māgha, Phālguna

Seasons: Spring, Summer, Rains, Autumn, Winter, Cool Season

Inner Sankrānti labels: Mesha Sankrānti Vaishākhi, Karka Sankrānti, Tulā Sankrānti, Makara Sankrānti Lohri, Pongal

Gregorian months (innermost): January, February, March, April, May, June, July, August, September, October, November, December

Key

- Names of months in full-moon system (North)
- Names and approximate dates of solar-timed festivals
- Gregorian months
- The relation between the inner and outer sides of this band varies by about 30 days in any given year
- Dark half-month
- New Moon
- Bright half-month
- Seasons
- Names of months in new-moon system (South)
- Full moon
- Dates and names of lunar-timed festivals

Above: The diagram shows the Hindu year, with months and the corresponding festivals. It is somewhat approximate, as the exact dates change yearly relative to the Gregorian calendar – with a month between the earliest and latest possible dates. A few festivals are determined by the sun alone, and their Gregorian dates are the same (or within one day) each year.

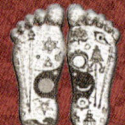

Pilgrimage

The estimated 80 million people visiting the 2001 Kumbha mela at Prayag made it the world's biggest-ever public event. It demonstrated the continuing importance of pilgrimage for the Hindu people. Not all holy sites, however, lie within India. Many Hindus have emigrated and have established their own sacred places, wherever they live. Nonetheless, India remains a special place and Hindus often combine pilgrimage with visits to relatives.

There are many reasons for pilgrimage. It is very popular because it enables people to link their natural desire for travel with spiritual goals.

Reasons for Pilgrimage

1. To remember special people (saints).
2. To fix the mind on God and to glorify Him.
3. For spiritual development and to gain spiritual merit.
4. For purification and atonement of sins.
5. For meeting and taking guidance from holy people.
6. To perform specific religious rites.
7. For self-reflection and contemplation.
8. For an uplifting and memorable experience (spiritual inspiration).

Scriptural Passages

"One who thinks the body to be the self, and the land of his birth worshipable, who desires an everlasting relationship with wife, relatives, etc., and who goes on pilgrimage simply to take bath, is no better than an ass or a cow (i.e isn't making proper use of the human form of life)."

Bhagavat Purana

Activities Performed on Pilgrimage

1. Taking *darshan* of specific deities (or saints).
2. Participating in worship and glorification (e.g. *kirtan*).
3. Charity, especially to priests and temples.
4. Austerities and penance (such as shaving the head, and following certain vows such as celibacy).
5. Listening to talks and receiving advice on spiritual life.
6. Specific rites (such as the *shraddha* ceremony in Gaya).
7. Circumambulation of holy places (shrines, towns etc.).

Is India Special?

Although Hindus have a natural affection for their home country, attempts to combine patriotism with religious sentiment are a relatively new phenomenon. These have given birth to various forms of Hindu nationalism.

For many, India is special purely for spiritual reasons. Its climate and atmosphere are considered especially conducive to spiritual life, and it is the land where many avatars and Hindu saints appeared. India is traditionally called 'Bharata' after a powerful king, renowned for his spiritual qualities.

Varanasi

Perhaps the most famous of all holy places is Varanasi, situated on the banks of the Ganga some 450 miles south of Delhi. It is also called Benares and Kashi. It may be one of the oldest cities in the world and is included in the list of India's 'seven ancient cities'. It is mentioned in the Epics and Puranas as 'the foremost city of Shiva'. Its most famous *mandir*, the Golden Temple dedicated to Visvanatha (Shiva), was destroyed and then rebuilt under Muslim rule.

Many Hindus retire to Varanasi in the hope of achieving liberation. The city is famous for its cremation *ghats*. Corpses are transported hundreds of miles for burning here. Relatives often bring the ashes of their loved ones and scatter them in the Ganges in the belief that this will benefit the departed soul.

Mathura and Vrindavana

Mathura, another ancient city of India, lies 95 miles south of Delhi. It is most famous as the place of Krishna's birth, which tradition dates to some five thousand years ago. Its main temple is the Keshava Deo Mandir, where Radha and Krishna are worshipped. The entire area, encompassing many holy sites and twelve sacred forests, is called Vraj. Most important is Vrindavan, the village where Krishna lived. It is now a bustling town with some five thousand temples, mostly dedicated to Krishna. Many elderly Vaishnavas retire to this sacred town in the hope of returning at death to the spiritual Vrindavan, where they can engage in eternal *lila* (pastimes) with their Lord.

Kanyakumari

Kanyakumari, one of the most important Shakta holy sites, is situated on the southernmost tip of India. The main temple is dedicated to Parvati, the eternal consort of Shiva. At the Bay of Bengal, where the Arabian and Indian oceans meet, many pilgrims come to bathe. On the beach there are seven different colours of sand, apparently transformed from the seven colours of rice thrown in celebration when the Goddess married Lord Shiva at this spot.

Puri

The Smartas are the fourth largest Hindu tradition, after the worshippers of Vishnu, Shiva and Shakti respectively. Most members of this community follow Shankaracharya (788-820 CE), who established four main 'maths' (seats) in the 'four *dhamas*', the four holiest places in India. The current Shankaracharya resides in the main seat at Puri, in the state of Orissa on the East Coast. The city is also central to Vaishnavas for its 900-year-old temple of Jagannatha, the Lord of the Universe, who is served by 6,000 priests. It is also famous for the annual Ratha-yatra (chariot festival), attended by thousands of pilgrims. Replica Ratha-yatras are also celebrated annually throughout the world.

Above top: *The Ganga at Varanasi, the city closely connected to Lord Shiva.*
Immediately above: *The town of Vrindavan particularly dear to the Gaudiya (Bengali) Vaishnavas who worship Radha and Krishna. This is one of their seven principal and historical temples.*

Special Places

- *Rivers (especially confluences) and lakes*
- *Hills and mountains*
- *Sites associated with particular deities (often with shrines and murtis there)*
- *Places connected with gurus, saints, and other religious leaders.*
- *Towns and villages mentioned in mythology*
- *Places considered to be replicas of, or gateways to, the higher realms*
- *Places where holy people congregate*

Holy Places

The 7 Ancient Holy Towns:
- *Ayodhya*
- *Mathura*
- *Haridwar*
- *Varanasi*
- *Kanchipuram*
- *Dvaraka*
- *Ujjain*

The 4 Holy Dhamas:
- *Puri (East)*
- *Rameshvaram (South)*
- *Dvaraka (West)*
- *Badrinatha (North)*

The 4 Maha Kumbha Mela Sites:
- *Prayaga (Allahabad)*
- *Haridwar*
- *Ujjain*
- *Nasik*

In India there are thousands of *tirthas* (places of pilgrimage) visited by millions of people every year. Each is somehow special, often associated with a particular deity or saint, and offering its own particular boon or blessing.

The most famous *tirtha* is Varanasi, also called Benares or Kashi. It is one of seven ancient holy towns (*see left*). There are four great *dhamas* (holy places) which correspond to the four points of the compass and near which the great teacher Shankara *(see page 138)* established his four main centres. Another key city is Allahabad, established on the site of the ancient city of Prayaga but renamed as 'The City of Allah.' It is the one of the four main sites for the twelve-yearly Kumbha Mela. The others are Haridwar, Ujjain and Nasik *(as shown to the left)*.

Personal Reflection
- What is it that makes a place sacred? What experiences do you have of sacred places (if any)? Are there tangible differences between a holy site and other places, or are they simply imaginary?

The table below lists the holy sites for the four main denominations:

Vaishnavas	Shaivites	Shaktas	Smartas
Mathura – Vrindavana	Varanasi	Kanyakumari	Puri
Dvaraka	Kedarnatha	Madurai	Rameshvaram
Badrinatha	Somnath	Vaishno Devi	Dvaraka
Puri (Jagannatha Puri)	Rameshvaram	Calcutta (Kali Temple)	Badrinatha
Tirupati	Chidambaram		
Ayodhya	Note: for more holy places dedicated to Vishnu or Shiva, see pages 134-135	Note: there are 51 principle Shakti sites throughout India	Note: these correspond to the four dhamas (most holy sites in India)
Nathdwar			
Udupi			

Glossary Terms

Tirtha - *literally means 'ford' and refers to places where one can cross from the material world to the spiritual. Many sacred places are considered gateways to the higher realms and to a higher consciousness. Some are thought to be replicas of places within the spiritual realm.*

The map below shows all the major holy places mentioned and also the main sacred rivers and mountains (*see over page*). Further details of most of these sites can be found in this chapter.

PAKISTAN

Indus River

Amarnath

Vaishno Devi

Amritsar

Badrinatha

Kurukshetra **Haridwar**

NEPAL

Delhi

Ganga River

Mathura & Vrindavan

Ayodhya

Yamuna River

Prayag

BANGLADESH

Varanasi

Nathdwar

INDIA

Saraswati River

Ujjain

Narmada River

Calcutta

Dwaraka

Somnath

Godavari River

Puri

Nasik

Mumbai (Bombay)

Arabian Sea

Bay of Bengal

Tirupati

Udupi

Chennai (Madras)

Kaveri River

Chidambaram

Madurai

Rameshvaram

Kanyakumari

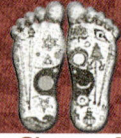
Holy Rivers, Lakes and Oceans

The Seven Holy Rivers

1. **Ganga** – *North India*
2. **Yamuna** – *meets Ganga in North*
3. **Godavari** – *South India*
4. **Sarasvati** – *underground river*
5. **Narmada** – *Central India*
6. **Sindhu** – *the Indus, now in Pakistan*
7. **Kaveri** – *South India*

Water is of special significance in Hinduism, not only for its life-sustaining properties, but also because of its use in rituals and because of the stress given to cleanliness. Bathing also has religious significance, especially in rivers considered sacred. Mother Ganga (the Ganges) is considered to purify the bather of sins *(papa – see page 12).*

There are seven principle holy rivers, although others, such as the Krishna in South India, are also important. Of the seven, the Ganga, Yamuna and Sarasvati are most important. According to different opinions, the Sarasvati is now invisible, extinct or running underground, and meets with the Ganga and Yamuna at Prayaga.

Most rivers are considered female and are personified as goddesses. Ganga, who features in the Mahabharata, is usually shown riding on a crocodile *(see left)*. Yamuna is shown in much iconography connected with the Pushti Marg sampradaya, and rides on a turtle. The famous story of the descent of Ganga devi is connected with Vishnu and with Shiva, who is depicted with the Ganges entering the locks of his hair.

Certain spots on the seashore are also holy. Puri is considered sanctified to Vaishnavas, and Cape Commorin (Kanyakumari) is sacred to followers of Shiva and devotees of Rama.

Some lakes and ponds are also considered especially sacred. Particularly in the South, tanks (man-made ponds) are constructed so that worshippers can bathe before entering the temple.

Above top: *The Goddess Ganga, riding her crocodile. She plays an important role at the beginning of the Mahabharata.*
Immediately above: *Bathers in the Ganga, which is considered to wash away accumulated sins.*
Above right: *Near Vrindavan, Radha-Kunda (the pond of Radha) is considered especially sacred.*

Related Stories

"The Descent of Mother Ganga" (STO-501)
        -*How Ganga came to earth.*

"Krishna Defeats the Kaliya Serpent" (STO-502)
        -*Krishna's dance in the middle of the Yamuna.*

Hills and mountains have special significance within Hinduism. Most important are the Himalayas, the vast range in North India to which countless ascetics have retired for a life of seclusion and austerity. Shiva is considered to reside on Mount Kailash and his spouse's name, Parvati, means "daughter of the Himalayas." Within the Himalayan range and its foothills are many places of pilgrimage such as Haridwar, Hrishikesh, Badrinatha and Kedarnath.

The Vindhya Mountains separate the North from the Deccan (South) and are mentioned repeatedly in the Epics and the Puranas. Another popular pilgrimage site is the cave of Vaishno Devi, north of Amritsar. Pilgrims climb many steps up to the cave, which is dedicated to three goddesses – Lakshmi, Kali and Sarasvati. It is the only temple in India where all three are worshipped together. Also famous, in the South, is Vyenkata Hill, whose 2,800-foot peak is crowned with the Tirupati temple (*see page 60*).

Perhaps India's most famous hill is Govardhana, which was raised by Lord Krishna to protect the inhabitants of Vrindavana from the wrath of Indra. The God of Rain was infuriated when child Krishna persuaded his father, head of the village, to stop the Indra-sacrifice and worship the hill instead. Indra sent torrents of rain but Krishna picked up the hill, and, holding it on the tip of the little finger of his left hand, used it as a giant umbrella. Govardhana Puja is still a popular festival and the story is central for the followers of Pushti-marg, who call Krishna "Nathji."

Related Stories

"The Lifting of Govardhana Hill" (STO-503)
"The Story of Vaishno-Devi" (STO-504)

Above, top: In a temple in Wembley, a murti of Shiva meditating in the Himalayas. These mountains are the home of numerous ascetics, many of whom consider Shiva their worshipful deity. Lord Shiva is called maha-yogi – the greatest yogi

Above: Govardhana hill as it looks today. Legend holds that it is slowly sinking into the ground by the width of a mustard seed each year. Pilgrims come annually to circumambulate the entire hill, covering a distance of some 14 miles.

Left: A traditional painting of Krishna, known as Nathji (in the centre). With the little finger of his left hand, Krishna held up Govardhana hill for seven days, whilst all the residents of Vrindavana sheltered from the torrential rain sent by Indra. In this painting, Nathji is worshipped by Vallabha (left), founder of the Pushti-marg tradition, and Yamuna (right), goddess of the sacred river that runs through Vrindavana.

Chapter 6
Rites of Passage

Hindu rites of passage are not mere formalities or social observances, but serve to purify the soul at critical junctions in life's journey. The word 'samskara' means 'mental impression', for the ceremonies help create a favourable mentality for stepping positively from one phase of life into the next. The *samskaras* are considered essential for the three higher (twice-born) *varnas*, and neglect of any ritual might render a member 'fallen' from his status. Significantly, the first *samskara*, called "purification of the womb", begins prior to conception. It aims at sanctifying the consciousness of both husband and wife before they try to beget a child. Scripture explains that the type of soul that enters the womb is largely determined by the mental states of both husband and wife, a notion graphically illustrated in the Mahabharata. If "members of the twice born" neglected this ceremony, and acted on sex impulse alone, then the child conceived might not develop the attributes to become a qualified member of a higher *varna*. Such offspring would then be called *dvija-bandhu*, "friends of the twice-born". This practice implies that the system of four *varnas* was not hereditary, but based on individual merit. The rites of passage were considered essential for preserving the purity of the individual and of the social system.

Although some traditions mention ten rites of passage, or up to sixteen – or occasionally even more – only four are currently popular, namely:

1. *Jatakarma* – birth ceremonies (plus others in childhood).

2. *Upanayana* – initiation (the sacred-thread ceremony).

3. *Vivaha* – marriage.

4. *Antyeshti* – funeral and rites for the dead.

These are discussed on the forthcoming pages.

Related Concepts
- The soul (atman).
- Reincarnation (life as one stage of an ongoing journey).

Related Values/Issues
- Life in the womb/abortion.
- Designer babies/cloning etc.

Personal Reflection
- What is the meaning of rites of passage in your own tradition or other faiths? How does Hinduism compare? What are the similarities and differences?

Above: Almost all rites of passage involve a havan ceremony. Here a bride and bridegroom throw grains into the sacrificial fire

Meaning and Purpose
The purpose of life's journey

Birth Ceremonies (Jatakarma)

The *jatakarma* ceremony welcomes the baby into the world. The father places a small amount of ghee and honey on the baby's tongue and whispers the name of God in his ear. On about the eleventh day after birth the parents celebrate the name-giving ceremony (*namakarana*) by dressing the baby in new clothes. The family astrologer announces the child's horoscope *(see page 101)*. Traditionally the child's name is chosen according to the position of the moon in the birth chart. Songs and sometimes a *havan* (fire sacrifice) accompany these rites, followed by the obligatory feast.

After these two ceremonies, various others follow, including:

1. *the first outing* (normally at around two weeks) the child takes darshan of the sun, then the temple deity and in the evening sees the moon.

2. *the first grains* (when teething begins).

3. *the first haircut* (called *mundan* – between 1 and 3 years).

4. *piercing the ear lobes* (normally 3-5 years).

Above right: Birth ceremonies go back at least to the time of Lord Krishna, which tradition dates to 5,000 years ago.

Right: A priest shaves the head of a young boy while his parents look on. The wood and utensils, visible in the foreground, are for a small havan (sacred fire ceremony). The ceremony is concluded with presenting a contribution to the priest and a vegetarian feast for relatives and other guests.

Related Value and Issues

■ Personality - inherent from birth or moulded entirely by our environment?

Personal Reflection

■ What is our perception of new-born babies? First time here? How might a Hindu perspective be different?

■ We of often talk about 'life after death', but what about 'life before birth'?

Meaning and Purpose

Why are we not born with equal opportunities?

Initiation - The Sacred Thread Ceremony

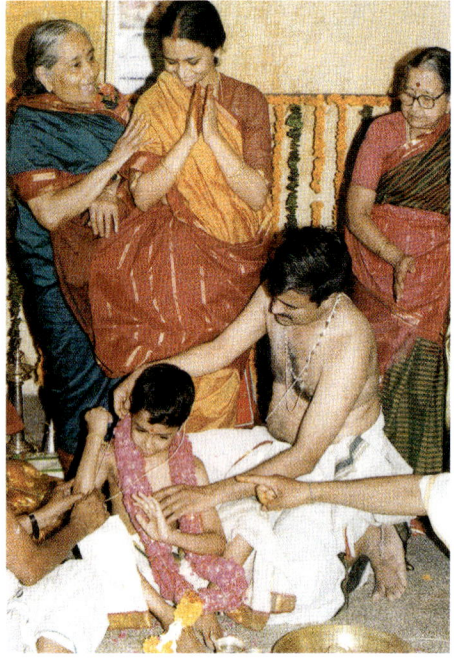

Above: A recent upanayana ceremony in the UK. The brahmachari ashram is not generally given as much importance these days, and more emphasis is given to secular education. Often the father himself performs the ceremony.

Below: The upanayana ceremony is very old, dating back to at least the time of Krishna. This painting shows Krishna and his brother Balarama at gurukula (the school of their spiritual teacher).

Glossary Terms

Dvija – *means "twice born", referring to full members of the three upper varnas. It also refers to birds and teeth.*

Jenoi – *a modern word for the sacred thread (it rhymes with 'annoy').*

This ceremony is essential to the members of the three higher classes and marks a boy's official acceptance into his *varna*. At this point he becomes 'twice-born'. Everyone has a first, biological birth, but when a young man seeks his spiritual identity he symbolically accepts a spiritual teacher as father and the Vedas as mother. He may also receive a new, spiritual name. At the ceremony, he receives the *jenoi* (sacred-thread), usually worn for his entire lifetime. It is replaced at intervals, but never removed until the new one has been put on. There is a separate *samskara* marking the beginning of education, but today the two ceremonies are often combined.

Upanayana means "sitting close by," referring to the boy's taking shelter of the guru (spiritual teacher). Traditionally, he would move away from home to the teacher's ashram, called 'gurukula'. Even members of the royal family were trained to live simply without luxury or sense-gratification, in order to keep their minds pure and unspoiled. When later married, they would remain attached to the spiritual values they imbibed during their school days. The emphasis at Gurukula was on the study of the Vedas and development of character.

The Ceremony

The ceremony itself involves shaving the head, bathing and wearing new clothes. The boy may also beg alms from his mother and from other relatives. There is a havan and the investiture of the sacred thread, which hangs over his left shoulder. The boy will then hear the Gayatri mantra from his priest or guru, who may give him a spiritual name to signify his "second birth" Thereafter, wrapping the thread round the thumb of his right hand, he will chant this prayer thrice daily, at dawn, noon and dusk. The boy takes vows to study the Vedas, serve his teachers and follow certain vows, including celibacy. He often concludes the ceremony by offering the traditional *dakshina* (gift) to his teacher.

Related Values/Issues

- The purposes of education
- Delaying gratification (austerity)
- Celibacy

Initiation for Girls

Traditionally this ceremony was open only to boys. With changing attitudes, some groups now initiate girls, although girls usually do not receive the sacred thread.

Marriage (*Vivaha*)

V ivaha (marriage) is perhaps the most important *samskara*. Traditionally it was the only rite performed for women, and for men in the fourth *varna* (*shudras*). A couple would stay together for life or until the husband took to the path of renunciation. Divorce was not allowed, and those who left their partners were often ostracised from society. Matches were usually arranged by the elders and based on astrological principles. Despite modern attitudes towards this practice, evidence suggests that these marriages worked relatively well.

Marriage was usually between members of the same *varna*, and the same *jati* (occupational sub-group). Scripture approved of a woman accepting a partner from a higher *varna* but the opposite was shunned. Men in some *varnas* could accept more than one wife provided they could adequately maintain them. Almost all marriages today are monogamous. Until more recent times, women were often married very early, to protect their chastity and because women were considered to mature much quicker than young men. So-called child marriage was often akin to a system of betrothal and marriage was only consummated when the bride reached adulthood. The giving of a dowry, as a symbol of the father's affection towards his daughter, is an ancient practice, apparently going back at least to the time of Lord Krishna. At that time, the wealth remained the bride's personal property. Because of more recent wide abuse, the Indian government declared the dowry system illegal in 1961.

Scripture lists eight types of marriage and current rituals fall within the 'Brahma' category. The ancient, elaborate and often lengthy ceremony is usually performed by brahmin priests. There is much regional and denominational variation, but certain features are common. These include:

1. **Welcoming the bridegroom.**
2. **Exchanging flower garlands.**
3. **The daughter being given in marriage.**
4. **Sacred fire ceremony.**
5. **Holding of hands.**
6. **Circumambulation of the sacred fire.**
7. **Marking the bride's hair-parting with kum-kum.**
8. **Taking seven steps together.**
9. **Tying the knot (the garments of bride and groom).**
10. **Viewing the Pole Star.**
11. **Receiving the elders' blessings.**
12. **Exchanging presents.**

Related Values/Issues

- Commitment.
- The purpose of marriage.
- Arranged marriage.
- Divorce and re-marriage.

Above: The bride & bridegroom, symbolically tied together, circumambulate the fire. Most ceremonies these days last two or three hours and are followed by a reception and wedding feast.
Below: A traditional painting of Shiva and Parvati, whose wedding ceremony was performed by Brahma.

Scriptural Passages

"As a person puts on new garments, giving up old ones, the soul similarly accepts new material bodies, giving up the old and useless ones."

Bhagavad Gita 2.22

***Below, top**: the coffin leaves for the crematorium during a funeral ceremony in Wembley.*
***Below, bottom**: in South India, an annual shraddha ceremony, in which pinda (rice balls) are offered to God and to the departed soul.*

After marriage, most Hindus spend the rest of their lives as householders. After children have left home, there is generally a period of gradual retirement from active life and an increased dedication to spiritual practice. This corresponds to the third stage of life (*vanaprastha*), which these days is rarely adopted formally and certainly followed less rigorously. A few men still take *sannyasa* and, leaving home, prepare for inevitable death. In one sense, the whole of life, with its various stages and *samskaras*, is a preparation for death and beyond.

The funeral rites are almost universally performed and follow similar patterns. Most Hindus cremate their dead. The exceptions are small children and saints, whose bodies are considered pure, and are therefore buried. The rationale is that burning enables the departed soul to abandon attachment for its previous body and move swiftly forward to the next chapter of life. Funeral ceremonies should therefore be performed as soon as possible – by dusk or by dawn, whichever occurs first. Therefore, in India a funeral takes place within hours of death. Regulations elsewhere mean that it may take much longer.

The Ceremony

The body is washed by relatives, dressed in fresh cloth, and bedecked with flowers. A few drops of Ganges water are placed in the mouth. The corpse is then carried on a stretcher to the cremation grounds accompanied by kirtan, chanting mantras such as "Ram Nam Satya Hai" (the name of Rama is truth). The eldest son lights the funeral pyre. For renunciates, it is considered important that the skull is cracked, and this is sometimes part of the ritual, apparently urging the departed soul to move on. Towards the end of the ceremony a priest or relative recites appropriate verses from scripture.

Usually three days later, the eldest son will collect the ashes and place them in the Ganges, or another sacred river. In the UK, relatives may travel to India for this purpose, though some are now using the Thames.

There is also a period of mourning, extending to about thirteen days after the funeral (varying according to *varna* and other considerations). During this time, the family is considered impure. They will not attend religious functions nor eat certain foods (e.g. sweets). It is a period for giving vent to one's grief, so that one can live unhindered by unreleased emotions. Significantly, though, these rites are more for the benefit of the deceased than for the bereaved. They are essential to ensure the smooth passage of the soul to a better level of existence. Most essential is the *shraddha* ceremony performed on the first anniversary of death. *Prasad*, often balls of cooked rice, are offered to God and in turn to the departed soul.

Dharma is roughly translated as 'religious duty'. There are two principle dharmas, namely *Sanatana-dharma* and *Varnashrama-dharma*. There are also general moral codes called Sadharana--dharma *(for more details, see pages 24-27).*

Sanatana-dharma refers to the soul's never-ending propensity to serve God. The concept of *Sanatana-dharma* underpins the Hindus' more inclusive approach towards life and "other religions" It is the basis for issues of equality, and tends to relate to overtly spiritual matters (e.g. worship).

Varnashrama-dharma defines duties for the individual, classified according to four divisions of labour and four stages in life. These specific duties change, for example as one passes through the different ashrams. *Varnashrama-dharma* is the basis for accommodating diversity, and attributing different social and spiritual standards to various sections of society. Although *Varnashrama-dharma* relates largely to social matters, it is not divorced from *Sanatana-dharma* but is a means of recognising a common goal approached from different starting points. Some Hindu thinkers consider that the current, rigid caste system is a result of neglecting the principle of spiritual equality inherent in *Sanatana-dharma*.

Sadharana--dharma, general morality, is often defined according to prohibitions *(yama)* and recommended practices *(niyama)*. Hindu opinion varies as to the exact number of each.

In practical terms, dharma refers to leading a righteous life in harmony with natural laws as defined in scripture. In pre-modern, rural India, this was regulated through stable, sustainable lifestyles and traditional norms of behaviour. Today, with emigration and globalisation, it is far more difficult for Hindus to discern what practices are consistent with dharma. They find themselves facing situations and moral dilemmas not directly mentioned in scripture, and must re-evaluate what practical behaviour constitutes righteous living.
Significant emphasis is placed on personal responsibility. This contrasts with the current world trend towards individual rights. The Vedic (Hindu) view is that execution of one's duties automatically fulfills the rights of others, and that stressing dharma fosters a climate of social and spiritual responsibility. The Hindus acknowledgement of interdependence thus differs from the individualistic, self-centred approach to life.

Related Values/Issues

- rights and responsibilities.
- the compensation culture.
- Who is to define what is right and what is wrong?

Above: *According to the notion of Sanatana-dharma, religion is not confined to a particular race or country. Here two white, British-born Hindus get married, thus entering the second stage of life according to the system of Varnashrama-dharma. This second ashram brings greater social and spiritual responsibilities.*

Quote

"Hinduism endorses the need for commensurate rights and responsibilities. However, it stresses responsibilities. If a person performs his or her duties, then another's rights are automatically fulfilled. However, the current trend towards demanding our rights is creating a culture of blame, compensation and irresponsibility. Placing the emphasis on dharma tends to promote responsibility. It's not wrong to demand legitimate rights, but without a culture of responsibility it creates problems. And it begins from the top, with the leaders. That is why many Hindu stories explain how leadership is based on character, not merely position."

Bimal Krishna

Related Stories

Many, especially fron the Epics and the Puranas. They include:

- *King Shibi* (STO-203)
- *Rantidevi* (STO-206)
- *Shravana Kumar* (STO-205)

The Four Varnas

Although every Hindu must follow general moral codes, each has individual duties according to his or her own nature. These are called *sva-dharma*, literally 'own duties.' They are regulated by the system of four *varnas* (social classes) and four ashrams (stages of life).

The ideal *Varnasrama* system is discussed here. (*For more information on actual practice and related issues of caste and untouchability, please see page 10*). Below we list the main duties of each of the four varnas:

Shudras (artisans and workers)

The *shudras* are the only section of society allowed to accept another's employment; other *varnas* are occupationally and financially self-sufficient.

■ To render service to others.
■ To take pride in their work and to be loyal.
■ To follow general moral principles, (e.g. not to steal).
■ To marry (the only compulsory rite of passage).

Vaishyas (farmers, merchants and business people)

The *vaishyas* are the productive class. They and the two *varnas* (*below*) are called twice-born, indicating that they accept the sacred thread (symbolising spiritual initiation) and must perform certain rituals and rites of passage.

■ To protect animals (especially cows), and the land.
■ To create wealth and prosperity.
■ To maintain workers with abundant food, clothes, etc.
■ To trade ethically.
■ To give taxes to the *kshatriyas* (ruling class).

Kshatriyas (warriors, police and administrators)

The *kshatriyas* are the nobility, the protectors of society. Though permitted a number of privileges, they are expected to display considerable strength of body and character.

■ To protect the citizens from harm, especially women, children, cows, brahmins and the elderly.
■ To ensure that the citizens perform their prescribed duties and advance spiritually.
■ To be the first into battle and never to flee the battlefield.
■ To be true to their royal word.
■ To never refuse a challenge.
■ To develop noble qualities such as power, chivalry and generosity.
■ To levy taxes (from the *vaishyas* only) and to never accept charity under any circumstances.
■ To take counsel, especially from the brahmanas.
■ To know the scriptures, especially the artha shastras.
■ To deal uncompromisingly with crime and lawlessness.
■ To take responsibility for shortcomings in their kingdom.
■ To conquer their own minds and senses and to enjoy only according to scriptural injunction.
■ To beget an heir.

Brahmins (priests, teachers and intellectuals)

The brahmins provide education and spiritual leadership. They determine the vision and values of any society. Traditionally their basic needs were fulfilled so that they could dedicate themselves to their spiritual tasks. They were expected to live very frugally.

- To study and teach the Vedas.
- To perform sacrifice and religious ceremonies, and teach others how to perform such rituals.
- To accept alms and also give in charity.
- To offer guidance, especially to the *kshatriyas*.
- To provide medical care and general advice free of charge.
- To know Brahman (spirit, the self, God).
- To never accept paid employment.
- To develop all ideal qualities, especially honesty, integrity, cleanliness, purity, austerity, knowledge and wisdom.

Related Stories

Many in the Epics. They usually relate to the warrior dharma, and also give insight into the characteristics of genuine brahmins. "Arjuna's Dilemma on the Battlefield" (STO-701).

Personal Reflection

- Is a classless society the only solution to social exploitation?
- Do these four *varnas* appear to apply to Hinduism only? As a teacher, do you need to develop particular values? How do they relate to the list given above?
- Do you agree that education is a leadership role, and should be given greater priority than administration? Why do you think that brahmins are not meant to accept a salary? What is the principle behind this?

Scriptural Passages

"It is better to perform one's prescribed duties, even though faulty, than another's duties. Destruction in the course of performing one's own duty is better than engaging in another's duties, for to follow another's path is dangerous."

Bhagavad Gita 3.35

"Brahmins, kshatriyas, vaishyas and shudra's are distinguished by the qualities born of their own nature in accordance with the three material qualities."

Bhagavad Gita 18-41

See also:
Bhagavad Gita 2.31-38, 4.13, 18.41-48

Common Misunderstandings

"The system of four varnas was a man-made structure based on one group exploiting others."

Hindu scholars contend that the original system was based on co-operation, mutual service to God, and commensurate rights and responsibilities. For example, although the warriors had great wealth and power, they were expected to be first into battle. The learned, brahmin class were given even greater respect but were required to have full control over mind and senses.

"Dharma is considered the ultimate say in moral issues".

This is true, but needs careful understanding. Dharma is to be applied with consideration (See Common Misunderstandings, page 39). The whole Mahabharata explores the nuances of dharma, and how difficult it can be to determine what is right action. When there is confusion, decisions are usually made in consultation with brahmins and other spiritual authorities

Related Values/Issues

- Duties, rights and responsibilities
- A classless society
- Moral dilemmas

ⓘ **For more information:**
Pages 26-27, 102-104

The Four Ashrams

Ashram means "a place of spiritual shelter". Each stage of life is not only a natural part of the journey from cradle to grave, but a time at which spirituality can be developed. The four *varnas*, starting with the *shudras*, traditionally accept 1, 2, 3 and 4 ashrams respectively, as depicted in the table below:

varna \ *ashrama*	1. Brahmacari celibate student life	2. Grihasta householder	3. Vanaprastha retirement to forest	4. Sannyasi renunciation
Shudra	no formal education	✔	no formal retirement	no formal sannyasa
Vaishya	✔	✔	no formal retirement	no formal sannyasa
Kshatriya	✔	✔	✔	no formal sannyasa
Brahmin	✔	✔	✔	✔

Today, only a few Hindus strictly follow all these four ashrams. Nonetheless, the idea of enjoying the world in a religious and regulated manner, followed by gradual retirement remains a powerful ideal.

Each of the four ashrams has its specific duties. The main ones are listed below.

1. Brahmachari (student life)

The *brahmacari* ashram, often away from the home (somewhat like a boarding school), was primarily intended for fostering spiritual values. Memorisation and skill development were subsidiary to character formation and self-realisation. Even sons of the royal family were expected to undergo this austere and rigorous training.

■ To be celibate and live a simple life, free from sense pleasure and material allurement.

■ To serve the guru (spiritual teacher) and collect alms for him.

■ To hear, study and assimilate the Vedas.

■ To develop all the appropriate qualities: humility, discipline, simplicity, purity of thought, cleanliness, soft-heartedness, and so on.

2. Grihasta (household life)

Traditionally some men remained lifelong celibates, either remaining as *brahmacharis* or immediately becoming *sannyasis*. Others were required to marry, extending their responsibilities to include wife, children, relatives and society in general. This ashram is the only one permitting sexual gratification.

■ To make money and to enjoy sensual pleasure according to ethical principles.

■ To perform sacrifice and observe religious rituals.

■ To protect and nourish family members (wife, children, and elders).

■ To teach children spiritual values.

■ To give in charity, and especially to feed holy people, the poor and animals.

Personal Reflection

- Do these stages resemble what happens in other societies? If so, what are the similarities? What are the differences?
- Are there any values which stand out for us, or with which we strongly agree or disagree? Why? How is our evaluation of these practices coloured by our own world view and our own culture and upbringing?

Meaning and Purpose

What does the system of four ashrams say about the purpose of life, according to Hindu thought?

Related Values/Issues

- family values / renunciation.
- the purpose of education.
- ageism.

3. Vanaprashta (retired life)

After the children have left home and settled, a man may gradually retire from family responsibilities and, with his wife, begin to focus his mind on spiritual matters. Often he goes on pilgrimage. His wife may accompany him, but all sexual relationships are forbidden. *Vanaprashta* literally means "forest-dweller".

- To generally devote more time to spiritual matters.
- To engage in austerity and penance.
- To go on pilgrimage.

4. Sannyasa (renounced life)

This position is traditionally available only to men who exhibit the qualities of a brahmin. The man would leave home and family and was prohibited from seeing his wife again. Considered civilly dead, he was free to wander, living a life dependent on God alone. The *sannyasis* are conspicuous in their saffron dress. They are often called *sadhus* (holy people) – although today not all are genuine!

- To fully control the mind and senses, and to fix the mind on the Supreme.
- To become detached and fearless, fully dependent on God as the only protector.
- To teach and preach the importance of self-realisation and God-consciousness, especially to the householders, who often become distracted from their spiritual duties.

ⓘ **For more information:**
Pages 26-27, 106-108

Women's Dharma

Above: Hindu women during the festival of Karva Chauth, during which they fast and pray for the well being of their husbands. Devotion to the husband is considered one of the traditional Hindu values, as exemplified in many stories.

Although women may be classified according to *varna*, they are also considered a section of society in their own right. They do not pass through the four stages available to men. Rather the Shashtra Manu Smriti talks of three stages for a woman:

1. As a child protected by her father
Traditionally, girls did not receive a formal academic education. A woman's role, considered essential in preserving social and cultural values, was learned in the home.

2. As a married lady, protected by her husband
Hinduism places great value on pre-marital chastity and this has significantly influenced practices. Girls were betrothed and married at a very young age. In married life, the wife's roles were centred on the home and she was not burdened with contributing towards the family income. Fulfilling one's responsibility as a loving and available parent was considered paramount.

3. As a widow, protected by the eldest son
If the husband died or took *sannyasa*, then the widow would be looked after by the eldest living son. Elder ladies were always treated with great respect.

According to tradition, women, more delicate than men, require and deserve protection. Hindu texts extol the virtues of womanhood and of the essential role women have in nurturing future generations. Though Hindus are themselves re-examining and restructuring the roles of women, there still remain powerful ideals, exemplified by ladies such as Sita, Gandhari, Draupadi, Mandodari and Savitri. Such idealism is often at odds with many prevalent attitudes in the West, and those now emerging in contemporary India.

Traditional female values and duties are listed below (please note that many similar practices such as the first one below also apply to males):

- As a child, to be obedient and respectful to her parents and elders.
- In household life, to serve a worthy husband and treat his friends and relatives with affection. To avoid mixing intimately with other men.
- To be fully conversant in religious principles.
- To be expert in household affairs, and to keep the home clean and well-decorated.
- To dress and decorate herself to please her husband. A wife should avoid dressing up if her husband is away from home.
- To control her greed and passions and to speak truthfully and pleasingly.
- To follow certain vratas (vows) such as fasting on days like Ekadasi (the 11th day of the moon).
- To love, protect and nurture children.
- In later life, to dedicate time to spiritual practices and to give counsel to younger family members.

Many related practices have been misused, and fossilised as part of the hereditary caste system. The bhakti traditions, which opposed casteism, have featured many women saints who broke away from stereotypical roles. Others remained faithful to their dharma and simultaneously developed their spirituality. Many Hindus acknowledge the need to reassess the practical role of women in society today, but strive to maintain the spiritual principles underpinning traditional practice.

Related Concepts

The basic foundation of equality lies in the notion of *atman*, the self beyond bodily designation. However, Hindus also acknowledge the need to recognise psychological and physiological differences as a practical reality. Equality is manifest through the concept of *Sanatana-dharma* and conditional differences through Varnasrama-dharma. Failing to recognise the spiritual equality of all and denying our external differences are both considered signs of ignorance and contrary to dharma. Spiritual equality is affirmed by discerning material differences, and recognising them for what they are – ultimately superficial but practically relevant.

Related Values/Issues

- women's issues.
- gender roles.
- feminism.
- equal opportunities.

Related Stories

"The Story of Draupadi" (STO-204; see also page 126)
       -*An example of a powerfully assertive woman.*
"Savitri" (STO-702)
       -*A wife's devotion saves her husband from death.*

Above: *In public places such as the temple, men and women are somewhat segregated. The prescribed roles and duties of women acknowledge that they have different tendencies from men.*

Common Misunderstandings

"Chastity, faithfulness and other traditional Hindu values mean that a woman will inevitably be exploited."

The scriptures feature stories of women who accepted the female dharma but remained influential and assertive. The above misconception may be based on the notion that social justice is achieved only through one means – complete equality. Hinduism holds that masculinity and femininity are intrinsic and complementary qualities, not merely products of social influence. The value of womanhood is expressed in many features of Hinduism, such as the respect it gives to motherhood, the many goddesses, and the practice of calling India "the Motherland". Some Hindu scholars consider much feminism to be, ironically, an asymmetric endorsement of male values.

"The Hindu notion of specific roles for men and women is sexist."

Dr. Werner Menski, a senior lecturer at the University of London, has written (1996) "It's too superficial to dismiss the Hindu approach to women merely as sexist." Hindu texts do not support the exploitation of any section of society, but they often differ with many currently popular solutions to such abuse.

Quote

"It is not that a chaste woman should be a slave while her husband is narad-hama, the lowest of men. Although the duties of a woman are different from those of a man, a chaste woman is not meant to serve a fallen [irresponsible] husband."

A.C. Bhaktivedanta Swami

ⓘ **For more information:**
Pages 96-97, 105, 106-107, 146-147

Caring for Others

Hindu Charities today

- Sewa International
- Food for Life (ISKCON)
- BAPS (Swami Narayana Mission)
- Ramakrishna Mission
- Friends of Vrindavana

Scriptural Passages

"Charity given out of duty, without expectation of return, at the proper time and place, and to a worthy person is considered to be in the quality of goodness.

Bhagavad Gita 17.20

Photos below:

Top Left: *A tree-planting project run by the 'Friends of Vrindavan' enviromental charity in conjunction with the World Wildlife Fund.*
Top Middle: *Indian children in a scheme to eradicate poverty. Religious organisations, such as the Swaminarayana Mission, run a number of such projects.*
Top right: *Bhaktivedanta Manor runs a cow protection and bull-power programme in conjunction with its farm. It also runs a 'Food for Life'* **(Bottom right)** *programme, daily feeding 450 poor and needy people in London.*
Bottom Left: *Sewa International is perhaps the largest Hindu charity worldwide.*

Hindu society recognises and values interdependence. According to Vedic theology, society can meet everyone's legitimate needs if the various individuals perform their respective duties. These duties embody the ideal of extending God's shelter to others. For this purpose, the system of *Varnashrama-dharma* allocated specific duties to each *varna* and ashram. For example, the *vaishyas* were considered responsible for the animals; women were especially entrusted with nurturing children; *kshatriyas* were obliged to ensure the physical safety of citizens; and *sannyasis* were required to remind everyone – especially householders – of their spiritual duties.

The less fortunate were cared for within the extended family. Religious obligations also included various forms of charity. For example, scripture obliges the householder to step outside the front door before each meal and to announce three times "Is anyone hungry? Please come to take your meal!" Only then would the family eat, with or without guests. Today, Hindu families are still renowned for their hospitality. Other acts of generosity include giving alms and clothing, and ritually feeding the poor, holy people and animals. A righteous life, whereby God is perceived in nature, naturally protects the environment. Planting trees and digging wells have long been considered to bestow considerable spiritual merit.

Social change and industrialisation have now meant that Hindus have established charitable organisations to adopt functions previously fulfilled more locally, within the community. These charities are often connected to religious institutions.

Part 3 - Lifestyle &
Expressions of Faith

 **Chapter 8 – Expressions of Faith**

 **Chapter 9 – Lifestyle**

In Part Three, we continue examining practices through those expressions of spirituality that influence everyday life. Much of the discussion in Chapter Eight revolves around Hindu culture, an important vehicle for nurturing and transmitting the Vedic ideals. Chapter Nine particularly examines Hindu lifestyles and their relationships to social phenomena.

Sanskrit and Sanskriti (Culture)

Above: Goddess Sarasvati: with two hands she strums the vina, and with another holds a book. Her fourth hand fingers prayer beads, symbolising the need for spirituality in both academic and artistic endeavours.

Above: The 48 letters of the Sanskrit alphabet. The language is extremely regular, almost mathematical in its grammar and formulation. It is considered a sacred and mystical language – 'the language of the gods.' The script is called Devanagari, meaning 'used in the cities of the gods.' Words are constructed from a number of roots, each considered to have an intrinsic quality that embodies the meaning itself, rather than being an arbitrary symbol. Sound is considered the subtlest of all five elements, and controlling sound can help manipulate matter, as through the chanting of mantras.

Hinduism is essentially a spoken tradition, and sound is the primary means of spiritual expression. Speech is personified as Vak, a form of goddess Sarasvati. As the deity of scholarship and the arts, Sarasvati *(left)* symbolises the intimate relationship within Hinduism between culture and religion, which until recently were practically inseparable.

There are 64 traditional arts which comprise a wide variety of skills, crafts and artistic activities including music, painting, sculpture, singing, cooking, architecture, creating colourful patterns, applying cosmetics, producing perfumes, flower arranging, and caring for trees. Their variety and the inclusion of practical crafts suggest art is an integral part of life, rather than a vocation aimed at pleasing the elite. These arts were part of the process of spiritual culture, of refining and uplifting the tastes, values and sentiments of human society. The word for culture is *sanskriti*, 'refinement', suggesting a means for extracting the spiritual essence of life (*brahman*). 'Sanskrit' similarly means 'the most refined language'. The similarity of the two words reflects the close relationship between (1) religious scholarship and (2) culture as a vehicle of spiritual expression.

The four Vedas were written in ancient Sanskrit, perhaps the oldest Indo-European language. It was largely spoken by brahmins and was less well understood by others, who spoke simpler variations called Prakrits, "natural languages." All the main Shruti and Smriti texts were subsequently written in Sanskrit. Parallel to these texts, there developed a large section-body of literature in the Indian vernaculars, often written by non-brahmin authors and intended for ordinary people.

The ancient rivalry between North and South extends to language. The North insists on the primacy of Sanskrit texts, and considers Sanskrit the only genuine 'sacred language.' The South claims that Tamil pre-dates Sanskrit and that certain Tamil texts are equivalent to the Sanskrit Shruti. Ramanuja and other scholars tried to synthesise the two traditions, and in Shri Rangam the Tamil poems of the Alvars are still recited alongside Sanskrit hymns. As the *bhakti* traditions emerged, they replaced much traditional Brahmanism and a huge body of vernacular literature evolved. It is still developing today. Important languages include Hindi (considered the national language), Gujarati, Avadhi, Tamil and Bengali.

Hindus have mixed opinions regarding the importance of their native languages. Some feel that without speaking Sanskrit, or another mainstream Indian vernacular, one cannot be considered a Hindu or properly study the tradition. Other teachers stress the universality of Hinduism and how the same truths can be expressed in any language. However, there are certainly difficulties in translation. English, for example, does not have equivalent words for some Sanskrit terms, such as 'dharma.' Sanskrit therefore retains its importance as a language of religious expression, especially as the language of liturgy and scholarship.

Story and Myth

Story and myth have always been part of *Sanatana-dharma*, but scholars ascertain that they rose to prominence in the Epic and Puranic periods. Since then, Hindu concepts and values have been transmitted more through story than through philosophical or theological exposition, and stories are central in disseminating popular Hinduism. Stories were customarily passed down through the family, particularly by grandparents. They were also popularised by musicians, dancers and travelling theatre troupes. More recently, they have been retold through books, film, TV and video. Hinduism is rich in meaningful stories. Western film-makers and playwrights have realised this, as illustrated by the Peter Brooks version (1989) of the Mahabharata.

A key element of story is the role of the hero and heroine, who embody exemplary values. Many narratives explore the nuances of dharma and the difficulties in its precise application. Although many of the stories are ancient, Hindu people talk of their hero figures with a sense of immediacy, as if they are alive today. These characters serve not as dated, tribal ancestors but as residents of a previously glorious age. Especially for children, the Panchatantra and Hitopadesh include allegorical animal stories with moral themes. Many of Aesop's fables are believed to be derived from the Panchatantra. *(For more information on story, please see pages 40-41 and 126-130)*

Above*: A Hindu parent reads traditional stories to his son and daughter. Many of these popular stories are also available in comic form, or on video.*
Below*: Draupadi, heroine of the Mahabharata. Many Hindus consider her, and other mythical and legendary figures, to be historical rather then fictional.*

Personal Reflection

- *(Previous page)* How does our own consciousness affect our use of language? Does language give any indication of a culture and its specific values?
- What impact have stories had on our own lives?

Glossary Terms

Myth – *a story, not necessarily fictional, which maps reality through understanding the higher dimensions of life*

Common Misunderstandings

"Hindu stories are entirely allegorical."

Some Hindus contend that the Epics, Puranas, etc. are historical accounts, but happen beyond our normal realms of comprehension. These narratives span vast periods of time and space, and occur within multiple dimensions. There may appear to be factual contradictions, but Hindus place greater emphasis on appropriate values than on exactitude in names, dates, and so forth. One should be careful in using terms such as 'myth' *(see Glossary Terms, right)*

"One can derive whatever message one wants from Hindu stories."

Although the tradition is liberal, and accepts that stories have multi-layered meanings, teachers should be careful about changing stories, or projecting their own values onto them without checking that they are actually consistent with Hindu thought. *(See also Common Misunderstandings, page 11)*

Dance and Drama

Above: A lady performing Bharata-Natyam at Janmashtami celebrations in England.
Below: An actor dressed as Rama at a presentation of the Ramayana by the Bhaktivedanta Players. This UK troupe performs both traditional and contemporary plays - this one to Welsh schoolchildren - using colourful costumes imported from India.

The earliest known treatise on the performing arts is the Sanskrit classic 'Natya Shastra,' written by the sage Bharata Muni. It is effectively a handbook for dance and theatre and details the techniques of dramatic expression. Early artistic performances were almost entirely associated with religion, and the first theatres were temples, where artists danced for the pleasure of deities. Later, during the time of the Moghul and British Empires, dance moved to the royal courts and became more associated with entertainment. However, many contemporary dances still accommodate spiritual themes derived from the Epics, Puranas and other Hindu texts. There are two main categories of dance – folk and classical, each with its own distinctive styles, as shown below.

Main Folk Dance Styles

Garba: a Gujarati clap-dance using circular movements and mainly performed by women during Navaratri.

Dandiya Rasa: a dance from Gujarat using wooden sticks to emphasise the rhythm. It was traditionally performed by men and women in November but is now popular after Garba during Navaratri.

Bhangra: an energetic and colourful harvest dance from Punjab mainly performed by men and boys.

Giddha: a graceful female dance from Punjab.

Main Classical Dance Styles

Kathak: the major northern style used to relate stories (*katha*) and employing intricate footwork.

Bharata Natyam: the name is derived from Bharata's Natyashastra and is the major Southern dance style. It is a graceful dance using facial expressions and hand gestures (*mudras*).

Kathakali: a powerful dance-drama discipline from the South, recognised by its elaborate and colourful facial masks.

Entertainment was a feature of ancient Indian life, but it rarely lacked a spiritual element. Drama was a principal form of entertainment, delivered by exclusively male troupes. This is now changing, and there are a number of mixed Hindu theatre groups currently performing in the UK.

Dance and drama were often interwoven (as in Kathakali, mentioned above) and integrated with other art forms. Especially popular were storytelling and poetry recitals, often with musical accompaniment. Still popular, especially during festivals, is the theatrical portrayal of lilas (divine pastimes), especially Rama-lila and Krishna-lila. In these performances, the actor is often considered to become the deity he is playing. Hindu dance and drama troupes have moved into the realm of contemporary theatre, expressing the ancient Hindu message in a way that is relevant and accessible to the post-modern world.

Music

Indian music, called 'sangeet,' is considered to have mythological roots and is associated with the heavenly singers, the
Gandharvas. The first recipient of this celestial art form was
the ancient sage Narada. The oldest musical texts are the 'Sama
Veda,' consisting of melodies for recitation of hymns during
ritual sacrifice. From very early days, music was considered a
means of moral and spiritual redemption rather than mere
entertainment. Indeed, the process of learning to play music
closely resembles traditional spiritual disciplines. According to
Ravi Shankar, it contains three key elements:

1. *The guru* - coming in parampara (disciplic succession).
2. *Vinaya* - humility (a key personal characteristic required
   in many spiritual disciplines).
3. *Sadhana* - regular and disciplined practice.

Bharata Muni, of the 2nd century BCE, laid the foundations
for two important principles upon which Indian music is now
based: *(1) raga*, the melodic scale, and *(2) tala*, the rhythm. Both
are carefully chosen to invoke the appropriate mood (*rasa*). In
discussing the aesthetics of dance and music, Bharata Muni
delineated *nava-rasa*, nine principle 'moods' or 'tastes.' Some
bhakti theologians, especially from the Chaitanya and Vallabha
schools, further developed the whole science of rasa to
encompass spiritual sentiment. Not surprisingly, these *bhakti*
movements, with their emphasis on spiritual emotion, integrated music into their worship. It was considered not only
adoration but a means towards a higher consciousness. Perhaps
the most famous musician was Tansen (1480-1575) accredited
with performing miracles simply through his singing.

Today music is evident in worship through *bhajan* (hymns)
and *kirtan* (the musical chanting of mantras). Common
instruments include drums, such as the *tabla* and *mridangas*, the
manjira (small hand-cymbals) and the harmonium, imported
and adapted from the West. Classical instruments, in addition
to tabla, include the *flute, vina, sitar, sarangi, santoor* and *shenai*.

Top: *Tansen, one of the 'nine jewels' in the court of Emperor
Akbar. Hindu music appears to have adopted elements of
other cultures, such as the Persian – although some consider
that these music forms originally came from India.*
Above: *Ladies from Manipur, in the far east of India, sing
bhajan. They are playing the harmonium and small hand-
cymbals.*
Left: *A musician playing tablas, which are used in classical
and religious music.*

Above: A painting of Radha and Krishna in the distinctive Kangra style.

Above right: A lady with a rangoli design she has created for the festival of Diwali. Rangolis, also called kolams, are lace-like patterns found on Hindu thresholds in Southern India. Women and girls paint them each morning before dawn, usually from rice flour. Rangoli patterns are thought to ward off inauspiciousness and invoke good fortune, and are therefore associated with the Goddess Lakshmi. On major festival days, large designs are constructed using coloured powders.

Below: An artisan carves a deity. Each murti must be carved according to dimensions specified in scripture.

Below right: Figurines decorating a temple tower in South India.

Hinduism is a richly visual tradition, illustrated by its paintings, sculpture and distinctive *rangoli* patterns. There are many of schools of classical art, such as Rajastani, Moghul, Kangra, Pahari and Kalighat. The subjects are usually of a religious nature, featuring pastimes of various deities. Puja, the worship of the temple image, in itself is a unique and complex art form *(see page 63)*.

One of the most enduring achievements of Indian civilisation is undoubtedly its architecture, whose roots derive from the Shilpa Shastra, one of the six Vedangas *(see page 124)*. Many large temples date back to the period 1000–1300 CE, when architecture flourished throughout India. The Moghul Emperors (1526-1857) added their own distinctive style, spending lavishly on forts, mosques and palaces. For Hindus, the carving of sacred images and figurines was an art form in itself, requiring years of disciplined training. In the UK, the intricacies of Hindu sculpture and architecture are visible in many new purpose-built *mandirs*, which are replacing the old converted buildings.

Hindu Symbols

Hinduism is rich in symbolism. Many acts of worship, such as *puja*, are symbolic, a form of visualisation in which worshippers simulate activities normally performed on higher planes of existence. Thus the scope of symbolism is broad and includes physical acts such as offering *pranam* (obeisances) with folded hands. Such physical gestures tend to induce the appropriate mood and awareness within the practitioner. Many symbols are considered auspicious, embodying the notion of inner purity. Sacred emblems are displayed in the home or temple to invoke good fortune. The most popular symbols are listed on the right.

Aum, also written 'Om' and called *pranava*, is the most important Hindu symbol. Its prolonged intonation is associated with the primeval sound through which the universe was created. It is thought to contain all things. It consists of three syllables: A–u–m, which are sounded progressively from the throat to the lips. The three sounds are considered to symbolise many items, but perhaps most importantly the three states of consciousness – waking, dreaming and deep sleep. The entire symbol represents the fourth state, which is the awareness of one's own spiritual identity. Aum is the most important *mula* (root) mantra and is thus chanted at the beginning of many prayers, mantras and rituals.

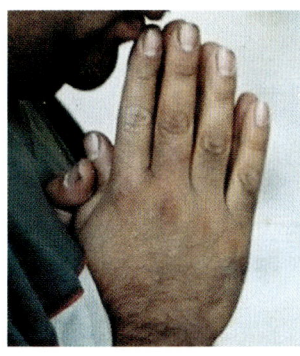

Hindu people greet each other by placing their two hands together and slightly bowing the head, whilst saying "namaste" or a similar phrase. They adopt the same posture when greeting the temple deity or a holy person. Thus when greeting another person, a Hindu is offering respect to the soul within (*atman*) and also to God within the heart (*Paramatman*).

Common Misunderstandings

"'Symbolism' means that a sign or emblem represents 'something else', and is special only to one who understands its significance". Many Hindus consider that religious symbols embody the divine, and are in themselves sacred. Hence the symbolic murti (sacred image) or prasada (sanctified food) not only point to transcendence but become that transcendence (brahman) if invoked with love and devotion (*see also Bhagavad Gita 4.24*).

Ten Important Symbols

1. **Om (Aum)** – *the most important Hindu symbol, often used as the emblem of Hinduism (see below left).*
2. **Hands in prayer** – *a sign of respect for the sacred, that which is dear to the heart (see bottom left).*
3. **Lotus (padma)** – *symbol of purity/ transcendence. Growing out of the mud, it is beautiful, and though resting on water, it does not touch it.*
4. **Conchshell** – *used during arati: one of the four symbols of Vishnu. The others are the lotus, club and disc.*
5. **Swastika** – *an ancient solar sign considered to invoke auspiciousnes.*
6. **Trident (trishul)** – *the symbol of Shiva; often carried by Shaivite sannyasis.*
7. **Kalasha** – *coconut circled by mango leaves on a pot. Often used in rituals such as the fire sacrifice.*
8. **Cow** – *symbol of purity, motherhood and ahimsa (non-violence).*
9. **Lotus feet (of guru or deity)** – *touching the feet of superiors shows an attitude of submission and service.*
10. **Diva/lamp** – *symbol of light.*

Symbols 3-10 (above) are shown here, in clockwise order from the lotus, top left

Scriptural Passages

"Of vibrations I am the transcendental Om."

Bhagavad Gita 10.25

Dress

Like other aspects of Indian culture, dress has religious as well as aesthetic significance. It demonstrates both elegance and simplicity, and can be produced by village workshops without the need for gigantic factories. Many clothes, such as a lady's sari and a man's *dhoti*, are simply pieces of cloth and do not require tailoring. For women there is an emphasis on modesty rather than sexual allurement, and simple elegance, rather than fashion. Saris come in a whole range of regional styles, and are made from cotton, silk or nylon. There are different regional ways of wearing a sari, although the "nivi" style has become very popular recently.

Left: The saffron clothes of this sadhu (holy man) indicates that he is a sannyasi. Tucked under his arm he holds the customary danda (staff).
Right: A married man dressed in a traditional white cotton dhoti. On the top he wears a generously cut shirt called a kurta. Men often wear a chaddar (shawl) which in cold weather can be wrapped around the shoulders and torso. When the weather is warm, it can be folded and slung over the shoulder. In Britain practically all Hindu men wear western clothes, except perhaps on important religious occasions. In India, men wear Western or Indian clothes and often a mixture of both.

Left: A Hindu lady dressed in a sari. In India most women still dress like this. In the early seventies, when Hindus started arriving en-masse in Britain, practically all women wore traditional costume. Western fashion is becoming increasingly prevalent in subsequent generations, although ladies often still wear saris when visiting the mandir. It is now not unusual to see photos of some Western dignitaries wearing an exotic silk sari. Some Muslims, such as those from Bangladesh, also wear saris.
Right: A Punjabi Hindu woman, dressed in the salwar-kameez. It consists of a tunic (kameez) covering loosely fitting trousers (salwar). Occasionally, a chunni (shawl) is used to cover the head and shoulders. Sikh women wear the same costume.

Personal Reflection

■ What significance does dress have for us? How does it affect or relate to our identity and self-worth?

■ Does dress reflect a person's nature, culture or values? Or do we feel that determining a person by his or her dress is being judgmental?

Cosmetics, Jewellery and Perfumes

Ancient Sanskrit texts laid down the concept of *sola singar*, the sixteen items with which every woman should adorn herself. They are: the *bindi*, necklaces, earrings, flowers in the hair, rings, bangles, armlets (for the upper arm), waistbands, ankle-bells, *kohl* (or *kajal* – mascara), toe rings, henna, perfume, sandalwood paste, the upper garment and the lower garment. Though modern life makes wearing all of these impractical, many women will dress up in most or all sixteen items for weddings, festivals and other special occasions.

Hindu jewellery and ornaments are now popular amongst non-Hindus. The nose-ring, or nose-pin, traditionally represented purity and was often adopted when a girl reached marriageable age. The word 'bindi' derives from the Sanskrit word 'bindu', meaning 'point' or 'dot'. Like *tilak* (*see page 132*), it is placed on the *agya-chakra*, often termed 'the third eye'. In some traditions, the *bindi* (also called 'sindoor') is the sign of a married lady. Customarily it is made from *kum-kum* vermilion), but as a fashion item it now comes in many shapes and colours.

Top: a Hindu bride just prior to the wedding ceremony. Her jewellery is made of 22-carat gold. After marriage, Hindu ladies should wear the bindi in between the eye-brows (see previous page, bottom left picture). A most important accessory for the bride is the mangala-sutra (auspicious necklace), made of black beads and a golden disc-shaped pendant.
Left: Filigreed patterns painted on the bride's palms with henna paste. The feet are similarly decorated. The paste is made from the powdered, dried leaves of the henna plant.
Bottom: A range of incense holders from India.

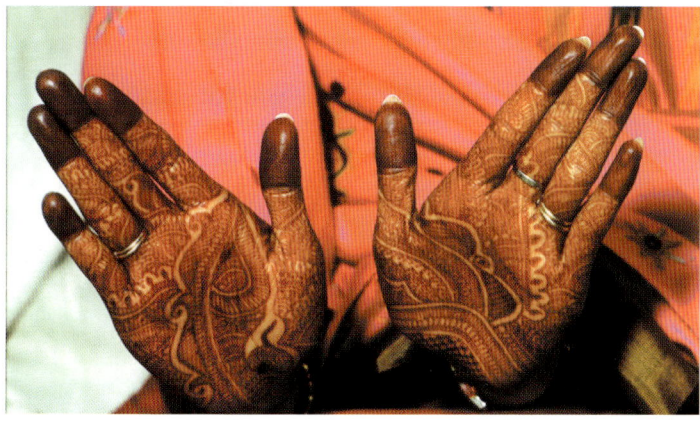

Hinduism engages all the senses in the pursuit of a higher pleasure, and aromas are particularly useful in invoking an appropriate mood. The distillation of fragrances goes back to ancient times, when there were two main preparations – pastes (ointments) and liquids. Sandalwood paste is still made by the long process of rubbing and grinding the wood on a flat stone with rose-water. In temple ceremonies, the paste is mixed with saffron and daubed on the forehead. It is especially cooling to the mind. Indian perfumes are usually pure essential oils - flower and herbal extracts without the addition of alcohol. They are used in *puja*, as well as for personal use. Popular fragrances include rose, jasmine, amber, kush and sandalwood. Camphor, an off-white crystalline powder, is often burned in lamps offered during the *arti* ceremony. One feature of Hindu aromatics - familiar to most Westerners and easily available - is incense. These are used during worship and to pleasantly scent the home. There are different forms such as sticks, cones, and resins burned on charcoal.

Food and Prasada

Above: cooking on a festival day in a temple kitchen. Feasting is often preceded by fasting, either totally or partially (by abstaining from certain foods, such as grains and beans on the Ekadashi day).
Below: A Hindu lady receives prasad, in the form of a meal. Customarily, in India meals are taken sitting on the floor, and without the use of cutlery.

Glossary Terms

Prasada - *literally means 'mercy', and refers to anything that has been sanctified through offering to God (e.g. flowers). It specifically refers to food offered to God.*

Hinduism places such great emphasis on the role of food that it has been called "the kitchen religion." No religious or public function is complete without the distribution of food, especially *prasada* (food offered to God).

There are many complex rules regarding the preparation and consumption of food. Vaishnavism has developed a sophisticated theology, which classifies all eatables according to the three *gunas*. Meat is usually shunned as it in considered *tamasic*, influenced by darkness. Shaivites observe fewer dietary restrictions and Shaktas are usually inclined towards meat, traditionally obtained from animal sacrifice. Although some Hindus eat meat, almost all avoid beef out of respect for the cow.

India has developed a vast vegetarian cuisine, beyond the imagination of most Westerners, who often picture vegetarians eating little more than nuts, fruit and salad. Milk products are considered essential to a vegetarian diet and *ghee* (clarified butter) is a widely used frying medium. Spices provide taste, aid digestion and promote good health. A typical meal consists of several preparations, but most often the main meal, at lunchtime, will consist of rice, *sabji*, dahl and chapattis (*see below*).

Food plays an important role in worship, and the food offered to the deities (*prasad*) is thought to bestow considerable religious merit, purifying body, mind and spirit. Temple cooks are usually brahmins and follow strict standards of personal cleanliness. There is widespread belief that the consciousness of the cook enters the food and influences the mind of the eater. Taking *prasada* that has been cooked and offered with devotion inclines the mind towards spirituality.

The *prasad* that has been on the altar is especially sacred, and is handed out to worshippers, either by the priest at the shrine or as worshippers leave the *mandir*. Prasad is also served in the form of a full meal, especially on festival days. Many Hindus have an altar at home and offer their food before eating.

Popular Foods

Rice – usually boiled, and served plain or garnished.
Sabji – any preparation made from vegetables and usually spiced.
Samosa – a fried pastry stuffed with spicy vegetables.
Dahl – a soup made from lentils or beans.
Puri – a flat, round bread, deep-fried in ghee or oil.
Chapatti (or Roti) – a flat, round bread toasted on a skillet.
Popadom – a crisp savoury (like a large potato crisp).
Barfi – a sweet made by condensing milk and adding sugar.
Laddu – a sweet made with chick-pea flour.
Dosha – a simple dumpling, popular in South India.
Chutney – often sweet and hot, made from fruit, coconut, etc.
Lassi - a refreshing drink of yoghurt and water; sweet or salty.
Googra – a sweet coconut pastry, popular at Diwali.

Hospitality

Offering hospitality is fundamental to Hindu culture and providing food and shelter to a needy stranger was a traditional duty of the householder. The unexpected guest is called the *atithi*, literally meaning "without a set time." Scripture enjoins that the *atithi* be treated as God. It was especially important to extend hospitality towards brahmins, *sannyasis* and other holy people. There are many stories regarding the benefits of offering a suitable reception and the sins that accrue from neglecting one's guests. Tradition teaches that, no matter how poor one is, one should always offer three items: sweet words, a sitting place and refreshments (at least a glass of water). The flower garland is offered to special guests and dignitaries, as a symbol of loving exchange.

Scripture also enjoins that one should treat visiting enemies so well that they will forget their animosity. A graphic example is that of the warrior class who would fight during the day and in the evening socialise with adversaries. Westerners visiting India (and other places in the East) are often astonished by the welcoming attitude towards guests and visiting strangers, strikingly different from the Western *"beware of the dog"* culture.

Above: Krishna sets the example of how to receive a respectable guest. Here, in a story from the Bhagavata Purana, he washes the feet of an impoverished brahmin.
Below: Offering food is an important and endearing aspect of hospitality in Hindu culture.

Related Stories

King Rantidev
> *- who set the ideal example for receiving guests.* (STO-206)

The Gift of the sun-god (STO-801)
> *- overcoming some of the problems created by guests.*

Related Values/Issues

- Valuing and caring for others.
- Magnanimity.
- Giving and receiving.

Personal Reflection

- What experience do we have of being well or poorly received? How did we feel?
- How do we receive others? What are the reasons that we receive guests well or poorly?
- Have we experienced the pleasure of giving? What different types of pleasure do we experience by receiving?

Scriptural Passages

"Even an enemy must be offered appropriate hospitality if he comes to your home. A tree does not deny its shade even to the one who comes to cut it down."

Mahabharata 12.374

"The uninvited guest should be treated as good as God."

Popular Proverb

Astrology

Astrology is one of the most important and widely used Vedic sciences. It is largely derived from one of the six Vedangas (see page 124) and is intimately related to the notions of reincarnation and karma (pages 10-13).

Attitudes towards this science reflect notable differences between the predominant Eastern and Western world views. Whereas most people in the West treat astrology with some scepticism, in India it is considered a respectable science, and texts eulogise authentic astrologers as the most learned brahmins. The West generally equates belief in subtle phenomena with superstition, whereas the East frames it within the context of 'subtle science.'

There are different schools of astrology, but Rishi Parashara is generally considered the foremost authority. Indians often claim that Western astrology, coming via the Greeks, was originally from India. Most Indian families still request a local brahmin to cast a chart for the new-born baby.

Above: A poster depicting murtis of the nine planets, at a temple in North London.
Below right: An astrological chart (Northern style). The first house (ascendant), in this case Libra, - is centre top and the other eleven houses proceed in an anti- clockwise direction. Each house is a complete sign. The nine planets are represented by their respective symbols.

The Uses of Vedic Astrology

- **Choosing a baby's name** The first syllable is determined by the position of the moon at birth.
- **Predicting important events** in a person's life and assessing the person's areas of potential (from the birth chart).
- **Choosing auspicious times** to perform rites of passage and other important ceremonies or to start new projects.
- **Assessing marriage compatibility** between prospective partners.
- **Answering specific queries** as an aid to personal counselling (by constructing a chart for the time of the query).

Meaning and Purpose

- *Freewill & Fate (pre-determination)*
- *Inequalities at birth*

Personal Reflection

- What influences of the moon do we know of? How do the phases influence the ocean, people's moods, crops, crime figures, and so forth?

Quote

"The law of nature is so subtle that every part of our body is influenced by the respective stars, and a living being obtains his working body to fulfil his terms of imprisonment by the manipulation of such astronomical influence. A man's destiny is therefore ascertained by the birthtime constellation of stars, and a factual horoscope is made by a learned astrologer. It is a great science, and misuse of a science does not make it useless."

A.C. Bhaktivedanta Swami

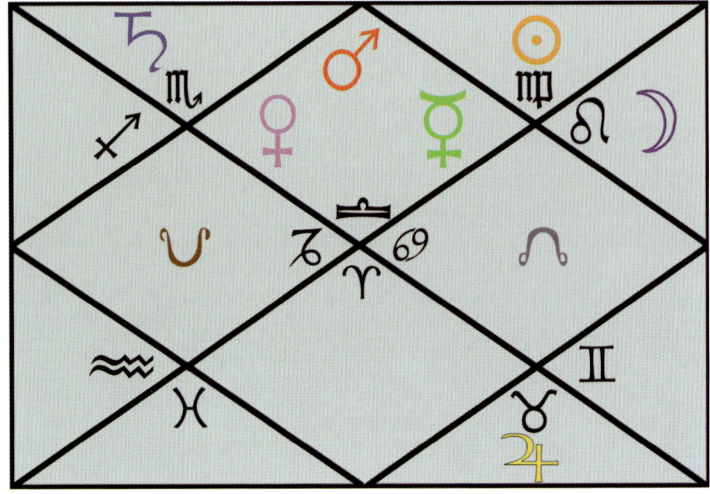

Other Arts and Sciences

India's arts and sciences are extensive and many may have predated their Western counterparts. These disciplines usually contained significant spiritual elements, and were not simply attempts to unethically exploit nature or improve the material standard of living. The relevance of Hindu art and science is increasingly recognised in the West.

Mathematics – India is often credited with contributing to the world, via Arabia, our current numerals and the concept of 'zero'. Hindu mathematicians certainly formulated an ingenious system of mental arithmetic used in astronomical calculations. This science of Vedic mathematics was revived quite recently by a prominent *sannyasi*, Swami Bharati Krishna Tirthaji (1884–1960). From only sixteen Sanskrit *sutras* (aphorisms) he expounded a whole mathematical discipline, by which normally lengthy calculations can be performed almost instantaneously. His writings include a concise proof of Pythagoras's theorem and a Sanskrit verse that codifies the value of pi to thirty-one decimal places. Vedic mathematics is currently taught in some British schools.

Vastu – the Indian version of Feng-Shui. Experts claim that it goes back 5,000 years, possibly pre-dating its Chinese cousin. It deals with the science of sacred space and with harnessing natural and beneficial energies in the design, construction and decoration of buildings. It is connected to the microcosm–macrocosm relationship illustrated in the story of the primal man found in the Rig-Veda. Much information on Vastu is derived from the architectural Shilpa Shastra. Many new books on this subject are now appearing on the market.

Ayur-veda (medicine) - Ayur-veda refers to a system of indigenous Indian medicine, mainly derived from the Sushruta and Charaka Samhitas. Mythologically, the science is attributed to Dhanvantari, an incarnation of Vishnu who appeared from the milk-ocean churned by the demons and demigods. He taught that sickness is rooted in an imbalance in three bodily humours – wind, bile and phlegm. Harmony is achieved by balancing these '*doshas*' through suitable diet, regulated lifestyle, positive mental attitude and prescribed natural remedies. The system advises preventative rather than reactive methods, and treats individuals according to their unique constitutions. It is still practiced throughout India, and is increasingly popular in the West.

Alchemy and Chemistry - Hinduism developed an alchemy based on two key elements – sulphur and mercury. These correlate with the tantric male-female symbolism of Shiva and Shakti. Some Hindus claim that yogis can transform base metals into gold. Today this science of alchemy is related to Ayurvedic medicine, and specifically the preparation of mineral remedies.

Above: A yantra, used to counteract negative energies in a building. The science of Vastu, related to Feng-Shui, is closely connected to other Vedic sciences, such as architecture, geometry and astrology. Yantras are diagrammatic representations of the various Hindu deities and are sometimes used as visual aids to meditation.

Below: Dhanvantari, an incarnation of Vishnu, who was born from the ocean of milk when it was churned by the gods and demons. He is credited with revealing the science of Ayurveda.

Above: Ashvattama, was the son of a powerful brahmin, but adopted the role of a warrior and fought at Kurukshetra. He could not maintain his duty, and transgressed all moral codes by killing unarmed warriors in their sleep. Krishna admonished him as "the unworthy son of a brahmin."
Below: Vishvamitra, who was born in a kshatriya family but later qualified himself as a powerful brahmin.

Hinduism has often been termed "a way of life" and in India spirituality is evident wherever one turns. Even the predominant social structure – often considered a mundane concern – is derived from religious sources. The Rig Veda enjoins that human society be divided into four *varnas (see page 82)*. The revealed nature of 'Veda' suggests that the *varna* system is therefore not man-made but of divine origin. Some traditions therefore conclude that the four *varnas* are natural divisions, inherent in every human society, and that each *varna* accommodates the corresponding type of person. Krishna teaches in the Gita that people are allocated to a specific *varna* according to two criteria, namely (1) *guna* (personal qualities) and (2) *karma* (aptitude for a type of work). He makes no mention of *varna* being determined by birth.

This differentiates the original *Varnashrama-dharma* from the current caste system. The term 'caste' originates from the Portuguese term *casta*, denoting purity of descent. It has come to refer not just to the four *varnas*, but to a whole system incorporating occupational sub-castes (*jatis*). In fact, current caste practices often give far more emphasis to *jati* than to *varna*. What really differentiates caste from *Varnashrama-dharma*, though, is its hereditary nature – possibly an imposition by brahmins attempting to consolidate their prestigious position. The fluidity of *Varnashrama-dharma* is acknowledged by numerous textual references to people changing their *varna* (see left and below).

"Gautama's Disciple"

A young boy approached Gautama Muni and begged to become his student. It was customary that only respectable brahmins would be accepted for such spiritual training. Gautama therefore asked, "Who is your father?" "That I do not know," the boy replied. "So, please ask your mother." The boy's mother subsequently admitted, "My dear son, I have known many men. I do not know who is your father." The boy returned to Gautama Muni and relayed the embarrassing message, "Sir, my mother also does not know who my father is." Gautama Muni concluded, "Yes, you are a brahmin. I accept you because you are thoroughly honest."

from the Jabala Upanishad

Common Misunderstandings
"Varnashrama-dharma and the caste-system are identical."
The two are not identical, though naturally inter-related. *Varnashrama-dharma* refers to a system which promotes social mobility whereas the caste system is rigid and hereditary.

The rigid, hereditary caste system has been prevalent in India for centuries, and some Hindu writers trace its origins to the beginning of Kali-yuga or beyond. The following are five of its main elements. Some of the underpinning principles are derived from the original *Varnashrama-dharma* structure. These practices, however applied, have certainly had significant influence on Hindu lifestyle.

1. Division of labour: the original *varna* system allowed men to adopt jobs different from their fathers, though generally they would follow in his footsteps. The later hereditary system forbade any mobility, and particularly prevented members of lower orders, whatever their real qualification, from securing prestigious jobs. Nowadays this practice is largely defunct, and many from lower classes enter reputable professions.

2. Social and economic interdependence: in the original system each *varna*, as part of the social body, served the others. Though lower *varnas* ministered to the higher, the over-riding notion was of service – to each other, to society and to the Supreme. The rigid caste system, however, has encouraged exploitation.

3. Purity: each *varna* was expected to strive for progressive degrees of internal and external purity. Thus they would seek congenial company, avoiding intimate dealings with the less spiritually mature. Possibly because of pride, these considerations degenerated into condescension. This was taken to the extreme when brahmins considered themselves polluted by the mere touch of another's shadow.

4. Regulation of dietary habits: commensality prohibited Hindus from eating with those of lower status. This was especially relevant when lower classes ate forbidden foods, such as meat, fish and eggs. At large social gatherings, the food was cooked by brahmins so as to be acceptable to all.

5. Inter-caste marriage: endogamy refers to marriage between members of the same *varna*. This was to produce cultured children of high pedigree. Scripture forbids inter-marriage where the groom comes from a lower *varna* than his bride, although the reverse is acceptable. In practice, parents often insist that their children's partners belong to the same *varna* and even the same jati. Children rejecting parents' wishes have caused the Hindu community to re-evaluate caste practices.

Personal Reflection

■ Reflecting on your own experience, do these features of caste appear in your own society? Are there rules - even unwritten - about whom to marry or with whom to mix? How do you feel about such notions? What are the merits and demerits?

Scriptural Passages

"According to the three modes of material nature and the work associated with them, the four divisions of human society are created by Me."

Krishna in Bhagavad-Gita 4.13

Quote

"I believe that Varnashrama-dharma is based on an appreciation of social and spiritual interdependence. Just as each part of the body has a specific function, so we all have a unique contribution to make to society. The brahmins, like everyone else, have a service role but are expected to be exceptionally pure in thought and deed. For example, I would never eat meat, even if really hungry."

Jaya Krishna, Hindu priest

Above:*Many Hindu marriages are now inter-racial and inter-religious. This still causes grief and concern to some parents, especially the highly caste-conscious. Modernisation has been instrumental in gradually eroding caste barriers.*

Caste and Untouchability

Above: *Untouchables would often do work considered too dirty by members of regular caste society.*

Above: *A Western-born non-caste brahmin performing a fire sacrifice. Many of the bhakti movements, such as the one to which this priest belongs have challenged rigid notions of caste and untouchability.*

Scriptural Passage

"A scholarly brahmin, expert in all subjects of Vedic knowledge, is unfit to become a spiritual teacher if he is not expert in the science of God consciousness. But a spiritually realised person, even if born in a family of untouchables, is fit to become a guru."

Padma Purana

The caste system has been mainly criticised for its treatment of outcastes or untouchables. This group has been termed the *panchama* (the fifth *varna*), collectively designating all who fall outside the regular four classes. The notion of untouchability may have been present in the original *varna* system, though it is not clear precisely how it operated. Puranic texts mention untouchables, stating that they should be well-supported, but intimate connection with them avoided. They also state that those who fell from their status within the higher 'twice-born' *varnas* were called *dvija-bandhu* ('friends of the twice-born') and were accommodated within the shudra class. In actual practice, some who abandoned key rituals or moral standards were altogether ostracised. Additionally, jobs deemed to be particularly contaminating were held only by outcastes. These include sweepers, leather workers and crematorium attendants. They were not allowed to live within the confines of regular village life, nor to share public facilities such as wells and temples.

Organised opposition to rigid caste practices began with the medieval bhakti movements. Some of them rejected both caste and its pre-runner, *Varnashrama-dharma*. Others considered the original *Varnashrama-dharma* to be the genuine system, though it usually took second place to a revitalised spiritual egalitarianism. Some contemporary bhakti traditions continue to initiate non-caste brahmins from amongst communities normally considered untouchable. This liberal practice has met opposition, particularly from caste-conscious brahmins.

Gandhi called the outcastes *Harijans* – the children of God – and wanted to accommodate them within the fourth *varna*. Ranji Ambedkar, another important reformer, was a member of the untouchable caste who succeeded in attaining a scholarship to study law. He later disagreed with Gandhi over the future status of untouchables, and advocated instead a classless society. He was one of the main architects of the new Indian constitution of 1950, which outlawed untouchability and gave equal status to all citizens. In practice many rigid caste values continue, and former outcastes have organised themselves as *Dalits* (the oppressed), fighting for social and economic equality. The struggle continues today, and though 'positive discrimination' is securing the outcastes equal opportunities, some claim that it is now displacing those who are actually more qualified.

Caste consciousness still continues, and is much debated amongst Hindu scholars and activists. Some advocate the mitigation of social injustice through the complete abolition of social divisions. Others attempt to redefine the ancient *Varnashrama-dharma* in a way that is relevant to post-modern society.

Related Values/Issues

- Negative discrimination.
- Equal opportunities.

Besides caste, many other well-advertised social anomalies have developed in India. Since the 19th century, increased recognition of social abuse has promoted ideas of reform. Some Hindus, possibly more inclined to Western thought, opted to purge Hinduism of what they considered dated and superstitious features. Others acknowledged the potential viability of ancient principles and practices which, according to their vision, had become degraded over time. The following are a few of the social practices and phenomena that prompted social reform and had a signicant influence on Hindu lifestyles.

Poverty: the affluent world often perceives a simple, rural life as abject poverty, and a sign of social retardation. Hindus traditionally considered it virtuous to voluntarily accept an uncomplicated life for spiritual purposes. With different views on wealth, poverty and success, the West is prone to hastily dismiss India's socio-religious practices as backward and irrelevant. Nonetheless, poverty remains a real problem in many areas.

The role of women: Hindu texts stress the importance of stable family ties and valuing and protecting women. Nonetheless, there has been – and there still is – wide abuse. Despite this, the tradition largely rejects the post-modern notion that social justice is achieved simply through promoting material equality.

Child-marriage: texts recommend marriage at an early age, particularly for girls in order to protect their chastity. Sexual transgression is considered particularly detrimental to spiritual life. Many so-called child marriages were actually a form of betrothal and marriage was not consummated until the wife was of age.

Sati was voluntarily performed on the basis of overwhelming affection for the partner and a desire to follow him into the next life. Hindu texts forbid its performance in Kali–yuga, the present age.

Polygamy was made illegal in 1952. It was previously considered essential for a limited number of responsible and qualified men to redress the gender imbalance in a society where practically all women were supposed to get married and significant numbers of men remained celibate.

The dowry system was originally a sign of affection by the father for his daughter. The dowry remained the wife's personal property, not that of her husband or his family. This system has been abused by unscrupulous in-laws who terrorise and even murder those brides who don't provide a sufficient dowry.

Personal Reflection

- How do we view India and the above-mentioned issues? Could there be any sense behind apparently dated practices?
- What is our experience of people confusing religion with materiality? Is religion a socio-political phenomenon or are there genuine spiritual forces at work? How do we recognise the difference?

Common Misunderstandings

"The principles behind Hinduism are now out of date, and contemporary Western values are helping address the resultant social anomalies."

Some Hindus now consider that Western researchers have unfairly dismissed many Hindu practices without sufficient consideration of any possible rationale behind them. Misuse of a principle does not negate it. One example is *Varnashrama-dharma*. Caste abuse has even prompted some writers to claim that *Varnashrama-dharma* is inherently racist. In fact, caste is quite different from *Varnashrama-dharma*, for the latter simultaneously promotes spiritual equality whilst acknowledging material diversity. Other phenomena require similarly sensitive treatment in order to understand them better. Naturally, even the purer spiritual principles, as distinct from later aberrations, may challenge or conflict with many post-modern values.

Above: *Vedic ideals suggest that women must be valued and protected. Some Hindus claim that practices such as early marriage, polygamy and dowry were based on these principles but in time became degraded. Others, including some Hindu reformers (see pages 140-141), rejected outright these practices as outdated and superstitious.*

Family Life

Family Relationships

Family position	Name (Hindi)
Paternal grandfather	Dada
Paternal grandmother	Dadi
Maternal grandfather	Nana
Maternal grandmother	Nani
Father	Bap, Pita
Mother	Ma, Mata
Brother	Bhai, Bhaya
Sister	Didi, Bhen
Father's brother	Chacha
Father's brother's wife	Chachi
Mother's brother	Mama
Mother's brother's wife	Mami
Mother's sister	Mausi, Massi
Mother's sister's husband	Mausa
Father's sister	Phuphi
Father's sister's husband	Phua, Bhua

Above: An extended family consisting of three generations shortly after arriving in the UK in the early 1970's. Even within family life, there was a degree of segregation, to help avoid over-familiarity.

Hindu attitudes towards family life can appear ambivalent. Some texts condemn it as 'a deep dark well', in which one loses all sense of spiritual direction and becomes hopelessly entrapped in maya. These texts are especially favoured by ascetic traditions. Other scriptural passages glorify responsible family life as the backbone of *Varnashrama-dharma* society. Ideologically, these two poles are reconciled within the notion of the grihasta (household) ashram, based on the principle that material facilities can be utilised to cultivate spirituality and detachment. Many popular traditions hold that the spiritual merit attained within sannyasa can also be achieved by properly executing household duties.

The basic building block of Hindu society is the joint or extended family, usually consisting of three of four generations living together. The women collectively cook and share domestic responsibilities, and the men provide the pooled income. Elders take important decisions and, based on their own experience in life, offer guidance to younger members, Within the family, property usually passes from father to son, and men make many of the decisions, though older ladies carry considerable influence. When women marry, they usually join their husband's family, though maintaining contact with their own.

Hindu families demonstrate firm ties of affection, strikingly different from many Western families. Hindu scripture has elaborately defined the dynamics of the various relationships within families. For example, a grandchild can tease and joke with a grandparent in a familiar way, not permissible with the father or mother. The different relatives are given specific terms of address, unlike the west where 'aunt' or 'uncle' refers to a whole host of relatives and family friends *(see top left)*.

The extended family traditionally provides shelter and support for the elderly, the disabled and the less well off. Children are expected to repay the debt owed to their parents by supporting them in their retirement and old age. An important aspect of Hindu family life is the inter-dependence between members. Marriage itself is a broad social and religious obligation, rather than just a relationship between partners. The extended family provides considerable practical and emotional support, as for example when children are born. One advantage is that marriage stability is not inordinately reliant on the state of the couple's emotional ties.

Despite these possible benefits, social trends indicate that the extended family is becoming less popular, especially outside India. Young couples often value the freedom that the nuclear family offers. They are also adopting other aspects of the Western lifestyle. TV is becoming more popular than worship, and is certainly strongly influencing family values.

Children

From early times the main purpose of marriage was to raise children. They were important not only in their own right, but also for continuation of the family lineage, and to perform the last rites for parents. In some circles, nurturing pious and emotionally stable progeny was considered a valuable socio-spiritual contribution. Some texts emphasise the crucial role that parents play in enabling their offspring to attain spiritual merit and liberation.

Overall, Hinduism emphasises that children should be loved and in no way neglected. The first chapter of the *Bhagavad-gita* alludes to the moral and social problems arising from 'unwanted children'. For this reason, Hindu texts condemn contraception (especially abortion), suggesting that it is children who should be wanted rather than sexual pleasure alone. Some members of the higher *varnas* still perform rites of passage before attempting to conceive children. Children are generally treated with much affectionate indulgence, especially before schooling begins.

Traditionally, only members of the three higher *varnas* received a formal education as brahmachari students. Shudra boys stayed at home and were trained by the father. Girls were also educated at home, largely in domestic skills, and were married at a relatively young age. Unmarried girls were not allowed to stay away from home to preserve their chastity. In today's societies these practices have changed considerably.

Despite this, the home still plays a central role in the transmission of values. Children take part in the daily worship and learn social graces, such as the procedure for properly receiving guests. Additionally, Hindu children, outside India especially, receive formal training within their community. Hindu UK temples and movements have their own Sunday schools to nurture children in the branch of their faith. Naturally as children grow, not all retain the same religious sentiment as their parents; on the positive side, globalisation means that many are actively researching their roots and trying to understand their religious heritage.

Top right: Children at the mandir. Children are naturally playful, and there are traditional Indian games. Many saints are still remembered for playfully performing puja and other acts of worship in their childhood. Hindu children today often have their own small altars where they imitate worship of the murti. There are many documented instances of boys taking sannyasa at an very early age much to the distress of even religious parents - showing again the tensions between two Hindu ideals - family affection and detachment.

Right: Many Hindu religious organisations have established their own day schools and Sunday schools, with particular emphasis on nurturing children in the values of their tradition.

Simple Living, High Thinking

Hindu spirituality has been largely nurtured in a rural setting, and scripture recommends a simple life, free from unnecessary complication. *Varnashrama-dharma* is closely associated with an agrarian culture, which fosters a mood of dependence on God. According to theologians, the village demonstrates the influence of goodness (sattva), the town is compelled by passion (rajas) and sinful places, such as many modern cities, are bound by ignorance (tamas). The whole system of *Varnashrama-dharma* is designed to bring everyone, step by step, to the level of goodness, more easily attained in a rural setting. Sustainability and a peaceful, regulated lifestyle are principal characteristics of *sattva guna*.

The early morning hours are also considered sattvic and in India people rise early, between 4 and 6 a.m. Practically everyone bathes upon rising, making use of a pond, river or handpump, or - if relatively well-off - a bathroom. It is common in the morning to see Hindus outside their simple dwellings, slowly cleaning their teeth with a twig from a tree, such as the antiseptic neem. Life is relatively slow, with morning hours dedicated to some form of worship. A light breakfast follows at around eight o'clock. Shops and stalls open quite late, around ten. The main meal is lunch - for the digestion is considered strongest when the sun is at its highest. People take a siesta in the sultry afternoons, and shops and stalls either close, or the shopkeeper takes a snooze. They often open late into the evening, when it is pleasantly cool, and people again throng to the streets and the temples.

Life is very much in contact with nature and the elements. Water is drawn straight from wells or rivers. Cooking is over open fires. Village homes have an earth floor, coated with a mixture of earth and cow-dung, which has antiseptic properties. Animals are very much a part of life. Dogs are not domesticated, and live quite differently than in the West. Cows roam freely and are given much leeway. Wild pigs, often part of the natural scenery, are valued for their function of waste disposal. Monkeys are notorious for their mischief and their stealing (eye-glasses are now a favourite!). Camels, ponies and buffalo are used for pulling carts. In the south especially, elephants are used in temple rituals. There are many stories about snakes, especially the cobra, which is considered to have mystical powers. Today, there are still many physicians who can cure a snake bite by chanting mantra rather than administering a serum. Mysticism and spirituality are woven into the colourful fabric of everyday life.

Left, from top down:
- *Women collect water from a well. A rural life involves much contact with the elements.*
- *This girl is cooking chapattis on an open fire. Many household chores are performed whilst squatting on the floor, a feat Indian people have little problem with.*
- *Animals are very much a part of a rural lifestlye.*
- *The sadhu (wandering holy man) typifies a simple life and the ability to focus the mind on an inner, spiritual wealth. Simplicity creates a mood of service and dependence upon God rather than an exploitative ethos and reliance on our own schemes to harness and control nature. Householders are also recommended to keep their lives and minds as uncluttered as possible.*

Village Life

The village is the natural centre of any rural community. Gandhi believed that villages were the key to happiness and prosperity, and pleaded for the de-centralisation of economic and political power through the organisation of village panchayats. The panchayat is a committee of five elders who effectively govern local life. The village was therefore the primary unit of social organisation.

Today, despite continuing urbanisation, many Indians still live in villages. Though modern technology is apparent everywhere, it appears incongruous, and life largely depends on the land as it has for thousands of years.

Top right: *A typical village scene in Bengal.*
Above: *Grinding flour and churning yoghurt in a village household*
Above right: *The bull, traditionally used for ploughing and transport, is gradually being superseded by the tractor.*
Right: *Disposable cups and plates are nothing new. These sun-baked clay pots and banana leaf plates are easily and effectively recycled. Village life, based on dharma (adherence to God's laws) helps to preserve the environment.*
Bottom right: *Many village still use cottage industries. Here a woman spins wool by traditional means.*

Personal Reflection

- What experience do we have of living a more simple life?
- What would be the advantages and disadvantages?
- Do we identify simplicity with backwardness?

Related Values/Issues

- Economics and the environment.
- Consumerism.

Top: The inner city in Puri.
Above: A typical indian lorry, complete with the distinctive artwork. India is a strange mixture of the traditional and the modern!
Below: Urbanisation is devastating the environment in many parts of India. Welfare organisations and the government are now taking measures to prevent further pollution of natural resources. Taking part in a school project, these girls show off their eco-friendly handicrafts.
Bottom right: Many Hindus outside of India have now happily adopted a Western lifestyle, whilst they still practice their religion. Here, a young couple from London learn about meditation using beads.

Today, India is a curious blend of ancient and modern, epitomised by the bhajan blasting from loudspeakers and the sadhu with his mobile phone. More people are moving into towns and cities, and in rural areas the bull is succumbing to the tractor. Industrialisation is taking its toll. Many holy sites are strewn with litter, especially plastic bags, which pose a threat to wildlife. Extensive deforestation and huge hydro-electric schemes have disrupted the flow of water in India's sacred rivers, causing flash floods after the monsoon and dried-up beds in summer. Some Hindu organisations are voicing their concerns, raising ecological awareness as India runs the path of modernisation. Television and the film industry are having their impact, evident even in the smallest of villages. The younger generation often considers the West its new source of inspiration.

What is noticeable, though, is that material progress and technology never seem to quite work in India! The recently constructed dual carriageway from Delhi to Agra is more accurately described as 'two parallel roads'. The driver continuously dodges cows, bicycles and tractors coming towards him on the wrong side of the road. Despite these anomalies – quite shocking to many Westerners – India somehow manages to maintain its sense of spirituality.

Many Hindus living outside India now have quite different lifestyles from their forefathers. Naturally, they tend to get up somewhat later in the day. The extended family is diminishing. Some remain strict about diet, whereas others adopt local eating habits. Unlike in India the temple has become a centre of social activity and an emblem of Hindu identity. Within the UK many multi-million complexes are being constructed in urban areas, replacing the old converted church-halls. Though these temples help Hindus maintain core spiritual practices, there are clear challenges in adjusting to rapidly changing lifestyles, and in applying to the modern context principles largely rooted in rural India.

Part 4 - Continuity & Change

 **Chapter 10 – Historical Perspectives**

 **Chapter 11 – Doctrine and Scripture**

 **Chapter 12 – Movements and Leaders**

This final part of the book relates to most elements of the ideals and practices we have covered so far, through Parts One to Three. In reading generalised statements, we should remember that no religion is static. Here, therefore, we consider the influence of time and how religion is a dynamic process, involving negotiated relationships between the individual, the broad and evolving tradition, and the various groups and sub-groups that constitute and enhance that tradition. The central theme here is 'authority' its role in ensuring the continuity of a tradition and its ability to successfully adapt to changing circumstances.

Chapter 10
Historical
Perspectives

"In Hinduism, the momentous event of a foundation at one point in time, the initial splash in the water, from which concentric circles expand to cover an ever-wider part of the total surface, is absent. The waves that carried Hinduism to a great many shores are not connected to a central historical fact or to a common historic movement."

Prof. K. Klostermaier
"Hinduism – A Short History"

To construct a reliable chronology of Hinduism is challenging, for the following reasons:

- Hinduism claims no identifiable human founder, nor a specific origin in history.
- It is so old that its past recedes into pre-history. Furthermore, the tradition itself claims to be eternal.
- Hinduism is extremely diverse, and only recently conceived of as a single, distinct religion. Hindus did not feel compelled to unify their many traditions, or define the common ground that distinguished them from 'other faiths'– not, at least, until these 'others' threatened to impose their own doctrines.
- Hindu people were little concerned with recording mere facts; they were interested in the meaning behind events, not a resume of the past. First hand records are therefore relatively rare.
- Within the accounts that are available, there is no clear divide between history and myth; written narratives span many eras of time and planes of existence. They are not limited to descriptions or eulogies of a single country, race or religion.

Nonetheless, researchers have drawn up a timeline for Hinduism, as they do for other religions. Most textbooks identify the roots of Hinduism with the Aryan migration into India, around 1500 BCE, and the subsequent composition of the Rig Veda. European scholars proposed this theory in the late 19th century. It was controversial from the start and some academics, especially from India, now consider it an example of colonial-missionary interpretation – a predominant culture projecting it own ideas, values and biases onto the politically dependent. Europeans considered India backward, thinking that anything valuable found there must have been imported from the 'civilised' West. Significantly, within ancient Indian texts there is no mention of any Aryan migration. The term Aryan *(see glossary)* was used, but not to refer to a specific race of people. As scholars continue to debate the theory, a new chronology is emerging, often reversing the paradigm by proposing India as the cradle of civilisation, and pushing dates further back. This is more consistent with Hindu versions of history, with their much earlier dates and numerous textual references to Vedic societies migrating westward.

The table below, although not completely consistent with the tradition's view, is a commonly presented picture. It has been simplified to include only more relevant elements and modified to accommodate results of more recent research. Naturally, all dates are somewhat tentative. The seven periods shown below are discussed over the next three pages.

A Hindu Chronology

3,000 – 1500 BCE	**Indus Valley Civilisation** (Old Chronology), or
6,000 – 1900 BCE	**Indus-Sarasvati Civilisation** (New Chronology)
1500 – 500 BCE	**Vedic Period** (some say, beginning with the Aryan migration)
500 BCE – 500 CE	**Epic, Puranic and Classical Ages**
500 CE – 1200 CE	**Early and Middle Medieval Period** Early development of *bhakti* (esp. in South India). Formation of *sampradayas* contesting internally and externally. Theological establishment of Vedanta.
1200 – 1757 CE	**Muslim Period** *Bhakti* saints and the cultivation of personal piety. Development of the theistic traditions.
1757 – 1947 CE	**British Period** The reform movements and birth of neo-Hinduism.
1947 CE – the present	**Independent India** Migration to Britain; Hinduism established as a world religion.

Ancient History

The Indus Valley Civilisation (prior to 1500 BCE)

Initially, little was known about the people living in the Indus valley before the supposed Aryan migration. Then, in the 1920s, archaeologists found the remains of two walled cities, Mohenjo-daro and Harappa, now both in Pakistan. Scholars assumed that the invaders destroyed these cities and forced the people to adopt the Aryan culture. Recent aerial photographs, however, suggest that by this time (1500 BCE) the Indus civilisation was already extinct due to the drying up of the river Sarasvati, a tributary of the Indus.

The ancient Indus-Sarasvati society appears to have been relatively civilised, with detailed town planning and sophisticated drainage systems. The inhabitants even developed a form of writing, depicted on various seals excavated from the site. To date, no one has been able to decode the script. Little is known about the people's religion, but scholars suggest that there was much emphasis on fertility rites and goddess worship, which may have been adopted by the migrating Aryans. There is also one seal (*right*) that appears to resemble Shiva as Pashupati, Lord of the Beasts.

The Vedic Period (1500 – 500 BCE)

Information about the Vedic religion apparently introduced by the Aryans is gleaned largely from the Vedas. Focus was on yajna, ritualistic performance of sacrifice, and on joining the ancestors in heaven. The pre-eminent doctrine was Purva Mimamsa, largely non-theistic and with some strands trying to prove that God is non-existent, or at least redundant. Uttara Mimamsa (Vedanta) emerged towards the latter part of the period with the compilation of the Upanishads. Scholars say that there was no clearly enunciated doctrine of reincarnation at this time. The predominant deities, different from those in later Hinduism, represented the forces of nature and were headed by Indra, god of rain. The central story of his killing the giant, Vrita, comes down in numerous versions up to the present. The migrating Aryans are accredited with introducing Sanskrit, and with the system of *Varnashrama-dharma*, though perhaps in a relatively simple form.

Epic, Puranic and Classical Periods (500 BCE – 500 CE)

From 500 BCE onwards, veneration of Indra, the main deity of the Rig Veda, was replaced by the worship of Vishnu, Shiva and Devi. Vedic *yajna* was largely superseded by *puja,* and the ritualistic Mimamsa *darshan* was pushed from centre-stage by the speculative philosophies of Vedanta. The emphasis shifted from the Vedas to the development of the Epics, the Ramayana and the Mahabharata, both written during this period. Although Vishnu was already a Vedic deity, only now his importance emerged. Shiva replaced his form as Rudra, and Devi replaced the fertility goddesses of the Vedic and pre-Vedic ages. This period also saw the rise of the Mauryan Empire founded by King Chandra Gupta, and extended by Ashok to include much of India. Under Ashok's patronage Buddhism spread throughout large portions of the sub-continent, and Jainism similarly flourished. The second Gupta Empire (circa 319-490) united large portions of the country, and nurtured a cultural renaissance within Hinduism and, a golden era for the traditional arts and sciences.

Above: A murti of Andal. She was the only woman among the twelve Alvars, the forerunners of Shri Vaishnavism, as later established by Ramanuja. She is still much worshipped in South India.

Below: Emperor Akbar, usually considered the greatest of the Moghul emperors.

Early and Middle Medieval Period (500 CE – 1200 CE)

From 500 CE onwards, several important developments laid the foundations for contemporary Hinduism, particularly the popular theistic and devotional elements. In the South, poet-saints recorded their spontaneous, spiritual outpourings. Most notable are the 12 Vaishnava 'Alvars' (6th – 9th centuries) and the 63 Shaivite 'Nayanars' (8th –10th centuries). Several key thinkers consolidated these teachings by developing new theologies transmitted through *sampradayas* (disciplic successions), which contested amongst themselves and with outsiders. Shankaracharya (780 – 812) travelled widely, defeating scholars of the *nastika* movements, Buddhism and Jainism, which around the turn of the millennium had established prominent seats of learning throughout India. He firmly reestablished the authority of the Vedic canon, propagated *advaita* and laid sturdy foundations for future Vedantic *sampradayas*. Abhinavangupta, Ramanuja, Madhva and others followed, writing their own scriptural commentaries, propounding new theologies and establishing their own successions. During much of this period, Shaivism was the prominent tradition in India, especially in the South.

The Muslim Period (1200 – 1757 CE)

From the 7th century onwards, Muslim Arabs had begun invading parts of India. Muslim political power began with the Turks during the rule of the Delhi Sultanate (1206-1526). The Moghuls subsequently came to power with the reign of Babur (1526-1520). However Akbar (1542-1605), third Moghul emperor of India (1556-1605), is generally considered the true founder of the Moghul Empire. He was liberal and broad-minded, patronising Hindu scholars and artists. In comparison, his puritanical great-grandson, Aurangzeb, reigning from 1658 until 1705, restricted Hindu practices and demolished many temples. During the entire Moghul period, Hindus were largely excluded from public life, compelling them to develop their spirituality without royal patronage. These restrictions, combined with the rigidity of the caste system, prompted a shift towards spiritual processes that circumvented authoritative religion. Leaders rose from amongst the people, emphasising the importance of personal piety. The *bhakti* saints flourished during this period, expressing their devotional sentiments through song, music and poetry, and propounding a theology of spiritual egalitarianism.

The British Period (1757 – 1948)

Robert Clive's victory at the Battle of Plassey in 1757 established British supremacy in India and heralded the collapse of the Moghul Empire. At first the British government adopted a lenient, 'hands-off' attitude towards Indian culture, drawing up regulations to protect "the natives in the free exercise of their religion". However, in the early 1800s, missionaries arrived to proselytise and they finally won the right to campaign without government licence. Shortly after, the first scholars arrived and, though initially sympathetic, were often motivated by a desire to "civilise the Hindoo" and save his soul from eternal damnation. Seats of Indology were established in Oxford, and important contributions were made to scholarship, although the research methods are now considered dated. Attempts to Westernise and Christianise India prompted some Hindus to defend their religion and culture. Others opted for Western values and practices. Most significantly, though, leading Hindu figures realised that India had to be more thoughtful, assertive and adaptable if she were to retain her identity. The resultant reform movements of the 19th and 20th centuries were effective in transforming Hinduism, not by attracting huge numbers of followers, but in stimulating the tradition to change and adapt. They were instrumental in sowing the seeds of Indian nationalism and a missionary spirit that later brought Hinduism to the West.

Above: British rule in India was often accompanied by much pomp and ceremony.
Below: Nehru, first PrimeMinister of independent India.

Independent India and Modern Hinduism (1948 onwards)

The partition of India in 1947, and the resultant bloodshed, served only to reinforce nationalistic tendencies and notions of India as "a Hindu country". Subsequently, the large number of Hindu movements imported into the West, and wide migration of Hindus themselves, meant that Hinduism was no longer simply "the religion of India." It was identified as one of the great world religions. As Hindus were increasingly exposed to members of other cultures and religions, at home and abroad, it raised the need for many to examine carefully their heritage. Teachings and practices that had been largely passed down by family tradition, begged for articulation. Hindus were increasingly invited to contribute to inter-faith initiatives and to present their opinions on the complex moral issues of the day. Although many still prefer the concept of 'Sanatana-dharma', Hinduism is a term that is here to stay. Though the tradition is undergoing many transformations, the elements of its ancient past are still evident, as for example through the fire-sacrifice and the continuing popularity of the Epics and Puranas. Although the exact meaning and nature of Hinduism remains a matter of discussion, it remains an overwhelming reality, a live and dynamic tradition that positively contributes to contemporary life.

Ancient History – the Tradition's Own Version

Hindu accounts of the ancient world and Indian history differ from most academic versions. However, the development of empathetic research methods and the emergence of 'new chronologies' is bringing together the two approaches (though school texts often present dated versions of academic theory). Conflicting opinions reflect the dynamics between different epistemologies – empirical and scriptural – and also between predominant Eastern and Western world-views. To better understand Hinduism, and its ways of seeing, interpreting and responding to the world, it is essential to examine its conceptual view of its own heritage.

Scriptural Quotes

"Because of the powerful influence of the age of Kali, mercy, religion, honesty, cleanliness, tolerance, memory, life-span and physical strength will diminish day by day. Wealth will be considered the sign of good birth, and justice will be won through power alone. A man will be known as a brahmin for his wearing a thread, and one expert at juggling words will be considered a scholar. Marriage will be arranged simply by verbal agreement and beauty will be thought to depend on one's hairstyle. Success in business will depend on deceit, and filling the belly will become the goal of life. As the earth thus becomes crowded with a corrupt population, whoever among any of the social classes shows himself to be the strongest will gain political power."

Bhagavat Purana 12.2.1-7
(selected passages)

- Hindus believe in 'Sanatana-dharma' – the eternal religion - encompassing the concepts of eternal time, universal truths and a human history that recedes indefinitely.

- Time is viewed as cyclical. History repeats itself not in every detail, but by perennially manifesting similar phenomena (much like the revolving seasons).

- Time is degenerative, in the same way that we only experience getting older. According to Hindu thought, upon death and rebirth the soul rapidly 'grows younger'; similarly, after prolonged moral and spiritual degradation, there is a rapid regeneration in the world. Therefore, with the passing of time, society is not necessarily becoming more civilised in terms of human and spiritual values.

- True religion, as expressed through Hinduism and other traditions, is ever existing, but subject to periods of degradation and revival. God reveals it in a manner suitable for particular social and cultural milieus.

- We are now half-way through the duration of this universe, consisting of 100 years of the creator, Brahma. His one year consists of 360 celestial days, each made up of 1,000 'great ages' *(maha-yugas)*. Each *maha-yuga* is 4,320,000 earth years.

- In the present *maha-yuga,* we entered the fourth age, Kali yuga, some 5,000 years ago. At that time the Vedic truths, previously transmitted orally, were first written down.

- Different ages feature suitable processes of self and God-realisation, and the appearance of particular incarnations of Vishnu. These are shown below:

Age	Predominant Spiritual Practice	Avatars
Satya Yuga 100% religious	**Meditation**	First five avatars – Matsya to Vamana
Treta Yuga 75% religious	**Yajna (offering of Vedic sacrifice)**	Parashurama and Ramachandra (Rama)
Dvarapa Yuga 50% religious	**Temple worship (puja)**	Krishna's descent and the Mahabharata war (at end)
Kali Yuga 25% religious, declining to complete degradation by the end	Personal practices that offer relatively quick effective routes to liberation often through specific mantra (prayers) or tantra, using techniques which emphasise the importance of Shakti, the feminine energy, expressed as Shiva-Shakti, Radha Krishna, etc.	Buddha and – still to come at the end of Kali-yuga – Kalki

The Hindu perspective on history is expressed in the following ways:

- Belief in a previous glorious age, as portrayed in many stories and myths. This has given rise to many types of spiritual idealism, including the notion of 'Rama-rajya,' the perfect reign of Lord Rama. Some nationalistic movements have adopted these ideals to further their political aims.

- Ancient heroic figures, both male and female, are still admired as relevant and timeless role models. Many Hindus consider them timeless archetypes.

- There is sometimes tension between traditional Hindu values and widely accepted post-modern views, including 'political correctness.' Hindus often consider their values eternal and universal rather than out-dated.

- Hindus often claim that India was 'the cradle of civilisation'. They reject the notion that India is only now emerging from a tribal, barbaric and superstitious past that is less civilised than the West. These different opinions reflect different criteria for defining 'civilisation.'

- Authors often claim that India was learned in many sciences well before the West. However, there is much debate regarding the compatibility of traditional Hindu values with those underpinning modern science. Some consider technology the antithesis of spirituality, based on the exploitation of nature; others, perhaps more modern in their approach, consider that the two disciplines, science and religion, are inter-dependent and entirely consistent.

- Approaches to Darwinian evolution range from passive acceptance to assertive confrontation. Traditionalists claim that real evolution is spiritual (through reincarnation) and that material evolution is not ascending (from lower life forms) but descending (from God and the progenitors.) It appears that the Hindu notion of a non-linear world history confronts Darwinian belief that human life is always progressing with time.

Related Values/Issues

- What differentiates civilised society from uncivilised?
- Do different nations maintain different versions of history?
- Why is Darwinian evolution largely accepted by most people today?
- What determines our values and our particular world view?
- Why do we tend to think that today's society is the most advanced it has ever been?

Quote

Gandhi, upon being asked, "What do you think of Western civilization?", replied, "It's a good idea!"

Above: Many Hindus do not believe that a non-technological past presupposes a necessarily poor and primitive one. This picture shows how one artist envisions a previous glorious age and a society based on performing dharma and relying on the natural gifts of God and nature.

Meaning and Purpose

The nature of time
The nature and purpose of human life

Chapter 11
Doctrine &
Scripture

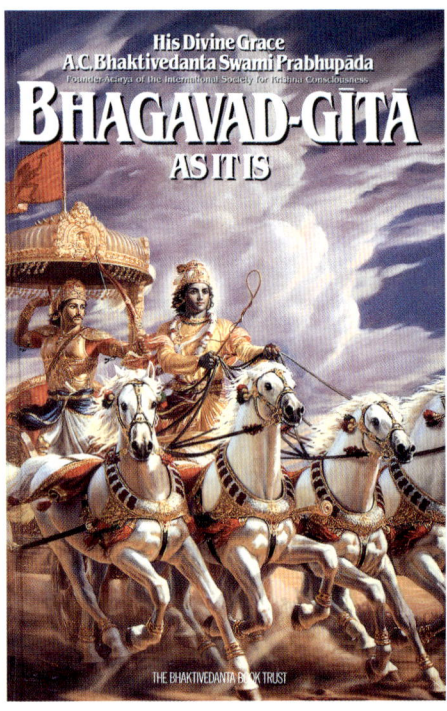

Above: *Of all the Hindu sacred books, Bhagavad Gita is perhaps the most popular. Although it principally supports the doctrine of Vedanta, it includes elements of the other five schools, especially sankhya.*

Hinduism has neither a common doctrine nor a single scripture as the source of its various teachings. It places more emphasis on orthopraxy than orthodoxy, encouraging relative freedom of thought within tightly defined codes of conduct and morality. More than Western traditions, it has succeeded in synthesising religion with philosophy, and religious commitment with a reflective search for truth. It does not generally exhort its followers to declare allegiance to a particular faith, belief or creed.

Many Hindus call their tradition 'Sanatana-dharma', the eternal law that governs everyone irrespective of belief. These truths regarding the universal law were divinely revealed to ancient sages. For many aeons they were passed down orally and only later written down, apparently around the start of the Kali-yuga when people's memories began to deteriorate. Perhaps the most important sage was Vyasa (Badarayana), generally accredited with writing the Vedanta Sutras, Mahabharata and Bhagavad-gita.

As Hinduism developed, it did not reject its parent traditions, but modified and assimilated them into newer schools of thought. For example, the ancient Vedic notion of sacrifice, and the later philosophies of Sankhya and Yoga, have all been assimilated into the more recent school of Vedanta. Even the more sectarian sampradayas do not entirely reject other doctrines, but claim that they demonstrate a less complete understanding.

Despite a relatively inclusive approach, Hinduism has rejected those doctrines that do not accept its scriptural authority. Most notably these include Jainism, Buddhism and the hedonistic philosophy of Charvaka. They are therefore called *nastika*, differentiating them from the accepted schools termed *astika*. There are six main *astika* systems, which are called *darshanas* ('ways of seeing'). The various groups and sub-groups within Hinduism usually subscribe to one or more of the six darshanas.

The Six Darshans Showing also the main teacher & the content of his teachings	
1. Vaisheshika *Kanada* Physics, especially atomic theory	2. Nyaya *Gautama* Logic and epistemology
3. Sankhya *Kapila Muni* Physics & Metaphysics	4. Yoga *Patanjali* Sadhana (spiritual practices)
5. Mimamsa *Jaimini* Hermeneutics and Ritual	6. Vedanta *Vyasa* Metaphysics

Related Values/Issues
- Fact, opinion and belief
- Doctrine versus dogma

Left: The six darshanas are grouped as three pairs of 'sisters'. Each pair consists of one darshan dealing with theory and the other explaining the corresponding practice and methodology. For example, Sankhya forms the doctrinal basis for the discipline of yoga. Each pair is further explored on the three subsequent pages.

Some groups consider these schools to be hierarchical, with Vedanta the culmination of Vedic philosophy. This is somewhat supported by the fact that Vedanta means "the end of the Vedas" or, less literally, "the ultimate conclusion of knowledge." Certainly, Vedanta today represents the more theologically developed strands of Hinduism, and forms the basis for many modern theistic traditions.

Vedanta and Mimamsa

Vedanta is closely aligned with its sister school, **Mimamsa** (meaning 'enquiry'). The two are often called Purva Mimamsa and Uttara Mimamsa, denoting the earlier and later schools of enquiry. The earlier Mimamsa deals with *dharma* and focusses on rituals, particularly for promotion to higher planets. Its main texts are from the Karma-kanda section of the Vedas. The later school, Vedanta, deals with *Brahman* and derives much from the Jnana-kanda section, especially the Upanishads and Vedanta Sutras (a.k.a. the Brahma Sutras). Members of these two doctrines are traditionally at logger-heads, but they are essentially complementary. Much of modern Hinduism, though philosophically grounded in its Vedanta, borrows its ritualistic practice from Purva Mimamsa.

There are ten principal schools of Vedanta. Of these, two are purely *Advaita*, one purely *Dvaita* and seven a synthesis of both. In Hinduism as represented in the UK, there are *four important schools* of Vedanta, as shown (*below right*).

Above right: Vivekananda widely popularised Vedanta in the West, but his teachings represent only one particular school, called Advaita (literally 'non-dualism', often called 'monism'). Vivekananda somewhat modernised the original Advaita doctrine of Shankara. The main antagonists of Advaita are the dualistic schools of Vaishnavism.

Right: For any tradition to be accepted as a genuine Vedantic school, the founder must present commentaries on three scriptures – the Upanishads, the Vedanta Sutras and the Bhagavad Gita, collectively called the 'prasthana trayi.'
This table shows four main branches of Vedanta along with: 1) its founding theologian, 2) the sampradaya, 3) the main representative movement in the UK. For details of leaders and movements, please see Chapter 12, page 132.

Common Misunderstandings

"Vedanta (and all Hinduism) is entirely monistic, believing only in the all-pervading world-soul, Brahman, rather than a personal God."

This advaita philosophy is certainly popular, and offers a simple explanation of the many deities. Nonetheless, many theologians have considered God to be a person. He is not merely an anthropomorphic representation, nor are the various deities and murtis simply incarnations or representations of an impersonal Supreme.
Thus Hinduism includes both monism and monotheism. It is misleading to call the Abrahamic religions, "the monotheistic traditions", implying that monotheism is absent from the Eastern traditions. Vedanta includes many monotheistic schools. They may accept the existence of many gods and goddesses, but strongly emphasise the pre-eminence of the Supreme Deity.

The Four Main Schools of Vedanta represented in the UK

1. Advaita (monism)
Theologian: Shankara
Sampradaya: Smartas
UK Movement: Ramakrishna Mission

2. Vishishtadvaita (qualified monism)
Theologian: Ramanuja
Sampradaya: Shri Vaishnavas
UK Movement: Swami Narayana Mission

3. Suddhadvaita (purified monism)
Theologian: Vallabha
Sampradaya: Pushti Marg
UK: Shree Vallabha Nidhi

4. Achintya Bheda-abheda
Theologian: Baladeva
Sampradaya: Gaudiya Vaishnava
UK Movement: ISKCON
(Hare Krishna Movement)

Above: Kapila, who founded the school of Sankya. Some Hindus claim there were two Kapilas, teaching theistic and atheistic versions of this doctrine.

Sankhya, derived from the word meaning 'to count', is a philosophical system of analysing matter established by Kapila. It aims to overcome suffering through cultivating discrimination and by releasing the soul (*purusha*) from its entanglement in matter (*prakriti*). Scholars say that it was originally a non-theistic system delineating 24 material truths (or elements), with the soul as the 25th. As theistic schools evolved, they added a 26th element, the *paramapurusha* or God. (*purusha* and *paramapurusha* are here synonymous with *atman* and *paramatman*). The later theistic notion of Shiva-Shakti is the equivalent of *purusha-prakriti*. Shiva is the male, the energetic, and *prakriti*, the complementary female energy. The Vedanta schools accommodated many of the terms and concepts of Sankhya, which are also mentioned in the Bhagavad-gita.

The 24 Elements of Sankhya Philosophy (shown in blue)			
Pradhana ▼	The Pradhana is the unmanifest three modes of nature (goodness, passion and ignorance). The three subtle elements constitute the subtle (astral) body, and the five gross elements constitute the outward body. They are listed here in order from subtle to gross. The living being has five knowledge-acquiring senses and five working senses, each of which relates to one of the five elements and the corresponding sense object.		
Three Subtle Elements			
False-ego			
Intelligence			
Mind			
Five Gross Elements ▼	Five Sense Objects ▼	Five Knowledge-acquiring Senses ▼	Five Working Senses ▼
Ether	Sound	Ear	Voice
Air	Touch	Skin	Legs
Fire	Sight	Eye	Arms
Water	Taste	Tongue	Reproductive organs
Earth	Smell	Nose	Evacuating organs

Scriptural Passage

Yoga means control of the contents of the mind. When thoughts are stilled, then the eternal soul experiences its own nature.

Yoga Sutras 1:2-3

The Eight Stages of Yoga

1. yama – *prohibitions and restraints*
2. niyama – *developing virtues*
3. asana – *physical postures*
4. pranayama – *breathing exercises*
5. pratyahara – *sense withdrawal*
6. dharana – *concentration*
7. dhyana – *meditation*
8. samadhi – *trance (absorption of the mind on one point)*

Patanjali–yoga, also called raja - or astanga-yoga, is intimately linked with Sankhya, its 'sister' *darshan*. The practice of yoga is based on the Patanjali Sutras, consisting of 194 aphorisms. They are divided into four sections – *samadhi* (trance), *sadhana* (the practice), *vibhuti* (mystic powers) and *kaivalya* (the ultimate aim). The process itself is divided into eight limbs (angas). Although popular hatha-yoga is related to astanga-yoga, particularly the third stage, the exercises in Patanjali's system are designed not for physical health but simply to facilitate meditation and self-realisation. The yogi must be able to sit comfortably, neither straining nor falling asleep, and have complete control over the breath. Patanjali also warns the yogi not to be allured by the mystic *siddhis* (perfections), but to keep in mind the goal of self-realisation. This involves discrimination (based on Sankhya), purging oneself of base qualities (lust, greed, illusion, etc.) and having complete control over the mind and senses. Patanjali also recommends scriptural study and surrender to the Lord, which bestow peace, illumination and *samadhi*. Kaivalya refers to the realisation that one is not the body but the soul within. It is achieved when the yogi is fixed in meditation on the Lord residing within the heart and no longer influenced by the three *gunas* (qualities of matter).

Doctrine – Vaisheshika and Nyaya

Vaisheshika, another orthodox school, was founded by Kanada (circa 600 BCE). In much the same way as the Greeks, he describes the elements, their characteristics and their interrelations. He mentions atoms and molecules and infers the existence of the *atman* through specific symptoms. Despite a philosophical approach, he stresses *dharma* as a means to both prosperity and liberation, and prescribes many traditional practices such as fasting, celibacy, and service to the guru.

Kanada states that since all material objects are constructed from atoms, they are products rather than causes, and the causes are the irreducible particles themselves. He introduces the principle of *adrishta*, an unknown invisible cause. Although Kanada's philosophy is non-theistic, later doctrines built upon the notion of *adrishta* to propose God as the remote cause of everything: it is God who orchestrates the dynamic interrelations between the innumerable atoms.

Above: The Greek philosopher Democritus (460 – 370 BCE) may not have been the first to propound atomism.

Nyaya systems trace their beginnings back to the disputations of Vedic scholars. At the time of the Upanishads, debate was cultivated as an art, following prescribed rules in which the elements of logical proof were contained. The school of Nyaya attempts to define a system of logic as a way to truth and liberation. It is a discipline aimed at reversing the folly and mistaken notions that bind the soul. The Navya-Nyaya (New School of Logic) developed from the twelfth century and specialised in epistemology. It acknowledges four legitimate means of obtaining knowledge:

1. *pratyaksha* – sense perception.
2. *anumana* – inference or deduction.
3. *upamana* – analogy.
4. *shabda* – literally 'sound', referring to scriptural authority.

These four are all considered valid, but without shabda the others are considered unreliable and potentially misleading. This rationale forms much of the foundation for the epistemological authority granted to Vedic writings.

Nyaya has also developed a sophisticated syllogism that has five stages as opposed to the three of Aristotle. Unique to Indian philosophy, and found in Nyaya texts, are arguments for the existence of Ishvara (God). Many of the currently popular theistic schools draw significantly from Nyaya. Of all the Hindu systems, Nyaya enjoys the greatest respect from Western philosophers, who are beginning to realise the subtleties and intricacies of Indian logic.

Above: Debate has played an important role within Hinduism, showing that spiritual commitment was not inconsistent with philosophical inquiry. Hinduism has little time for armchair philosophy, and demands high standards of personal integrity. If a scholar lost a debate, he would often become the student-disciple of the victor. This painting shows a debate between the bhakti revivalist, Chaitanya, and a famous religious leader of the day. The scholar was defeated, and became one of Chaitanya's leading followers.

Related Values/Issues

■ Stating our case/opinion reasonably.
■ Faith and reason.

Hindu Sacred Books

Key Points:

- Hinduism has no single scripture but many.
- They include the Vedas and their corollaries sometimes called collectively 'the Vedic scriptures'.
- There are two main divisions:

    (1) **shruti** – that which is heard (revealed truth).

    (2) **smriti** – that which is remembered (realised truth).

- Sanskrit is the language of most canonical texts, but many subsidiary texts are written in the vernacular.

Sacred texts are sources of:

1. Philosophical concepts.
2. Information on personal values.
3. Practical injunctions.
4. Story and myth.
5. Prayers and mantras.
6. Details of worship/liturgy.
7. Various arts and sciences.

The concept of Hinduism being a single monolithic religion is recent, dating back only to the 19th century. Many scholars liken Hinduism to a family of religions, with all affiliated members bearing a family resemblance. Thus any definition of Hinduism is somewhat arbitrary and requires qualification. One such definition is "the followers of Vaidika Dharma", or those who follow the religious teachings outlined in the Vedas and their corollaries.

Hindu religious literature is divided into two main categories:

(1) **Shruti** ("that which has been heard")
(2) **Smriti** ("that which has been remembered")

Shruti is canonical, consisting of revelation and unquestionable truth, and is considered eternal. It refers mainly to the Vedas themselves.

Smriti is supplementary and may change over time. It is authoritative only to the extent that it conforms to the bedrock of Shruti.

There are different opinions about the relative validity and importance of each. Some Hindus stress the foundational importance of Shruti, whereas others say that in making truths accessible, Smriti is more important today. Belief in universal truth suggests to some Hindu thinkers that any teaching that corresponds to real knowledge can also be accepted as 'Veda'. Hence there are numerous writings considered to be 'Vedic', including many vernacular works. It is important to note that:

(1) the divide between Shruti and Smriti is often contested.
(2) the divide is not discrete but can be represented as a continuum, with some texts more canonical than others.

Most key texts are written in classical Sanskrit, considered the sacred language of the gods.' The script itself is termed 'devanagari'- literally 'from the cities of the gods'. *(For more information on Sanskrit, please see page 90).* Many subsidiary texts, particularly by medieval *bhakti* writers, are in local vernaculars, such as Tamil, Brajbasi, Gujarati, Bengali, etc.

The content of Vedic scripture is divided into three main sections, though the last one, as shown below, is sometimes omitted:

Karma-kanda: largely dealing with ritual sacrifice aimed at enjoyment *(world-accepting).*
Jnana-kanda: philosophical texts aimed at knowledge through renunciation *(world-denying).*
Upasana kanda: texts focusing on worship of God and service to him *(world-accommodating/transcending).*

These three largely correspond to the three main paths – karma-yoga, jnana yoga and bhakti yoga *(see pages 44-45).*

The most important books in the Shruti and Smriti are listed to the right. They are here grouped into ten categories to aid memorisation. The main texts within both Shruti and Smriti are explored in subsequent pages.

For popular purposes in the UK, the Ramayana, the Mahabharata, the Puranas and the Bhagavad-gita are most commonly used.

Related Practices

■ Sacred texts are treated with respect; they are never placed directly on the floor, nor touched with feet or dirty hands.

■ Prayers are often recited before using or consulting them.

■ Texts are often wrapped in silk cloth.

■ Sometimes they are placed in a shrine and offered worship.

■ Ancient texts were etched on leaves, such as palm.

■ Books are used for recitation, personal study, theological training, pravachan *(see page 58)* and consultation on matters of spiritual and secular law.

Related Values/Issues

■ The differences between belief, opinion and truth.
■ The need for authority.

Personal Reflection

■ In what ways does secular literature fulfill a similar role to scripture e.g. as a means to information? Are there any parallels in the need to accept the opinion, advice or judgment of others? How should it be accepted?

■ How important is it for a teacher to make any topic accessible to students (as Smriti attempts to do)? What are the benefits and possible pitfalls in doing this?

Ten Principal Texts

Main Shruti Texts (3)
- **The Four Vedas**
- **The 108 Upanishads**
- **The Vedanta Sutra**

Main Smriti Texts (4)
- **The Itihasas** ('histories' or epics)
- **The Bhagavad-gita** (philosophy)
- **The Puranas** (stories and histories)
- **The Dharma Shastra** (law books)

Other Texts (4)
- **The Vedangas** ('limbs of the Vedas')
- **The Upavedas** ('following the Vedas')
- **Sectarian texts** (e.g. agamas, tantras)
- **Vernacular literature** (e.g. in Tamil)

Notes:
1. The Epics are the **Ramayana** and **Mahabharata**

2. The 'other texts' are usually classified as Smriti. Some consider the Vedangas to be Shruti.

3. The sectarian texts mainly deal with ritual procedures, and include:
   - the **Vaishnava** Pancharatra,
   - the **Shaiva** Agamas and Tantras,
   - the **Shakta** Devi Shastra and Tantras.

Glossary Terms

Veda – *knowledge, from the root vit, 'to know.'*

Vedic – *often refers to the period of compilation of the Rig Veda (i.e. the Vedic period). Hindus themselves often use the term to describe anything co nected to the Vedas and their corollaries (e.g. Vedic culture).*

Meaning and Purpose

How do we determine the meaning and purpose of life? Does written authority play a role?

Shruti - the Four Vedas

Scriptural Passage

"We meditate on that most adorable, most desirable and most enchanting effulgence of the Supreme Lord, who is the source of creation, inspiration and eternal happiness. May His light inspire and illumine our intellect."

Gayatri Mantra (from the Rig Veda)

(a) The six Vedangas (limbs of the Vedas) are:
1. Kalpa *(ritual detail)*
2. Siksha *(pronunciation,*
3. Vyakarana *(grammar)*
4. Nirukti *(etymology)*
5. Chandas *(metre)*
6. Jyotisha *(astronomy/astrology)*

(b) the four Upavedas *('following the Vedas')* explain arts and sciences:
1. Ayur-veda *(medicine)*
2. Gandharva-veda *(music and dance)*
3. Dhanur-veda *(warfare)*
4. Shilpa-veda *(architecture)*

The Vedas are considered the oldest Hindu texts. Scholars believe that they were written down some 2,500 years ago, though the tradition often dates them to the beginning of Kali-yuga (circa 3000 BCE). Some Hindus say that there was originally only one Veda, the Yajur, which was later divided into four. Scholars, however, usually consider the Rig Veda the oldest of all Hindu writings. The following is an overview of the four Vedas.

The Rig Veda – the most important and, according to scholars, oldest of the Vedas. It is divided into ten books (called mandalas) and has 1028 hymns in praise of various deities. These include Indra, Agni, Vishnu, Rudra, Varuna, and other early or 'Vedic gods'. It also contains the famous Gayatri mantra and the prayer called the Purusha Shukta (the story of Primal Man).

The Yajur Veda – a priestly handbook for use in the performance of yajnas (sacrifices) It is divided into two sections, the earlier 'black' and the more recent 'white.'

Sama Veda – this consists of chants and melodies to be sung during worship and the performance of yajna.

The Atharva Veda – contains hymns, mantras and incantations, largely outside the scope of *yajna*.

Within each of the four books there are four types of composition, or divisions, as shown below. In the narrowest of senses, only the Samhitas comprise the true Vedas. The first two divisions relate to the performance of sacrificial rituals (the karma-kanda section), whereas the second pair consists of philosophy (and belong to the jnana-kanda section).

1. *The Samhitas* – literally "collections," in this case of hymns and mantras. They form the Veda proper.

2. *The Brahmanas* – prose manuals of ritual and prayer for the guiding priests. They tend to explain the Samhitas. They also contain early versions of some stories.

3. *The Aranyakas* – literally 'forest books' for hermits and saints. They are philosophical treatises.

4. *The Upanishads* - books of philosophy, also called 'Vedanta', the end or conclusion of the Vedas.

There are also two important bodies of supplementary literature, related closely to the Vedas themselves. They are:
(a) *The Vedangas*, which expound the sciences required to understand and apply the Vedas.
(b) *The Upavedas* (usually considered Smriti) which deal with the four traditional arts and sciences.
The different divisions are shown on the left.

Upanishads

Upanishad means "sitting near," alluding to the tutorials given by a guru to his disciples (who would traditionally sit 'at his feet'). The Upanishads are philosophical texts delineating some of the key concepts within Hinduism, including notions of the soul, reincarnation, karma, Brahman and liberation *(see Chapter One)*. The Upanishads are sometimes considered the beginning of direct spiritual instruction within the Vedas. The traditional number of Upanishads is 108, though there are many more, especially of recent origin. Of these, 13 are usually considered most important.

Vedanta Sutras

The Vedanta Sutras (also called the Brahma Sutras) are an attempt by the sage Vyasa (Badarayana) to systematise the teachings of the Upanishads. There are a total of 550 aphorisms divided between four chapters. Various authors wrote lengthy commentaries upon them, giving rise to the many different and often conflicting schools of Vedanta *(see page 119)*. Important commentaries – considered Smriti – include the Shariraka Bhasya by Shankara, the Shri Bhasya by Ramanuja, the Shrikara Bhasya by Shripati and the Govinda Bhasya by Baladeva.

Because people are less philosophically inclined in Kali Yuga, the Upanishads and Vedanta Sutra are considered difficult to understand without the guidance of the supplementary Smriti literature, as explored overleaf.

Scriptural Passages

"Do not stay in illusion, go to the eternal reality. Do not remain in darkness, approach the light. Do not remain in this place of death - become immortal!"

Brihad-aranyaka Upanishad 1.3.28

"The Personality of Godhead is perfect and complete, and because He is completely perfect, all emanations from Him, such as this phenomenal world, are perfectly equipped as complete wholes. Whatever is produced of the Complete Whole is also complete in itself. Because He is the Complete whole, even though so many complete units emanate from Him, He remains the complete balance."

Shri Ishopanishad, Invocation

Scriptural Passage

"Now (while one has a human birth), one should inquire into Brahman."

Vedanta Sutra 1.1.1

Glossary Terms

Sutra *means 'thread' and refers to an aphorism that needs unpacking to understand its full import. The logic is that when one takes the small tip of a roll of thread, one can unwind it more and more. Similarly, the sutras themselves are small but profound, containing almost unlimited insight.*

Above: Krishna, cousin of the Pandavas, and Arjuna's charioteer during the great battle.
Below: Dhritarashtra, Pandu's elder brother. He was not qualified to rule on account of his blindness, but became regent after Pandu's early demise.
Bottom: Arjuna, the third son of Pandu, to whom Krishna spoke the Bhagavad Gita. Here disguised as a brahmin, he wins the hand of Draupadi.

Mahabharata, "the history of greater India," was originally composed by the sage Vyasa. Handed down over thousands of years, its present form of 110,000 verses makes it the longest poem in the world. The plot is gripping, with many twists and turns, and intertwined with intricate sub-plots. It focuses on the political tensions between the Pandavas and the Kauravas, and culminates in the fratricidal battle of Kurukshetra. The book also includes narrations of other historical tales, and several philosophical discourses. The story particularly explores many of the intricacies of *dharma*, especially for the warrior and priestly classes.

The Mahabharata is a favourite subject of art and drama. One film version, screened on TV in the early 1990s was so popular that it practically brought the whole of India to a stop! The plot is interlaced with intrigue, romance, fighting and chivalry. Tradition holds that it is especially meant to capture the attention of people in Kali-yuga, who prefer entertainment to philosophy. Nonetheless, the message of Mahabharata is ultimately spiritual and at the heart of the epic is the Bhagavad Gita, narrated as the two sides stood poised for battle.

Brief Summary of the Story

The story tells of a struggle for the throne between the five sons of Pandu (the Pandavas) and their impious cousins, the Kauravas (sometimes called the Kurus). Pandu was the second of three princes, and took the throne in preference to his blind elder brother, Dhritarashtra. As the result of a curse, Pandu died tragically while his sons were minors. Pandu's younger brother, Vidura, though pious and learned, was born of a maid-servant and could not ascend the throne. It thus remained vacant and by the law of succession should have passed to Pandu's sons, headed by the pious Yudhisthira. As the boys grew up, alongside their cousins, Dhritarashtra acted as regent. However, his one hundred sons, headed by Duryodhana, were increasingly resentful that fate had deprived them, as well as their father, of the vast Indian empire.

The Kauravas therefore plotted to kill the teenage Pandavas and their widowed mother, Kunti, by burning them alive. The princes were tipped off and escaped the burning palace via a tunnel. Now aware of their cousins' treachery, they opted to remain in the forest. During this time, the third brother, Arjuna, won Draupadi as a bride in an archery contest. Due to a benediction gained in a previous life, Draupadi became the wife of all five brothers.

The blind king, feeling repentant, arranged to return to his nephews half the kingdom – but by far the worst half. However, with the help of their friend Krishna, the Pandava kingdom flourished and became opulent in all respects.

Hearing of Yudhisthira's fame and popularity, Duryodhana seethed with envy. He threatened and cajoled his blind father to arrange for a gambling match between the two groups of cousins. The weak and affectionate Dhritarashtra reluctantly consented. Duryodhana ensured that the dice were rigged, and Yudhisthira lost everything.

One of the Kurus even tried to strip Draupadi naked, but Krishna protected her by supplying an endless length of *sari*. None of the warriors intervened, sowing the seeds of their future destruction. The five brothers took terrible and irrevocable oaths to destroy the offenders. Nonetheless, according to the terms of the contest, they and Draupadi were exiled to the forest for 13 years. During the final year they were to remain incognito and if discovered were to remain in exile for a further 12 years.

The five princes and their wife again entered the forest. After many adventures, they adopted disguises for the final year, trying to avoid the spies sent by their cousins. They remained undetected and finally returned to reclaim their kingdom. The Kauravas refused, and the two parties prepared for war on the plains of Kurukshetra. The carnage lasted 18 days and the Pandavas came out victorious, but with very few soldiers left. Yudhisthira was crowned emperor. His kingdom flourished for 30 years, after which the Pandavas retired to the Himalayas, leaving their grandson on the throne.

Above*:A pivotal point in the Mahabharata. In this painting Krishna protects Draupadi, as one of the Kurus tried to disrobe her. According to Hindu theology, the abuse of a woman incurs heavy 'bad karma'. None of the nobles intervened and in this way they precipitated their destruction on the field of Kurukshetra.*

Related Values/Issues

- good over evil/justice.
- the legitimate use of violence.
- duty and personal inconvenience.
- the qualities of a real leader.
- chivalry/the warrior ethic.
- abuse of women (Draupadi's story).

Personal Reflection

- Where is the notion of a 'spiritual warrior' found in our own heritage, or other world cultures? How does the warrior compare to today's soldiers and freedom fighters?

- Is war entirely wrong or is there legitimate use of violence?

Scriptural Passage

"One who is free from sin suffers calamities, while sinners are living happily. A rich man dies young and a poor fellow drags on his existence, weighed down by decrepitude. All this is the work of destiny."

Mahabharata 12.28

The Bhagavad Gita

Meaning and Purpose

- *The purpose of life and how to achieve it.*
- *Why do we suffer?*

Scriptural Passages

"Dhritarashtra said: 'O Sanjaya, after my sons and the sons of Pandu assembled in the place of pilgrimage at Kurukshetra, desiring to fight, what did they do?" (1.1)

"Now I am confused about my duty and have lost all composure because of miserly weakness. In this condition I am asking You to tell me for certain what is best for me. Now I am Your disciple, and a soul surrendered unto You. Please instruct me." (2.8)

Arjuna said: "My dear Krishna, O infallible one, my illusion is now gone. I have regained my memory by Your mercy. I am now firm and free from doubt and am prepared to act according to Your instructions." (18.72)

[Sanjaya concludes] "Wherever there is Krishna, the master of all mystics, and wherever there is Arjuna, the supreme archer, there will also certainly be opulence, victory, extraordinary power, and morality. That is my opinion." (18.78)

The Bhagavad-gita, the "Song of God", is the best-known Hindu scripture in the world. Forming two chapters of the Mahabharata, it is a spiritual treatise spoken by Krishna to Arjuna as they sat on a chariot between two armies poised for battle.

Blind King Dhritarashtra, sitting in his palace, was worried as to how the proposed battle-site, Kurukshetra – even then a place of pilgrimage – might favour the righteous Pandavas standing opposite his own sons. Doubtful and perturbed, he confided in Sanjaya, his secretary. Sanjaya, by mystic vision, saw events unfolding in Kurukshetra and thus narrated to the blind king the entire Bhagavad Gita.

The king was pleased to hear of Arjuna's perplexity upon seeing friends and relatives on both sides. Arjuna dropped his bow, refused to fight and implored Krishna to become his teacher.

Lord Krishna then explained how Arjuna's affection for his kinsmen was based on the bodily concept of life. Under this illusion, Arjuna considered the body to be the self and those connected with his body to be his kinsmen. In the first six chapters, Krishna explains how the real self (*atman*) is different from the body and can be elevated to self-realisation through different types of yoga, culminating in *bhakti* (devotion). The middle six chapters discuss the Supreme Lord, his service and his devotees. In the third six chapters, Krishna explains about the soul's entanglement within the three *gunas,* and how it can be liberated. Upon hearing these instructions, Arjuna again took up his bow, determined to fight. In the final verse of the Gita, Sanjaya plunges Dhritarashtra back into despair, informing him that his sons, fighting opposite Krishna and Arjuna, had no chance of victory. The whole Gita is completed in 700 verses. There are now thousands of editions, translated into all major languages and usually published with extensive commentary on the text.

Related Values/Issues
- How to cope with dilemmas, such as Arjuna's.
- Many others (*for a useful list of cross-references relating verses to issues/concepts/topics, please see FCT-1102*).

Personal Reflection
- Are there any other stories of soldiers who found friends and relatives on the opposite side? We very often de-humanise 'the enemy' – why?
- What experiences do we have of the benefits and disadvantages of considering our material relatives as somehow special?

Related Concepts
The Bhagavad Gita discusses all the major concepts explored in Chapter One of this book

Smriti – the Ramayana

The Ramayana, "the Journey of Rama", is a Sanskrit epic compiled by the poet-sage Valmiki. Scholars say that it received its present shape perhaps as late as the second century CE, but that it contains much older material. Indian scholars date Valmiki to the third millennium BCE. Though academics consider the Ramayana a mythical account, Hindus consider Rama a historical figure, and an avatar of Vishnu. Some date him back to the Treta Yuga, whereas others consider him far more recent. There are two principal vernacular versions; the Hindi 'Ramcharitmanas' by Tulsidas and a Tamil version by Kambha. Tulsidas's version is extremely popular, but is shorter than Valmiki's, excluding the final chapter about Sita's banishment, the birth of her twin sons and her disappearance. The Ramayana is the subject of many art forms, particularly drama, and is increasingly well known outside the Hindu community.

Scriptural Passage

"If one surrenders unto Me sincerely, saying, 'My Lord, from this day I am fully surrendered unto You,' I always give that person protection. That is My vow."

(Ramayana, Yuddha-kanda)

Below: *A scene from the Ramayana. Sita becomes enchanted by a magician diguised as a deer. Rama goes to catch the deer and Ravana kidnaps Sita.*
Bottom: *A painting of Hanuman shortly after finding Sita. Ravana's men subsequently captured Hanuman. They set fire to his tail, but he escaped and burned down much of the city.*

Brief Summary of the Story

The story tells of how Rama was cheated out of his throne and unfairly banished to the forest. His wife, Sita, and brother, Lakshmana, chose to go with him. Despite the hardships, Rama actually enjoyed forest life, for it allowed him to keep company with the many sages and saints who lived there. Ravana, king of the Rakshasa race (man-eaters), heard of Sita's beauty and kidnapped her. Rama was beside himself with grief, but resolved to rescue his wife. He eventually formed an alliance with a race of Varnaras (monkey-like people). Their general, Hanuman, eventually found Sita on the isle of Lanka. Thereafter, Rama ordered his army to throw boulders in the ocean. Miraculously they floated, and the monkey warriors constructed a floating bridge to Lanka. The two armies met outside the city gates. Rama's army managed to gain the upper hand and many of Ravana's sons were slain. Eventually Rama killed Ravana, was reunited with Sita, and returned to his capital, Ayodhya. During his reign everyone was freed from misery.

The triumphant restoration of Lord Rama to his own kingdom is celebrated during the famous festival of lights, Divali. Rama, with Sita, Lakshman, and his entire army, returned on the night of the new moon. It was pitch dark, and the jubilant citizens lit the way with thousands of divas (lamps).

Related Values/Issues

- Duty/*dharma* (of husband, wife, leader, son, brother, etc.).
- Stewardship and 'secondary proprietorship'.
- Good over evil.

Personal Reflection

- Sita, although a princess, chose to go with Rama to the forest, despite the hardships. Have we ever loved someone, or felt so good in their company, that we would accept so much personal hardship just to be with them? Or do we tend to love only when the going is good?

The Puranas are an important source of popular Hinduism. Purana means 'very old' or 'ancient', and the books themselves claim greater antiquity than the Vedas. Nevertheless, scholars consider them to be more recent scripture, dealing with what they term the 'later deities' – Brahma, Vishnu and Shiva. There are many books but eighteen main or *maha* ('great') Puranas. These form three sets of six books, with each set connected to one of the *trimurti* – Vishnu, Brahma and Shiva. Some Hindus say that each set is suitable for readers influenced by the corresponding *gunas* (goodness, passion and ignorance). There are also eighteen *Upa* ('following' or 'subsidiary') Puranas.

The Puranas deal with creation, genealogies of deities and patriarchs, rules for living, descriptions of various worlds, and many of the popular myths and stories. Some of them, such as the Vishnu-, Bhagavata- and Devibhagavata-Puranas are often recited publicly.

Of them all, the Bhagavat Purana (Srimad Bhagavatam) is most popular. It consists of over 18,000 verses divided into 12 cantos (volumes). It specifically glorifies Lord Vishnu, twenty-two of His incarnations, and His devotees. Especially popular is the tenth canto that tells the much-loved stories of Lord Krishna, both as the cowherd boy of Vrindavan and later as the powerful king of Dvaraka.

Top: *Rameshbhai Oza delivering one of his popular recitations of the Bhagavat Purana.*
Above: *Krishna performing one of his famous lilas (pastimes). Here he defeats Kaliya, the many-headed serpent, by dancing on his hoods.*
Below: *This poster depicts the popular story of Durga slaying the buffalo demon.*

Common Misunderstandings

"The stories in the Puranas are all allegorical."

The word myth is often used to refer to the stories found in the Puranas. The word should be used with discretion, and we should be careful not to equate it with 'fairy tale'. Some Hindus believe that the events described are allegorical, but others believe that they are factual, happening beyond our realm of direct perception and comprehension (i.e. they happen on higher dimensions).

"Hindu stories can be interpreted however one likes."

Stories are often presented to teach a specific lesson. Though there is room for flexibility, and deeper understanding, we should be careful not to exploit the stories, or trivialise them, simply to promote our own values, or in the name of making them more accessible.

The Dharma Shastras

The Dharma Shastras include the law codes of Hinduism, both secular and religious (since both were very much inseparable). They deal with three main subjects: codes of conduct, civil and criminal law, and punishment and atonement.

Most important is the **Manu Smriti** (or Manu Samhita), still consulted in Indian law. It was written by Manu, an administrative demigod (the "ruler of mankind") and the first lawgiver. The word "man" is said to derive from Manu. There are fourteen Manus during each creation of the world. The Manu Smriti contains 2,700 verses divided into twelve chapters. Most scholars claim that it was written between 300 and 600 BCE. Other important dharma texts were written by Yajnavalkya, Parashara and Narada.

The Manu Smriti establishes the Hindu way of life. It specifically outlines the duties of the four *varnas* and four *ashramas*. It extols the virtues of the brahmins, but clearly states that the *varna* divisions are based on individual merit and capacity rather than birthright. The text also deals with rules of inheritance and adoption, and with law and the science of government.

Closely related is the **Artha Shastra**, a text that discusses the science of acquiring wealth and power. One such popular work is the Artha Shastra of Chanakya (a.k.a. Kauntila), who was the prime minister of King Chandra Gupta, reputed to have defeated Alexander the Great.

Chanakya also studied many scriptures and compiled an anthology of popular wisdom in the form of proverbs. It is part of the **Niti-shastra**, which also includes the famous animal fables of the **Panchatantra** and the **Hitopadesha**.

Scriptural Passages

"A man should not associate with a woman in a solitary place, not even with his mother, sister or daughter, for the senses are so strong that they lead astray even a person advanced in knowledge."

Manu Smriti 2.215

Above: *An illustration of the "blue jackal" from a popular version of the Panchtantra.*

Related Values/Issues
- Citizenship.
- Crime and punishment.
- Capital punishment.
- Morality.
- Rights and responsibilities.
- Classless society/equal opportunity.
- Righteous war /chivalry.

Personal Reflection
- How does the quote from Manu (*above*) relate to popular opinion today? Is it out of date, or could it be relevant?

- Do any of the proverbs relate to our experience? Are there any similar proverbs from our own background? What do they really mean?

Verses From Chanakya

- *A pigeon today is better than a peacock tomorrow.*
- *The union of even small people can become irresistible. The elephant is tied up with rope made of grass.*
- *As the gardener plucks each flower without destroying its root, so should the ruler collect revenue without harming its source.*
- *Excessive courtesy should never be trusted.*
- *Flies go after open wounds, bees after flowers, good people after good qualities, mean people after faults.*

Chapter 12
Movements & Leaders

The Four Main Denominations

1. Vaishnavas *worship Vishnu (usually as Krishna or Rama).*

2. Shaivas *worship Shiva (often in the form of the linga).*

3. Shaktas *worship Shakti a.k.a. Devi (especially Parvati, Durga, Kali).*

4. Smartas *worship five deities i.e. Vishnu, Shiva, Devi, Ganesh and Surya.*

Note 1: In the UK, many individuals and temples will not specifically align themselves to one (or more) of these traditions. They worship deities from all these traditions. They often describe themselves as 'Sanatanist' to reflect their more inclusive nature. Under-pinning them, there is often a leaning towards the monistic Smarta conclusions of Shankara.

Note 2: Shaivism and Shaktism are often closely related, especially within trantric traditions, which explore the male-female symbolism of Shiva-Shakti.

Classifying the many groups within Hinduism is a challenge, and not so easy (as, perhaps, with other religions.) In so doing, we may inadvertently promote the idea that Hinduism is a single monolithic religion. It is, more accurately, a family of religions, with each family member autonomous but sharing distinctive family features.

In discussing all religious groups, we may imply that they are static, homogeneous and well-defined 'wholes'. In actual fact, they are fluid and evolving traditions, internally diverse and contested, and hazy at the edges. In trying to discern specific strands within Hinduism, therefore, we are also in danger of over-generalising, promoting stereotypes and creating false boundaries. Nonetheless, it is useful - even necessary - to establish a somewhat tentative framework for categorising the numerous groups and sub-groups. Over this spread we have categorised them according to three criteria – (1) focus of worship, (2) doctrine, and (3) preferred process or practices.

Four main communities can be identified, each according to its respective focus of worship (*these four communities are discussed on pages 134-137*). Each community, which we loosely term here a 'denomination', favours its own specific deity or deities (*as shown top left*).

Top Left: A lady wears the V or U-shaped clay mark (tilak) that denotes a follower of Vishnu. Her neck and prayer beads are made of wood from the sacred Tulsi plant.

Top Right: Tilak consisting of three horizontal white lines denotes a worshipper of Shiva. The young priest shown here has added a fourth, horizontal line in yellow (perhaps denoting his specific tradition). Shaivites wear Rudraksha beads, of which their rosaries are also made.

Bottom Right: A sannyasi of one of the ten orders founded by Shankara. Although aligned to the Smarta practice of worshipping five deities, they often tend to favour Shiva. This man's staff is a single rod (eka-danda) to distinguish him from the Vaishnava sannyasis whose staff is made of three rods (tri-danda).

Bottom Left: Worshippers of Durga (Shakti), who do not usually bear any clear distinguishing marks, though they often wear the red dot ('chandlo') in between the eyebrows.

Six Doctrines and Four Paths

Although Hinduism can be primarily classified into four main denominations according to their respective focuses of worship, there are two other criteria that help account for the tradition's diversity. They revolve around (1) the different doctrines, and (2) the various processes of realisation.

1. Doctrines

There are six orthodox *darshans* (ways of seeing) to which the various groups and sub-groups subscribe. (*They are outlined in detail on page 118*). Of these, Vedanta is often considered the culmination and represents the theologically developed strands of contemporary Hinduism. Vedanta, however, has not entirely rejected the other five schools, but has tended to accommodate and assimilate them.

Vedanta is often exclusively associated with the Advaita Vedanta of Shankara. However, there are two main approaches, as shown to the right. These two poles are combined in various ways to form ten main schools of Vedanta (see page 119). For most purposes, teachers would best familiarise themselves with the basic notions of these two schools, the impersonal and the personal. They can also be termed monism and monotheism, keeping in mind that the latter is almost always 'inclusive monotheism' (*see page 22*).

> ### 1. Advaita – monists or impersonalists
>
> *who believe that:*
> - *God is ultimately impersonal.*
> - *the soul is entirely non-different from God (but has yet to realise/develop his Godhood).*

> ### 2. Dvaita – dualists or personalists
>
> *who believe that:*
> - *God is ultimately personal.*
> - *the soul remains eternally distinct from God (though both are usually considered Brahman).*

2. Processes/Paths

Within Hinduism there are diverse practices, but most fall within four main paths or *margs*. Since these are aimed at union (with God) they are also termed 'yogas'. They are:

> 1. **karma yoga** - *the yoga path of action*
> 2. **jnana yoga** - *the path of knowledge*
> 3. **raja (astanga) yoga** - *the path of meditation*
> 4. **bhakti yoga** - *the path of devotion*

Some authorities list only three paths by excluding Raja yoga, which is often closely associated with Jnana-yoga, because of the common emphasis on renunciation (*see also page 44-45*).

The four main denominations often favour one or more of these processes, and will also lean towards a particular doctrine, (*see right*).

The Four Denominations and their Favoured Doctrine/Path

- **Vaishnavas** *are mostly personalists and favour the path of bhakti-yoga.*
- **Shaivas** *are often impersonalists with tendencies towards jnana- and astanga-yoga (closely linked to sankhya-yoga). There are, however, notable personalistic, bhakti strands, especially in South India (e.g. the Lingayats).*
- **Shaktas** *tend to be impersonalists, and their worship often focusses on material benefit (karma-yoga). Their theology tends to be less developed and draws largely on Shaivism.*
- **Smartas** *follow the impersonal (advaita) doctrine of Shankara and favour the path of jnana, featuring renunciation and philosophical inquiry.*

Main Writings

- *Mahabharata*
- *Ramayana*
- *Bhagavad Gita*
- *Bhagavat Purana*
- *Vishnu Purana*
- *Hymns of the Alvars (Tamil poet-mystics)*
- *Vedanta Sutras*

The largest community within the family of religions called Hinduism worships God under the name of Vishnu ('one who is all-pervading'). Vaishnavas are divided into many smaller divisions, often focussing on one form or *avatar* (descent) of Vishnu. There are also a number of prominent theologians, who established their own *sampradayas* (preceptoral successions) teaching different forms of Vedanta and contesting the purely monistic doctrine of Shankara. There are four main branches of Vaishnavism and the various *sampradaya* often claim orthodoxy on the basis of belonging to one of these. The two main focuses of veneration are Krishna and Rama, who are usually considered God, with other deities allocated relatively subordinate positions. Vaishnavas tend to be personalists, associated with the devotional, *bhakti* traditions.

History

Vaishnavism claims to go back millions of years (in keeping with its own historical worldview). Worship of Krishna dates back at least 5,000 years, though Western scholars suggest it emerged more recently. Between the 6th and 9th centuries, the twelve Alvars (poet-mystics) laid the foundations for the Shri Vaishnavas based in Shri Rangam, South India. Their founder–theologian is Ramanuja (1017-1137). After him emerged three other *sampradayas* headed by Nimbarka (1125-1162), Vishnuswami (1200-1250) and Madhva (1238-1317). From the twelfth century onwards a bhakti renaissance swept across India, bringing waves of devotional sentiment. Centres of devotion were rediscovered and revived in places such as Ayodhya and Vrindavana. The *bhakti* traditions broke through caste barriers and attracted millions of followers. Among the many *bhakti*-saints are a number of notable women such as Andal and Mirabai. Vaishnavas remain the largest Hindu community, both within India and the UK. The four *sampradayas*, each named after a specific deity shown below.

Above*:Shri Rangam, the headquarters of the Shri sampradaya.*

Important Stories

- *Those of Krishna*
- *The Ramayan*
- *The Ten Incarnations (BUK-301)*

Important Places

- *Mathura/Vrindavana*
- *Ayodhya*
- *Nathdvar*
- *Udupi*
- *Kanchipuram*
- *Guruvayor*
- *Pandhapur (Maharastra)*
- *Puri*
- *Shri Rangam*
- *Mayapur*
- *Tirupati*
- *Dvaraka*

Name of Sampradaya	1. Lakshmi	2. Brahma	3. Kumara	4. Rudra
Theologian/Founder	Ramanuja	Madhva	Nimbarka	Vishnuswami
Other Prominent Leaders	Twelve Alvars	Caitanya (Bengal)		Vallabha
Broad Traditions	Shri Vaishnavas (S. India)	Gaudiya (Bengali) Vaishnavas Madhavites (S. India)	Hamsa sampradaya (mainly Vrindavana)	Pushti Marg (Gujarat)
Modern Movements in Britain	Swami Narayana Mission	ISKCON	none of prominence	Shree Vallabha Nidhi

Shaivism

Shaivism is the second largest religious community in contemporary India. It has several distinct and important branches, and is commonly associated with asceticism. Lord Shiva himself is often depicted as a yogi sitting in meditation in the Himalayas. Shaivism includes the principle of *avatar*, but the concept is less developed than in Vaishnavism. Shiva has important forms as Rudra (in a fierce and angry mood), Nataraja (the King of Dance) and the Linga. Shiva's followers often consider him the Supreme deity, above all others.

History

The roots of Shaivism are anchored in pre-historic India. Evidence of the worship of Shiva has been found in ancient archaeological sites, such as Harappa and Mohenjo Daro. In the Rig Veda, he is referred to by the name Rudra. The oldest story about Shiva concerns his destruction of the sacrificial arena of Daksha after Shiva's wife (Sati) voluntarily gave up her life upon being insulted by her father, Daksha.

Between 700 and 1,000 CE there lived sixty-three Nayanmars (singer-saints) whose poems are still recited today. Thereafter, Shaivism became the prominent religion of India, particularly in the South. The rulers of many major kingdoms became Shaivites and patronised its representatives. Magnificent temples were built in Shiva's honour and many impressive sculptures were inspired by him. Shiva is mentioned in the four Vedas, and particularly the Svetashvatara Upanishad, the Shaivite equivalent to the Vaishnava Bhagavad-gita. There are numerous references to Shiva in the epics and Puranas. Most Shaivite theology though, derives from later scriptures, particularly the Agamas. There are five main traditions, shown below.

Main Writings

- *Svetashvatara Upanishad*
- *Shiva Purana*
- *The Agamas*
- *Tiru-murai (poems)*

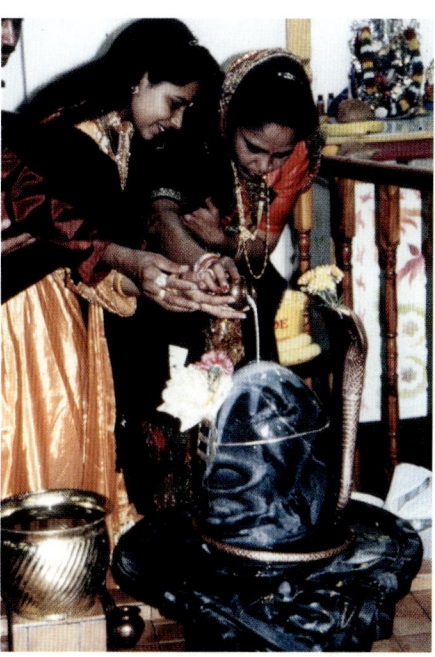

Above: *worshippers at a temple in Wembley, London, pour milk on the linga. It represents Shiva as the male, creative principle.*

Important Places

- Benares
- Kedarnath
- Somnath
- Rameshvaram
- Chidambaram
- Amarnath

Important Stories

- Shiva drinks poison.
- Shiva destroys the three cities of the demons.
- Killing Andhaka and other demons.
- Daksha's Sacrifice.

Pasupatis	Shaiva Siddhanta	Kashmiri Shaivism	Virashaivism (the Lingayats)	Shaiva Asceticism
Perhaps the oldest school within Shaivism. The school of Shaiva Siddhanta (right) is a continuation of this tradition.	Followed by many intellectuals. It has a personal doctrine, stressing the plurality of souls (as opposed to the advaitic idea that all souls and God are ultimately one).	Almost defunct today. Its most prolific writer is Abhinavagupta (c. 960 –1020). The goal of this movement is to 'become Shiva' and regain one's universal nature. It is also called Shiva-advaita.	Closely associated with the twelfth century reformer, Basava. It opposed caste differences. Followers wear a small Shiva-linga round the neck. The present community is centred round Karnataka.	Shaiva has long been connected with rigorous asceticism. Well –known are the naked Nagas. Many yogis are Shaivites. Prominent are the Nathapatnis, followers of Gorakhnatha, and the Aghori who deliberately contravene moral norms.

Shaktism

Main Writings

- *Devi Purana*
- *Kalika Purana*
- *Devi Bhagavata Purana*
- *Mahabhagavata Purana*
- *The Tantras*

Important Places

- *Bengal*
- *Calcutta (Kali Temple)*
- *Kanyakumari*
- *Madurai*
- *Vaishno Devi*

Above*: A deity of Devi worshipped during the Navrati festival. The two other principal goddesses, Lakshmi and Saraswati, are sometimes considered to be her daughters.*

Meaning and Purpose

Where does the distinction between male and female come from? Is it an ontological reality or social construct?

Shaktism focusses on the goddess generically called 'Devi'. She is worshipped most often as the consort of Shiva, but has also been raised to the status of the Supreme. Although some books equate Shaktism with all major female deities (the "shaktis" of their respective consorts), the Shakta tradition specifically worships Shiva's consort, in her various forms such as Parvati, Durga, Kali, etc. The worship of Sita (with Rama) or of Radha (with Krishna) is not strictly part of Shaktism, but does point to the ubiquitous role that the female deity plays within Hinduism.

Within Shaktism, there is little emphasis on doctrinal *sampradayas*, and much ideology comes from Shaivism. Since Shiva embodies the male principle and Shakti embodies the female, the two principles of Shivism and Shaktism are complementary. Shakti doctrine tends to emphasis the non-difference between matter and spirit, and looks to the creative impetus of matter rather than its ability to delude and entangle. For this reason, Shaktas worship for material benefit as well as final liberation. A notable aspect of Shaktism is animal sacrifice and even documented accounts of human sacrifice.

History

Archaeological finding suggest that Shaktism goes back to pre-historic times. The Goddess does feature in the Vedas themselves, but scholars suggest that mainstream worship comes from other sources. She appears in the Epics and Puranas, especially the Markandeya Purana. It is in the Tantras that she appears to take the role of the Supreme.

There appear to be no strong sampradayic links, and Shaktism may have been passed down in a broader fashion, largely through local and village customs, and through connections with other schools such as Shaivism. Shaktism has greatly influenced modern thinkers such as Ramakrishna and Aurobindo. Not surprisingly Devi in her fiercer forms has become the patron deity of women's liberation movements. Wherever Hindus have settled throughout the world, there are now a number of prominent Devi temples.

Related Values and Issues

- Is God male, female, neither or both?
- (Possible) innate differences between male and female.

Personal Reflection

- What is our reaction to the large number of goddesses within Hinduism? How does this relate to ideas of a purely masculine God? How does the feminine appear in our faiths/non-faith traditions?

Related Stories

- Durga Kills the Buffalo Demon (STO-313)
- Devi Kills other Demons.

The Smarta Tradition

There is a fourth mainstream Hindu community. For its emphasis on Smriti, its followers are known as Smartas. They are traditional, very strict about rules and regulations, and emphasise the universality of Hinduism by distancing themselves from the exclusive worshippers of Vishnu, Shiva or Devi. They worship five deities – Vishnu, Shiva, Devi, Ganesh and Surya, as introduced by Shankara. The ten orders of *sannyasa* (Dasanam), founded by Shankara, also follow the same system of panchopasana (five types of worship). Some of these *sannyasis* (renunciates) tend towards special veneration of Shiva, of whom Shankara is considered an incarnation.

The Smarta tradition is a relatively new development in Hinduism. Many Hindus may not strictly identify themselves as Smartas but, by adhering to Advaita Vedanta as a foundation for non-sectarianism, are indirect followers. Nonetheless, other traditions dispute the claim that the notion of an impersonal God is the only basis for non-sectarianism. These controversies over the nature and identity of the Absolute were spearheaded by prominent theologians *(as discussed overleaf)*.

Quote

"In these three worlds, it is only the association of saintly people that serves as the boat to carry one across the ocean of repeated birth and death."

Adi Shankaracharya

Main Writings

■ *Vedanta Sutra*
■ *Upanishads*
■ *Shariraka Bhasya*

Important Places

■ *Badrinatha*
■ *Puri*
■ *Sringeri*
■ *Dvaraka*
■ *Kanchipuram*

Above: Adi Shankara (or Shankaracharya), who is reputed to have started the system of worshipping five deities. He is founder of the Advaitin School of Vedanta philosophy (monism), which underpins the widespread notion that all deities are equal.

Above: Madhva (or Madhvacharya). There has been some tension between the various denominations and schools of thought, most often between Vaishnavas and Shaivas/Shaktas. There has also been much theological controversy. Discussion and debate is an important and welcomed aspect of Hinduism. Madhvacharya was a Vaishnava theologian (see next page) and most strongly contested Shankara's monistic doctrine. Madhva propounded that Vishnu is Supreme. Some teachers within the Shaivite and Shakti traditions have also propounded that their respective worshippable lords are the Supreme (God). Smartas consider all deities equal, simply different attributes of an impersonal Supreme.

Personal Reflection

■ What do we know of religious disagreements, similar to those between Madhva and Shankara? When is it appropriate to express these differences, and in what manner should it be done?

Founders and Theologians

When exploring 'key figures', Hinduism poses a particular challenge for several reasons. Firstly, it is impossible to trace the exact beginning – if indeed it had one! It has no single founder, but contains many leaders who reformed and revived existing traditions, either breaking them into innumerable sub-groups or consolidating them. The rather vague boundary between man and the immortal makes the subject even more complex. Almost universally, God is considered the ultimate Father of religion, and many of the *sampradayas* consider their founder an *avatar*.

Tradition holds that in ancient times there were seven great rishis (poet-sages) born from the mind of Brahma. They are often associated with the seven stars of the Big Dipper constellation. Hindu families claim to trace their dynasty (*gotra*) to one of them. They are *Bhrigu, Gautama, Bharadvaja, Vishvamitra, Vashishta, Atri* and *Angira*. Though lists given by various sources vary, the names of these and other *rishis* appear repeatedly in the stories of the Puranas, Epics and other texts. Despite their inconceivable age, living from the time of creation, some are reputed to still be alive.

Theologians

Much current Hindu thought is based on theological foundations laid down by prominent scholars from the medieval period. Most important are those who established the ten main branches of Vedanta and corresponding *sampradayas* (disciplic successions). They are often awarded the suffix 'acharya', 'one who teaches by example'. Here we outline some important *acharyas*.

Shankara (780 – 812), a great Hindu reformer, was born in Kerala and took sannyasa as a youth. He travelled widely defeating Buddhists and other members of the *nastika* movements, thus re-establishing the authority of Vedic texts throughout India. He founded the *advaita* school of Vedanta, ten orders of *sannyasa*, and monastic centres in four strategic locations. He is often called Adi Shankara, to differentiate him from the later pontiffs, who to this day are also called 'the Shankaracharya'. Adi Shankara is often considered an incarnation of Shiva. His contemporary followers in the UK include the Ramakrishna Mission.

Abhinavagupta (c. 960 –1020) was a representative of Kashmiri Shaivism and is perhaps its most prolific writer. He propounded a form of Advaita Vedanta and wrote the multi-volume Tantra-loka. Further Shaivite theologians were **Shrikantha** (13th century) and **Shripati** (1350 – 1410).

Ramanuja (*shown left*) is the most important acharya amongst the Shri Vaishnavas, and the founder of the Vishishtadvaita school, which qualified Shankara's monistic doctrine. Ramanuja (1017-1137) taught devotion to a personal God, Vishnu, and proposed that the universe is the Lord's body. Salvation is earned largely by grace and entails entering Vishnu's abode (Vaikunthaloka) where one receives a body almost identical to the Lord. Tirupati and Shri Rangam, important centres of Sri Vaishnavism, are headquarters of the two main branches, the northern and southern schools. **Sahajanand Swami**, founder of the Swami Narayana Mission, came in Ramanuja's line and modified his Vishishtadvaita doctrine. **Madhva** (1238-1317), another important Vaishnava scholar, opposed Shankara's Advaita doctrine far more vehemently than Ramanuja, founding the Shuddha-dvaita (pure dualism) school of Vedanta. **Chaitanya** (1486-1534) claimed to come in Madhva's line, and his teachings were consolidated by Baladeva (1600-1768).

The Bhakti Saints

Bhakti initially flourished in South India through the great Vaishnava saints known as the twelve Alvars (6th - 9th Centuries). Shaivism also has its bhakti traditions and during roughly the same period 63 Nayanars (*bhakti* poets) wrote songs that now form the twelve books of the Tirumurai. Shortly after, and especially from 1500 CE onwards, a great devotional renaissance swept through the entire sub-continent. The *bhakti* saints largely rejected the hereditary caste system and its emphasis on prescribed ritual, stressing instead the need for morality, purity of heart and an attitude of selfless service. They expressed their sentiments through song, poetry and music, often attracting thousands of followers. Their preference for the spirit of the law rather than its letter enabled many followers of apparently lower birth to partici-pate. These include a number of famous women saints. The considerable influence of the *bhakti* saints continues up to the present time.

Above: *Chaitanya and his followers displayed symptoms of ecstasy as they sang and danced in praise of Krishna.*

Common Misunderstanding

"The Bhakti traditions are for emotional and sentimental people and place little emphasis on philosophy."

Not true. Many *bhakti* traditions, for example those connected with Chaitanya*(above)* and Vallabha, have developed highly sophisticated theologies, emphasising both knowledge and devotion. Devotion without wisdom is considered of a lower order.

Quote

"My dear Lord, when will my eyes be beautified by filling with tears that con-stantly glide down as I chant your holy name? When will my voice falter and all the hairs on my body stand erect in transcendental happiness as I chant your holy name?"

Chaitanya

Kabir (1440-1518)	He is famous for his songs and poems used by Hindus, Sikhs and Muslims alike. His followers are called the Kabir Panthis.
Surdas (1479-1584)	Born blind, he became renowned for his beautiful songs glorifying Krishna. He was a follower of Vallabha.
Vallabha (1481-1533)	A brahmin from Telegu, he founded the Pushti-Marg (path of nourishment), which affirms the role of grace in reaching salvation. He taught that sannyasa is not possible in the current age. There are a good number of his Gujarati followers in the UK.
Chaitanya (1486-1534)	Founder of Bengali Vaishnavism, whose followers express devotion through singing and dancing. He was later considered a dual avatar of Radha and Krishna. His influence still extends through various groups including the Hare Krishna movement.
Tulsidas (1511-1637)	He wrote the popular version of the Ramayana known as the 'Rama Carita Manas' perhaps the most popular book of North India.
Mirabhai (1547-1614)	Possibly the most famous woman saint within Hinduism (*see page 147*). She was a Rajastani princess who considered Krishna her real husband and was consequently persecuted by her own family. Her songs and poems are still recited by Krishna devotees.
Tukarama (1608-1649)	A saint from Western India who worshipped the famous deity of Vishnu known as Vitthala (or Vitobha) in Pandhapur, Maharastra. He was part of an important Vaishnava tradition known as Dasa Kuta and which is still influential today. Other poet saints such as Namdev (1270-1350) also came in this line.

1. Bramho Samaj
Ram Mohan Roy
Devendranatha Tagore
Keshab Chandra Sena

2. Arya Samaj
Dayananda Saraswati

3. Ramakrishna Mission
Ramakrishna
Vivekananda

4. 'Satyagraha'
Mahatma Gandhi

Most Hindus today still adhere to traditional teachings and practice passed down via the four main communities. What has been termed 'modern Hinduism' has grown largely out of a number of quite radical reform movements of the nineteenth and early twentieth centuries. These movements had a relatively small number of followers and by no means replaced or superseded the major traditional forms of Hinduism. Some specific reform movements, like the Arya Samaj and the Ramakrishna Mission, still continue to be influential.

The reform movements largely emerged from the growing contact that Hindu thinkers had with Western thought, culture and religion. Below are the four most important movements and the names associated with them.

The Brahmo Samaj

The Brahmo Sabha was founded in 1828 by **Rama Mohan Roy** (*left*) and in 1843 was restructured and renamed Brahmo Samaj by **Devendranatha Tagore**, father of the well-known poet, Rabindranatha Tagore. Rama Mohan was extremely learned and strongly influenced by Christianity. He disagreed with the doctrine of reincarnation and fought to abolish certain traditional practices, some of which had been grossly misused. These included caste, polygamy, image worship, *sati* and child marriage. His ideas of worship were drawn largely from Christianity. Devendranatha Tagore was greatly influenced by the western philosophy of Locke and Hume. He tried to reform the Brahmo Samaj but lacking support eventually left. **Keshab Chandra Sen** joined the Samaj in 1857 and initially worked with Tagore. But later disagreeing with Tagore's ideas, he left to establish his own movement.

Today the Brahmo Samaj has but a few thousand members and little visible influence on the Hindu community. It failed to fulfil the hopes of those who saw the future religion of India as a blend of Christianity and Hindu metaphysics.

The Arya Samaj

The Arya Samaj was founded by **Swami Dayananda Sarasvati** (*left*) in 1875 as a radical reform movement. Dayananda wanted to halt the Christian missionary onslaught and to return to the ancient Vedic tradition. He therefore sought to purge Hinduism of what he considered later additions, such as image worship, pilgrimage and ritual bathing. Although emphasising the ancient Vedic tradition, Dayananda also sought to modernise Hinduism and to re-absorb Hindus who had converted to Islam or Christianity. His movement, with its concerns over the influence of other religions sowed the seeds for the many political parties that desired to re-establish Hindu rule in India. The Arya Samaj is still an active organisation, both world-wide and in the UK. Its members agree to follow its 'Ten Principles' and worship largely through *havan* (the sacred fire ceremony) and recitation of the Gayatri mantra.

The Ramakrishna Mission

Ramakrishna (*right*) was born Gadadhar Chatterji in a poor but orthodox Bengali Brahmin family. As a young man he became the priest at the Kali temple near Calcutta. He was later initiated as a *sannyasi* and experienced mystical visions, especially of Devi. He was profoundly influenced by Christianity and Islam and emphasised the universality of religion. He preached that "Jiva is Shiva" (the soul is God). He met many contemporary reformers and it was Keshab Chandra Sen who made him first known to the world.

It was **Vivekananda** (1863-1902), however, who made Ramakrishna really famous. Born into the wealthy Dutt family, he was named Narendranath. He joined the Brahmo Samaj but later became Ramakrishna's favourite disciple, receiving the name Swami Vivekananda. He was expert in presenting Advaita Vedanta and greatly impressed the Western world in his presentation to the World Parliament of Religions in Chicago in 1893. He travelled extensively, promoting wide reform, claiming that other reformers "played into the hands of Europeans". He established the Ramakrishna Mission, today well known for its social and educational programmes.

Gandhi's 'Satyagraha'

Mohandas Gandhi (1869–1947) is probably the best known Indian of the twentieth century. He was primarily an educator and reformer. His ultimate aim was to re-establish Rama-rajya, the reign of Lord Rama – or, in more Western terms, the 'kingdom of God on Earth'. He, was opposed to British oppression and particularly the way Indian cotton was sent to Manchester and the clothes returned for sale in India. He tried to free his country from this unhealthy economic dependence and campaigned for India's independence from British Rule. His means to do this was *satyagraha* – grasping the truth – based on *ahimsa* (non-violence), with an unswerving faith in God. He followed many orthodox practices and was particularly fond of the Bhagavad Gita. He often referred to the "still small voice within". He is most well known for his support of the untouchables. He died at the hands of an assassin, disappointed with the partition of his beloved India.

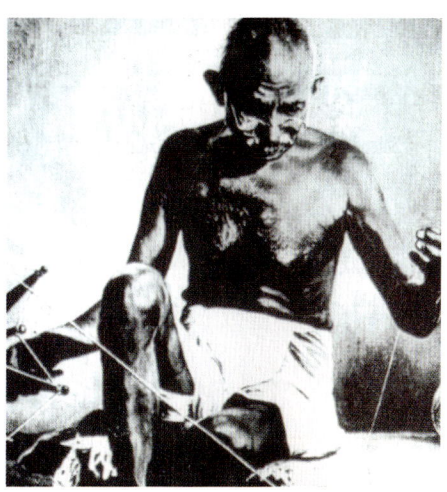

Common Misunderstandings

"Mahatma Gandhi was opposed to the system of Varnashrama-dharma and proposed a totally classless society."

Although Gandhi fought against the rigid and exploitative caste system, he maintained a strong conviction in the need for dividing society according to the four *varnas* and four ashramas. He sought to bring the untouchables (Dalits, as they are now usually called) within the shudra *varna*. For this reason, he differed with Ambedkar, who proposed a totally classless society.

Quotes

"My patriotism is not an exclusive thing. It is all-embracing, and I should reject that patriotism which sought to mount the distress or exploitation of other nationalities".

"The truest test of civilisation, culture and dignity is character, not clothing".

Mahatma Gandhi

Within the reform movements *(see last spread)*, the Brahmo Samaj and Ramakrishna Mission accepted and assimilated many Western ideals. Gandhi, though in many ways traditional, was also amenable to Western influence. The Arya Samaj, however, rejected and opposed Westernisation and modernisation, and sought to reclaim those who had converted to other faiths. Thus they planted the seeds for Hindu nationalism.

The Hindu Mahasabha and the BJP

In 1909, Mohan Malaviha and other leading Arya Samajists founded the Hindu Mahasabha, the Great Hindu Assembly, to give Hindus a political voice apparently denied to them by Congress. The Mahasabha declared 'Hindustan' as the land of the Hindus and demanded the right to govern themselves according to Hindu law. After the partition of India in 1947, it championed its reunification, expressed through the term Akhand Bharat, 'Undivided India'. Its greatest advocate was Vir Savarkar (1883-1966) who coined the word 'Hindutva' (Hindu-ness) to refer to the socio-cultural aspects of Hindu India differentiating them from 'Hindu dharma', the religion itself. The Hindu Mahasabha demonstrated a pro-Hindu leaning that only increased with partition in 1947. After the creation of East Pakistan (now Bangladesh), and the reported violent eviction of many Hindus, the Jana Sangha (People's Party of India) was formed with a strong pro-Hindu bias. In 1980, a number of its splinter groups came together to form the Bharatiya Janata Party (BJP), which became a pre-dominant political force in India. Some reports at the time suggested that it played a major role in the upsurge of popular feelings that sparked the destruction of the Babhri Mosque in Ayodhya in 1992. It has repeatedly utilised the religious theme of Rama-rajya, the ideal rule of Lord Rama as narrated in the Ramayana and advocated by Gandhi.

The RSS (Rashtriya Swayamsevak Sangha)

Many members of the BJP are also closely connected to the RSS – The Rashtriya Swayamsevak Sangha ("National Self Help Association") - It was founded in 1925 by K.V. Hedgewar, a long-serving member of the Hindu Mahasabha. He was succeeded by M.S. Golakwar who declared that the Hindu nation had a divine mandate to re-spiritualise the world through the agency of the RSS. Today, it has grown into perhaps the most powerful Hindu organisation. It now claims a membership of over five million and declares its aims cultural rather than political.

The VHP (Vishva Hindu Parishad)

The Vishva Hindu Parishad, "Hindu World Council", was founded in 1964 by Swami Chinmayananda in conjunction with other religious leaders. Its organisational structure was determined in 1982 in Delhi, now home to its headquarters. The VHP aims to reawaken Hindu consciousness and to promote co-operation between Hindus throughout the world. It pro-pounds a kind of universal Hinduism drawing extensively on the teach-ings of Vivekananda. It is ideologically conservative but in practice quite progressive. Its writers often attempt to show that Hindu thought is entirely consistent with modern technology and science, and even predated them. The VHP, through its numerous initiatives worldwide, continues to have major influence on the emerging identity of post-modern Hinduism.

Above: K.V. Hedgewar, founder of the still influential RSS.

Besides the reform movements themselves, there are a number of notable leaders who sought to revitalise Hinduism from a mainly spiritual platform and who prepared the way for propagating it beyond India and making it accessible to the modern world. Three of the most influential are listed below:

Aurobindo Ghose (1871-1950)

After graduating in Cambridge, England, Aravinda Ghose returned to India with strong sympathies for the Indian nationalist movement. He spent a year in jail, where he is said to have heard God exhorting him to dedicate his life to the spiritual upliftment of India and the world. After his release, he went into self-imposed exile in the French colony of Pondicherry, where he devoted his life to yoga and to writing on spiritual matters. His ashram attracted many people from India and abroad. Aurobindo, as he became known, attempted to formulate an integral yoga which synthesised Hindu spirituality with modern ideas and an active role within the world. His ideas stimulated great interest amongst intellectuals and artists. After his death, his disciples planned to develop Auroville as a model city for the modern world. Their work continues today.

Ramana Maharshi (1879 – 1950)

Ramana Maharshi, 'the sage of Arunachal', was a widely recognised Hindu mystic who attracted many followers from both East and West. As a boy of fourteen, he had a near-death experience and, perceiving the self as different to the body, left home to become a sannyasi. Despite his taking a vow of silence, many people sought his advice. He established an ashram, which was visited by many influential people. Ramana Maharshi was considered an extraordinary personality and his ashram became renowned for giving all its inhabitants a deep sense of peace and tranquillity. Ramana Maharshi is credited with establishing the relevance of the Advaita philosophy to the modern world.

A.C. Bhaktivedanta Swami Prabhupada (1896 – 1977)

Unlike the previous two saints, Bhaktivedanta Swami initially had little apparent success in India. Born into a traditional Bengali Vaishnava family, he became a follower of Gandhi. He entered householder life and was deeply affected when he met his spiritual master, who instructed him to preach the message of Chaitanya in English. He later took *sannyasa* and at the age of 70 begged passage to New York on a cargo ship. Despite obscurity and poverty, he established ISKCON, which became perhaps the most successful of all the new Hindu-related movements springing up in the 1960s. Bhaktivedanta Swami, known affectionately as Shrila Prabhupada, established over 100 ashrams world-wide, and translated more than 70 Vedic texts into English. He passed away in 1977, having established a governing body of his senior disciples to manage the movement after him. He emphasised the practice of devotion to a personal God, in the form of both Radha and Krishna, and the chanting of the now-famous Hare Krishna mantra.

Modern Hindu Groups and Leaders

Main Groups in the UK

There are many different Hindu groups in the UK, and it would be misleading to consider one as more representative than another. Nonetheless, while keeping this in mind, it is important to know and teach about the main ones, briefly described below.

Swami Narayana Mission

Swami Narayana Hindus are largely from Gujarat and follow teachers in the line from Sahajananda Swami *(1781-1830)*, considered by his followers as an incarnation of God. The group claims heritage from the Shri Sampradaya of Vaishnavism. There are now various Swami Narayana *sampradayas* reflecting different views on the identity of the guru and the genuine line of succession. The largest is the Swami Narayana Mission, whose current leader is Pramukh Swami *(left)* and whose centre is a magnificent traditional temple in Neasden, London. Another major group, looking to the leadership of Acharya Tejendraprasad Pande, is based in Willesden Lane, London.

The Hare Krishna Movement (ISKCON)

The International Society for Krishna Consciousness is a strand of Gaudiya (Bengali) Vaishnavism following the *bhakti* saint Chaitanya *(1486-1534)*, considered an incarnation of Radha and Krishna. He opposed the rigid caste system by widely popularising the congregational chanting of the Hare Krishna Mantra and by creating brahmins from those born of lower *varnas*. His theology was developed by the six Goswamis of Vrindavana and consolidated by Baladeva. The Bengali saint, Bhaktivedanta Swami Prabhupada, who appeared in the line of succession from Chaitanya, founded ISKCON in 1966. The Society's UK Headquarters are at Bhaktivedanta Manor in Hertfordshire.

Ramakrishna Mission

The Ramakrishna Mission was founded by the Bengali saint, Vivekananda Swami (1863-1902) in the name of his guru, Ramakrishna (1836-1886). It teaches the Advaita version of Vedanta coming from Shankara. It is headed by a well-disciplined and organised body of *sannyasis*. It is still particularly popular in Bengal. Its UK Headquarters are near Slough in Berkshire.

Quotes

"God's grace is like a strong wind that's always blowing. But we have to raise our own sails."

Paramahamsa Ramakrishna

"The Indian people are forgetting their glorious tradition, their culture, their religion and it is a big problem for the children"

Indira Bettiji

Pushti Marg

The Pushti Marg (path of nourishment) tradition descends from the *bhakti* revivalist Vallabha (1479-1531). Its followers worship Krishna in his form as an infant and as Nathji, holding up the Govardhana Hill. Most of its members are from the Lohana *jati* (community) from Gujarat. They believe that entering the Lord's *nitya-lila* (eternal pastimes) is a higher goal then even liberation. They are largely represented by a group called the Shree Vallabha Nidhi. There are several successions from Vallabha, and a popular guru who visits Britain regularly is a lady called Indira Bettiji.

The Arya Samaj

Members of the Arya Samaj follow the teachings of the reformer Dayananda Sarasvati (1824-1883) who rejected the practices of caste and *murti* worship. The main ceremony performed is the *havan* (sacred fire) ceremony. The Arya Samaj remain influential worldwide and in Britain, where most followers come from the Punjabi community.

Visiting Holy People

Many holy people from India regularly visit the UK. Murari Bapu *(right),* who speaks from the Ramayana, is most popular with worshippers of Rama. Rameshbai Oza is famous for his "bhagavat-katha", a recital of the Bhagavat Purana *(see page 130)* which usually lasts seven days and is attended by thousands. Many other sadhus (holy men) frequently visit the UK. Many temples also rely on India for priests to perform their regular worship. Musicians, dancers and other performers also regularly visit Britain.

Other Hindu and Hindu-related Groups

There are several organisations which do not always classify themselves as Hindu but which are somehow related. These include the Satya Sai Baba Organisation, headed by Sai Baba. He was born in 1926 in India and is considered a reincarnation of the saint Kabir. The organisation understands itself as a spiritual organisation which embraces all faiths. It has centres throughout the world.

Transcendental Meditation rose to popularity in the 1960's under the leadership of the Maharishi Mahesh Yogi *(right).* He taught mantra meditation that remains popular today. Many other Hindu-related groups became popular during the same period, including Rajneesh (1931–1990), whose movement is now called 'Osho'. The numerous yoga organisations in Britain also derive much theory and practice from Hindu scripture. A popular group is The Divine Life Society with its Shivananda Vedanta Yoga Centres.

Representative Groups

There is no single representative organisation for Hindus in the UK, though the National Council for Hindu Temples (NCHT) has perhaps the widest membership. In 1994 it was instrumental in forming the Hindu Council of the UK, which now appears to be becoming a leading voice for Hindus in the UK. The national branch of the VHP (Vishva Hindu Parishad) has centres throughout the UK. There are also regional umbrella groups and numerous groups based on caste, regional or linguistic affiliations, or performing some type of charity work.

Other Prominent Groups / Centres

There are many other organisations in the UK. For details of further groups, please consult Religions In The UK – A Multi-faith Directory published by The University of Derby in conjunction with the Interfaith Network.

Eight Types of Hindu Figures

As we have studied in this chapter:

1. *Deities (God/Goddess and gods and goddesses)*
2. *The ancient rishis (seers), including the Seven Rishis*
3. *Mythological figures (may also be historical)*
4. *Theologians & founders of sampradayas*
5. *The bhakti saints*
6. *Socio-political leaders and reformers*
7. *Recent cultural and religious leaders*
8. *Contemporary gurus and leaders*

Famous Women within Hinduism

Hindu scripture, particularly of the earlier period, places great value on contributions of women. The much-reported abuses of women in India demonstrate a falling away from traditional practice. Many famous women serve as lasting role models, though with the influence of feminism such values are less popular with the younger generation or need reinterpretation to suit the current social context. Such famous figures are extremely diverse and include deities (such as Sita and Parvati), historical or mythological figures (such as Draupadi from the Mahabharata), political activists (for example, the Queen of Jhansi), and saints and spiritual leaders (e.g. Mirabai and Anandamayi). A more complete list is given below, with three life sketches on the following page.

Above: Queen Kunti, heroine of the Mahabharata, is famous for her heartfelt prayers to Lord Krishna. She wears the white sari of a widow
Below: Today, Hindu women are prominent in all walks of life. Worldwide popularity has favoured a number of female gurus, such as Mother Meera, Nirmila Devi, and Amritanandamayi Devi. Indira Bettiji is particularly well-known in Britain. Mother Gayathri, a popular guru in Britain, is shown here.

Sita – The wife of Lord Rama, considered part of the Godhead. For many Hindus, Sita is the ideal example of womanhood and a dutiful wife.

Kunti – The mother of the five Pandava princes. Her devotion to Lord Krishna never faltered even in great adversity. She is one of the 'five virtuous women.' The others are Draupadi (*see below*), Mandodari (the wife of Ravana), Ahalya (wife of the sage Gautama), and Tara (the wife of Vali, the monkey king killed by Rama).

Draupadi – The wife of all five Pandavas. She was insulted in the royal court and, as a result, millions of warriors perished on the plains of Kurukshetra. A chaste yet powerfully assertive woman, she displayed both fiery anger and remarkable compassion.

Damayanti – Wife of Nala. Together they demonstrated unflinching devotion to each other.

Savitri – By her selfless devotion she saved her husband from the court of Yama, the Lord of Death.

Andal (725-755) – The only woman amongst the South Indian Alvars (poet mystics). Andal was so overwhelmed with love for Vishnu that she refused to marry anyone else. According to tradition she merged into the deity of Vishnu after being formally married to him.

Akka Mahadevi (12th century) – A medieval women saint with an unusually modern outlook. She was devoted to Lord Shiva. The Lingayats venerate her as a symbol of the equality of women and as an early exponent of women's emancipation.

Mirabai (1547-1614) – Great saint, born in a royal family and famous for her songs and her devotion to Lord Krishna, whom she considered her eternal husband.

The Queen of Jhansi (1835-1858) – Famous for fearlessly fighting against the British.

Kasturaba Gandhi (1869-1944) – Wife of Gandhi; still greatly honoured as a devoted wife by the Hindu community.

Helena Blavatski (1831-1891) – One of the early foreigners (from Russia) to take up Hinduism, she co-founded the Theosophical Society in 1875. Annie Bessant (1847-1933), an English woman and prolific writer, became the society's president in 1907.

Anandamayi (1896-1982) – a well-known female yogi from Bengal with a large following and many centres throughout India. She is credited with many miracles.

Sita was the daughter of King Janaka. She is the heroine of the Ramayana. As Rama's only wife, she resolved to undergo the hardships of forest life rather than leave her husband. Out of infatuation for her, the tyrant Ravana met his ignoble end. After he kidnapped her, she refused to submit to his adulterous advances. Sita is considered to embody all the virtues of a traditional Hindu woman and has been held up as a role model for Hindu girls to follow. Some modern feminists have objected to this notion as being sexist.

Draupadi is a central figure in the Mahabharata. Born of the sacrificial fire in King Drupada's court, she became the common wife of all five Pandava brothers. King Jayadratha tried to kidnap her, and she fought like a true warrior queen (*see right*). She demonstrated how a traditionally devoted wife can also be powerfully assertive.

Once, Yudhisthira lost her in a rigged gambling match and the Kauravas tried to disrobe her before the entire royal assembly. In the attempt to strip her, the kings present failed to intervene, and thus sowed the seeds of their destruction on the plains of Kurukshetra. The Mahabharata thus illustrates the ancient ideal of valuing and protecting women, and the terrible consequence of neglecting or exploiting them.

Mirabai: Although many Hindu heroines exemplify the traditional role of women, others have opposed or transcended tradition when it declined into abuse. Mira was one such example. Born in 1547 in a Rajput (warrior) family in Rajastan, she became an ardent devotee of Krishna. At a young age, she resolved that only he could be her future bridegroom. She was, however, duly married into a Shakti-worshipping household. She refused to abandon the worship of Krishna for the Goddess, and was victimised by her husband. She left for Vrindavana, but returned when her husband reformed. Upon his death, she refused to perform sati and was persecuted by her husband's family. The new king tried to kill her but by Krishna's grace she survived. She finally abandoned her husbans's palace to lead the life of a wandering saint. She sang and danced in public, unconcerned for social decorum and finally it is said that she mystically entered a murti of Krisna. Her poems and songs express her intense feelings for Krishna and are still sung and recited by devotees today.

Personal Reflection

■ How well do we understand traditional Hindu attitudes towards women?

Common Misunderstandings

"Traditional Hindu attitudes towards women must be wrong (since they are dated). Identifying differences between men and women is sexist."

Not necessarily - there may be assumptions that need re-examining here.

Quote

"Worldly comfort is an illusion, No sooner you get it, it goes. I have chosen the Indestructible for my refuge."

Mirabai

Hinduism in Britain Today

Key Points:

- There are about 1,000 million Hindus in the world, of whom about 750 million live in India.
- There are about 800,000 Hindus living in Britain today.
- Most are of Gujarati origin (70%), and a significant number from Punjab (15%).
- Others are from Bengal, South India, Shri Lanka, Guyana, Fiji, Mauritius and parts of Africa.
- Most came here via East Africa or from India itself.
- Throughout the UK, there are about 135 Hindu temples conducting regular worship.
- There are significant Hindu communities to be found in Leicester, London (Wembley, Southall and Harrow), Coventry, the West Midlands, Bradford, Preston and Greater Manchester, with smaller communities in many other towns and cities.

Hindus first started arriving in Britain in significant numbers shortly after the Second World War. However, the main wave of immigration, from East Africa, spanned the late sixties and early seventies. Most Hindus settled in inner-city areas, and were often relatively poor, many having lost their wealth upon expulsion from Uganda. They often became menial workers or started small businesses as grocers, newsagents and clothing manufacturers. The natural centres of these fledgling communities were the first austere temples, converted from old buildings such as church halls.

Settling in a foreign county had its obvious challenges. There were initial problems with diet, climate, and acceptance into the host community. As the second generation emerged, some youngsters felt unclear about their identity. Hindu parents, concerned to preserving their heritage, recognised the need to articulate teachings previously handed down by family and cultural tradition. Temples and religious groups established formal education classes, in language, scripture, and the performing arts. Despite the different appeals for continuity, the cultural aspects of Hinduism have, quite naturally, undergone significant changes. Young ladies are now less likely to wear traditional dress, and Hindu youth have developed their own brands of popular music. There is evidence that many young Hindus have integrated well and developed high degrees of social and cultural competence in a pluralistic society.

The Hindu diaspora in Britain appears to be flourishing. Members are well established in professional fields - law, media, medicine, engineering and accounting - and in many branches of business. Hindu students top the charts in academic achievement. Many magnificent, purpose-built mandirs, replacing the converted church halls, testify to the growing prestige and influence of the Hindu community. The tradition, with its rich culture, accommodating nature, and emphasis on personal spirituality, not only endures but makes a positive contribution towards contemporary British life.

Below: The Preston Mandir in Lancashire.
Right: A modern Hindu couple, whose grandparents moved to the UK in the late sixties.

Further Reading

This selection focuses on books for teachers and for student research. A more comprehensive list (with ISBNs) features on the CD-Rom (Tab 9) within the Heart of Hinduism Resource Pack.

Academic Books (especially for Secondary RE teachers and Libraries)

◆ *Hinduism – A Short Introduction* by Klaus. K. Klostermaier (Oneworld, Oxford)

◆ *A Concise Encyclopedia of Hinduism* by Klaus. K. Klostermaier (Oneworld, Oxford)

   These books are academically sound and very readable. Klostermaier writes with an unusual combination of sympathetic insight and intellectual rigour. There are further books in the same series.

◆ *A Very Short Introduction to Hinduism* by Kim Knott (Oxford University Press)
   A succinct and accessible introduction to the tradition.

Faith Books (for Libraries)

◆ *The Mahabharata and The Ramayana* by Krishna Dharma (Torchlight, Badger CA, USA)
   Krishna Dharma's brisk-moving style transforms the Hindu Epics into an easy but absorbing read, without losing their original spirit. For schools, the best translations available.

◆ *A Tale of Gods and Demons* by Sharma and Prime (Mandala Publishing, San Rafael, CA)
   A beautiful book, conveying the dignity of the tradition through a retelling of the Ramayana.

◆ *Panchatantra* retold by Krishna Dharma (Torchlight, Badger CA, USA)
   A very accessible rendering of these famous stories from the Panchatantra.

◆ *Bhagavad-Gita As It Is* by A.C. Bhaktivedanta Swami Prabhupada (BBT, Los Angeles)
   An easy to understand version from one of the leading bhakti traditions.

◆ *Creation from the Bhagavat Purana* by Ananta Shakti (publication, Autumn 2003)
   Promises to be the best book around on Hindu creation. Over 24 full colour illustrations. Written for 8-12 year olds, and highly suitable for to Key Stages 2 & 3.

◆ *Meeting Hindus* edited by Gwyneth Little (Christians Aware, Leicester)
   Includes much ethnographical-type material from Hindus themselves. Particularly useful as research material.

Teacher's and Student's Books

◆ *Beliefs, Values & Traditions*, by Anne Lovelace and Joy White (Heinemann, Oxford)
   An accessible and interesting pupils' book, dealing with Hinduism's relevance to the contemporary world.

◆ *Teach Yourself World Faiths – Hinduism* by V.P. Kanitkar and W. Owen Cole (Hodder Headline, London)
   Kanitkar's books are informative and contain many first hand accounts. Cole is a reputable author.

◆ *The Hindu Priest* by Rasamandala Das (Franklin–Watts)
   A very personal way into the tradition for Key Stage 1.

◆ *Hindu Stories* by Anita Ganeri (Evans Brothers)
   Stories Suitable to Key Stage 2. From a writer experienced in the Hindu tradition.

◆ *The Complete Idiot's Guide to Hinduism* by Linda Johnsen (Alpha, Indianapolis)
   Loads of information, presented in a mood and manner accessible to most Westerners.

Auxiliary Books (to supplement the Heart of Hinduism)

There are two books that we highly recommend (and supply) to complement your Teachers' Pack. The first includes many recommended stories, and the second covers the topic of moral issues.

◆ *Vedic Stories from Ancient India* by Ananta Shakti (Ahimsa books, Borehamwood, UK
   A very popular anthology of stories, many with moral themes. Especially suitable for Key Stages 3 and 4.

◆ *Moral Issues in Hinduism* by Rasamandala Das (publication date, September 2003)
   In the same style as this book, this promises to be one of the best studies of the subject.

Glossary

Many proper names, usually with only one significant entry, are listed under this glossary with the page reference. These include names of places, people, festivals, organisations and sacred texts. Some terms are also listed, or alternatively listed, under the index (*see page 159*).

Adi Shankara 138 – well-known theologian and founder of the advaita school. Also called Adi Shankaracharya.
Advaita 6 – non-dualism, the name of the theology equating the soul with God.
Advaitin 131 – a follower of the advaita school of thought founded by Adi-Shankara.
Agamas 123 – a generic name for sectarian literature, particularly the 28 Shaiva Agamas.
Aghori 129 – a group of ascetics whose deliberate practice is to contravene social and moral norms.
Agni 53 – the god of fire, particularly prominent in the Vedic period.
Ahalya 146 – wife of the sage Gautama, and one of the 'five virtuous women'.
Ahimsa 37 – non-violence, a key Hindu principle.
Akhand Bharat 136 – 'undivided India': a term used in championing the re-unification of India.
Akka Mahadevi 146 – famous medieval woman saint from South India.
Allahabad 70 – the Muslim name for the city of Prayaga, the site of the main Kumbha Mela.
Alvars 108 – the South Indian Vaishnava poet-saints of the early medieval period. Twelve are considered principal.
Ambedkar, Ranji 104 – a reformer from the untouchable class who converted to Buddhism with many followers.
Anandamayi 146 – well-known female guru from Bengal (1896-1982).
Andal 128 – the only woman amongst the twelve Alvars.
Angira 138 – one of the seven great rishis (sages of old).
Anjali 95 – hands folded, to make an offering.
Anuman 121 – deduction or inference; one of the means of acquiring knowledge.
Antyesthi 74 – the last rite of passage, the funeral.
Apsaras 53 – the celestial dancing girls, well-known for their ability to divert renunciates from the path of spiritual life.
Aranyakas 124 – "the forest treatises", one of the four sections of the Vedas.
Arjuna 126 – the third son of King Pandu. He heard the Bhagavad-gita from Krishna.
Artha 28 – economic development, one of the four aims of life.
Artha Shastra 131 – texts that discuss how to acquire wealth and power; considered related to the Dharma Shastras.
Arti 57 – the most popular Hindu ceremony, in which a lamp and other articles are offered.
Arya Samaj 145 – one of the main 19th century reform movements, still extant today.
Aryan 112 – 'noble': traditionally refers to any people, irrespective of race, who have a culture based on spiritual values.
Ashok, King 113 – monarch who patronised Buddhism; under his influence it spread throughout much of India.
Ashrama 26 – a place where spirituality is cultivated; also, stage of life (of which there are four).
Ashvattama 102 – son of Drona, martial teacher of the five Pandavas; he notoriously slaughtered their sleeping sons.
Astanga Yoga 44 – the eightfold path that culminated in meditation and samadhi (trance). One of the four paths.
Astika 118 – 'orthodox': refers to the six darshans. Non-orthodox schools are called nastika.
Asuras 53 – the demons. Materially elevated but impious beings, constantly at loggerheads with the gods.
Atharva 124 – the fourth of the four Vedas.
Atithi 99 – literally 'without any time'; the unexpected guest.
Atman 8 – literally 'self': it can mean body or mind, but ultimately refers to the soul.
Atri 138 – one of seven great rishis (sages), each of whom have a gotra (dynasty) from which Hindus claim descent.
Avadhi 90 – popular language for vernacular texts, especially in the area of North India around Ayodhya.
Ayodhya 129 – the capital city of Koshala, the kingdom of Rama.
Ayurveda 101 – the indigenous science of Indian medicine; the texts which explain this science.

Badanarayana 118 – a name for Vyasa, attributed with writing key texts such as the *Mahabharata* and *Vedanta Sutras*.
Badrinatha 72 – a holy spot in the Himalayas. One of the four dhamas (especially holy places).
Baladeva 138 – key theologian for Bengali Vaishnavism; his commentary on the Vedanta Sutra is the '*Govinda Bhasya*'.
Basava 135 – influential reformer within the Lingayat tradition of South Indian Shaivism.
Benares 70 – another name for Varanasi, perhaps the most famous of all Indian holy towns.
Bhagavad Gita 128 – the Song of God, spoken by Krishna to Arjuna.
Bhagavad katha 130 – the public recitation of the Bhagavat Purana, often over seven days.
Bhagavat Purana 130 – one of the most popular Puranas, containing the famous stories of Krishna.
Bhajan 54 – a hymn, from the root 'bhaj', to worship with adoration.
Bhakti 45 – the path of loving devotional service (also Bhakti yoga).
Bhakti yoga 116 – the path of loving devotional service; also called bhakti marg.
Bhaktivedanta 143 – name of the founder of ISKCON. It means "bhakti is the conclusion of all knowledge".
Bhangra 92 – an energetic dance style from the Punjab.
Bharadvaja 138 – one of the seven great rishis (sages) of ancient times.
Bharata 68 – the ancient name for India, called after the king of the same name.

Bharata Muni 93 – author of musical texts delineating nine rasas (tastes) upon which much music is based.
Bharata Natyam 92 – the name of the most popular Southern Indian style of classical dance.
Bhava 93 – emotion. A word used in the classical performing arts and also in much bhakti theology.
Bhrigu 138 – one of the seven great sages. According to some texts, he tested the trimurti to see who was the Supreme.
Bindi 95 – dot, usually of a red colour, traditionally worn by married women on the forehead.
Birbal 42 – the witty minister of Emperor Akbar; many legends have developed around his exploits.
Blavatski, Helena 146 – Russian lady who co-founded the Theosophical Society.
Brahma 48 – the creator (or, some say, secondary creator); one of the trimurti, three main deities in this world.
Brahma Sutra 119 – another name for the Vedanta Sutra.
Brahmachari 84 - a celibate student. A member of the first stage of life (called the brahmachari ashrama).
Brahman 6 – the Supreme or spirit; that which pervades and supports everything.
Brahmanas 124 - one of the four main divisions in the Vedas themselves.
Brahmin 83 – a member of the highest varna; a priest, teacher or intellectual.
Brahmo Samaj 140 – the reform movement started by Rama Mohan Roy.
Brighu Muni 138 – one of the seven ancient sages (rishis).

Chaddar 94 – a cotton or woollen shawl worn by men and women.
Chaitanya 139 – the founder of Bengali Vaishnavism; one of the medieval saints.
Chakra 48 – the disk weapon usually associated with Vishnu, and one of his four symbols.
Chanakya 43 – a brahmin, advisor to King Chandragupta, who wrote on statecraft and popular wisdom.
Chandra 53 – the Moon; the presiding deity of the Moon. Also known as Soma.
Chappati 98 – a round unleavened bread toasted on a skillet and then puffed over an open flame.
Charaka Samhitas 101 – one of the texts explaining the science of Ayurveda.
Charanamrita 62 – the water collected from the feet of the murti after bathing, and later sipped by worshippers.
Charvaka 118 – scholar who proposed that the purpose of life is to obtain ghee (i.e. good food by any means) and enjoy.
Chidambaram 72 – a Shaivite pilgrimage town, the state of Tamil Nadu.

Daksha 135 – one of the chief progenitors; father of Sati, Shiva's wife, who killed herself by self-invoked mystic fire.
Dalit 104 – 'the oppressed'; a title assumed by the class previously called 'untouchables'.
Damayanti 140 – wife of Nala and one of the famous women of Hinduism.
Danda 96 – staff, particularly as carried by the sannyasi.
Dandiya rasa 92 – a Gujarati stick dance popular in the UK at Navaratri.
Darshan 54 – literally 'seeing'; the act of taking audience of the deity or a holy person.
Dasa Kuta 133 – a Vaishnava tradition centred around Pandapur in Maharastra.
Dasanam 131 – 'ten names'; the ten orders of sannyasa founded by Adi Shankara.
Dasharatha 41 – the father of Rama.
Dayananda Sarasvati 140 – founder of the Arya Samaj.
Deva 53 – god; sometimes translated demigod. God is often called deva-deva, 'gods of gods'. Devi means 'goddess'.
Devanagari 90 – "used in the cities of the demigods"; it refers to the Sanskrit script.
Devi 50 – "goddess"; used to refer to any female deity, but most specifically Shakti, wife of Shiva.
Devi Bhagavat Purana 130 – perhaps the second most popular Purana; it includes the stories of Shakti.
Devi Purana 130 – another Purana dealing largely with the Goddess.
Dhanvantari 101 – incarnation of Vishnu who appeared out of the Milk Ocean and gave humankind the science of medicine.
Dharma 24 – the religious duties that sustain humans and all living beings.
Dharma Shastra 131 – the law-books of Hinduism dealing with morality and the judiciary.
Dhoti 96 – a piece of cloth about 4 metres long and worn by Hindu men to cover the loins and legs.
Dhritarashtra 126 – blind brother of King Pandu; his bias towards his own sons fostered the Kurukshetra conflict.
Diwali 67 – the festival of lights (October/November). For most Hindus it heralds the New Year.
Doshas 99 – the three bodily humours which constitute the conceptual basis of Ayurvedic medicine.
Draupadi 41 – the common wife of all five Pandava princes, and heroine of the Mahabharata.
Durga 52 – a warlike form of Devi, usually with many arms carrying weapons and riding on a lion.
Duryodhana 126 – the first son of Dhritarashtra. His avarice caused the Kurukshetra War.
Dussehra 67 – the festival that celebrates the victory of Rama over the evil Ravana.
Dvaita (dualism) 138 – the theology that the soul and God are different, specifically as taught by Madhva.
Dvaraka 72 – a holy spot in Maharastra, on the West coast of India. Krishna lived there as a king.
Dvapara-yuga 32 – the third age in every cycle of four ages (yugas). It ended some 5,000 years ago.
Dvija bandu 102 – 'friends of the twice-born'; those born in the three higher varnas but who fall from the standards.

Ganapati 50 – a name of Ganesh, the elephant-headed son of Shiva.
Gandharvas 53 – residents of the heavenly planets who are particularly expert in singing and music.

Ganesh 50 – one of the two sons of Shiva. He has a rotund body and an elephant's head.

Ganesh Caturthi 67 – the festival that celebrates Ganesh's birthday (on the fourth day of the waxing moon).

Ganga 74 – the River Ganges, held by many to be the most sacred; name of the river goddess.

Garba 92 – a form of circular dance from Gujarat and popular at Navaratri.

Garba griha 63 – the inner sanctum of the temple.

Gaudiya Vaishnavism 134 – the Bengali worshippers of Vishnu (specifically Radha and Krishna together).

Gautama 138 – an ancient rishi (sage), often considered one of the principal sapta (seven) rishis.

Gaya 70 – a pilgrimage place in Bihar, especially important for offering rites to the departed.

Gayatri 59 – the mantra chanted thrice daily by brahmins; a wife of Brahma.

Giddha 92 – a Punjabi dance performed by women.

Godavari 74 – one of the seven most holy rivers, in Central India.

Golakwar, M. S, 142 – former leader of the Rashtriya Swayamsevak Sanga (RSS).

Gopuram 92 – gateway to temples, especially in the South; they are often decorated with ornate figurines.

Gorakhnatha 135 – important historical figure amongst the Nathapatnis sect of Shaivas.

Gotra – dynasty originating with one of the seven great rishis (sages of old).

Govardhana 75 – the famous hill lifted by child Krishna.

Govinda 52 – a name for Krishna meaning, "one who gives pleasure to the cows and the senses".

Grihasta 84 – a person in the second stage of life; the householder.

Guna 14 – literally 'rope'. It refers to the three material qualities that pervade and control matter.

Guru 31 – a spiritual teacher; a regular teacher may also be called guru.

Gurukula 107 – the school of the guru. A traditional Hindu school.

Hanuman 50 – the monkey-like deity; he is a devotee of Rama, but also worshiped in his own right.

Hanuman Jayanti 67 – the birthday festival of Hanuman.

Harappa 113 – one of two walled cities unearthed in the 1920s; evidence apparently supported the Aryan invasion theory.

Hare Krishna 144 – a popular mantra chanted by members of ISKCON, therefore called the Hare Krishna Movement.

Haridvara 72 – an important pilgrimage site on the banks of the River Ganges.

Harijanas 104 – 'the people of God'; a term used by Gandhi to denote what some call the 'fifth varna', the untouchables.

Havan 59 – the sacred fire ceremony dating back to Vedic times, but still used in many ceremonies/rites of passage.

Hedgewar, K.V. 140 – founder of the Rashtriya Swayamsevak Sanga (RSS).

Hindu Mahasabha 140 – the political party established in 1909 and forerunner of many nationalistic movements.

Hitopadesha 131 – a text containing moral stories; considered part of the Dharma Shastra.

Holi 67 – the spring festival in which participants throw coloured water and powders over each other.

Homa 59 – another name for havan

Hrishikesh 75 – a pilgrimage spot on the River Ganges in the Himalayan foothills.

Indra 53 – the deity in charge of rain; he was most prominent during the Vedic Period.

Indira Bettiji 144 – a contemporary women guru of the Pushti-marg sampradaya.

Indus 106 – river now in Pakistan, from whose name the words Hindu and Hinduism are apparently derived.

Ishvara 20 – literally 'controller'. It refers to a deity, or the Supreme Deity.

Itihasa 123 – 'history'. The Mahabharata and Ramayana constitute the two Itihasas.

Jaimini 118 – the founder of the Mimamsa school (one of the six darshans).

Janaka 147 – legendary King of Mithila and father of Sita, Rama's consort.

Janmashtami 67 – the birthday festival of Krishna, falling on the eigth day (asta) of the dark moon.

Japa 59 – the practice of reciting mantras quietly or silently on prayer beads.

Jatakarma 76 – a name for the rite of passage performed just after a child's birth.

Jati 102 – sub-castes, or occupational sub-groups, which form part of the caste system.

Jayadratha 147 – notorious warrior who tried to kidnap Draupadi. He was slain by Arjuna during the Kurukshetra war.

Jiva 135 – 'that which lives'; a term for the individual soul, also called the 'atman' or 'jivatman'.

Jnana 44 – knowledge. Jnana yoga is the path of wisdom, one of the four main spiritual processes.

Jnana-kanda 122 – one of three broad sections of the Vedic literature. It deals with knowledge.

Kabir 139 – the medieval bhakti saint who is revered by Hindu, Muslims and Sikhs.

Kaivalya 114 – realisation of 'oneness' with God and a spiritual identity beyond the subtle and gross bodies.

Kalasha 95 – a waterpot, an auspicious symbol used in many rituals.

Kali 52 – a fierce form of Devi. It is pronounced 'car-ley'.

Kalika Purana 136 – an important Shakti text dedicated to the Goddess Kali.

Kali-yuga 32 – the fourth age, the iron age or age of quarrel and hypocrisy. Kali in this case rhymes with 'gulley'.

Kalki 116 – the last of the ten Vishnu incarnations. He appears on horseback, wielding a sword, at the end of Kali Yuga.

Kama 28 – lust and gratification of the senses. It is pronounced 'car-ma'.

Kanada 121 – founder of one of the six orthodox systems, namely Vaisheshika (atomic theory).

Kanchipuram 72 – important centre of Shri Vaishnavism in South India.

Kanyakumari 71 – a holy site on the southern tip of India and connected with Goddess Parvati .

Kapila 120 – the founder of Sanhkya, one of the six main philosophies and dealing with physics and metaphysics.

Kapila Muni 112 – founder of the school (darshan) of Sankhya.

Karma 12 – literally 'action', but often used to imply 'reaction', as in 'the law of karma'. Pronounced 'cur-ma'.

Karma kanda 122 – one of the three broad divisions of Hindu scriptures. It deals with rituals for material elevation.

Karma-yoga 116 – the yoga of selfless action. One of the four main yogas, also called the four margs (paths).

Karna 121 – tragic anti-hero of the Mahabharata. At Kurukshetra he fought against his step-brothers, the Pandavas.

Kartikeya 50 – a name of Murugan, one of the two sons of Shiva and Parvati.

Kashi 71 – another name for the city of Varanasi.

Kathak 92 – a classical dance school of Northern India.

Kathakali 92 a form of dance-drama from South India that features elaborate costumes and face masks.

Kauravas 126 – the descendants of King Kuru. It specifically refers to the cousins of the Pandavas and their allies.

Kaveri 74 – one of the seven main holy rivers flowing through the sacred town of Shri Rangam in South India.

Kedarnatha 72 – an important Shaiva shrine in the Himalayas.

Keshab Chandra Sena 140 – reformer who spent some time with the Brahmo Samaj.

Kirtan 58 –'glorification'. It usually refers to the chanting of mantra to musical accompaniment.

Kohl (or kajal) 97 – mascara. Also called 'anjana'.

Konarak 73 – site on the east coast of India famous for its ancient temple dedicated to the Sun.

Koshala 129 – the kingdom of Rama, of which Ayodhya is the capital.

Krishna 50 – a principal deity, usually considered an avatar of Vishnu. Many worship him as the Supreme.

Kshatriya 82 – literally 'one who protects'; member of the second varna; a warrior-administrator.

Kumbha Mela 70 – mela means 'fair'; kumbha means 'pot'. A huge gathering that takes place every three years.

Kunti 146 – the wife of King Pandu and mother of the five Pandavas. One of the heroines of the Mahabharata.

Kurta 96 – a loose fitting collar-less shirt worn by men. Usually made of cotton or silk.

Kuru 126 – dynasty in which the Pandavas appeared. The term is specifically used to refer to their wicked cousins.

Kurukshetra 126 – the site of the great eighteen-day war described in the Mahabharata.

Kuvera 53 – the deity who is considered 'the treasurer of the demigods'.

Lakshman 129 – the brother of Rama who went with him to the forest. He worshipped with Sita, Rama and Hanuman.

Lakshmi 50 – the goddess of fortune. She is the eternal consort of Vishnu.

Linga 135 – a vertical stone column worshipped as a form of Shiva. It represents him as the supreme male principle.

Lingayats 135 – a popular South Indian Shaiva tradition. Members wear a small linga around their necks.

Madhva 137 –Vaishnava theologian who founded his own disciplic succession and taught a highly dualistic theology.

Madurai 71 – an important temple in South India dedicated to Parvati.

Maha Shiva Ratri 67 – the night festival celebrating Shiva's marriage to Parvati.

Mahabharata 126 – literally 'the History of Greater India'. One of the two Epics and the longest known poem.

Mahadeva 52 – a name of lord Shiva, meaning 'great god'.

Maharishi Mahesh Yogi 145 – leader of the Transcendental Meditation organisation established in the late 1960s.

Mahasabha 142 – 'great assembly'; the Hindu Mahasabha was established in 1909.

Maha–yuga 116 – 'great age'; a complete cycle of four ages lasting a total of 4,320,000 years.

Mahenjo Daro 120 – one of two walled cities unearthed during archaeological excavations in the 1920s.

Mahesh 52 – another name of Shiva.

Mandir 60 – temple.

Mandodari 146 – celebrated wife of Ravana. She was loyal to her husband but urged him to return Sita to Rama.

Manjira 93 – small hand cymbals used in singing hymns and mantras.

Manu 131 – a demigod considered the ruling deity of mankind. The Manu Smriti is attributed to him.

Manu Smriti 131 – an important and ancient text, the 'codebook for mankind'; the principal Dharma Shastra.

Mataji 49 – 'respected mother'; a form of address for any lady, but also an affectionate name for Devi.

Mathura 72 – an ancient town and the birthplace of Krishna. It is one of the seven ancient cities of India.

Matsya 116 – the first of the ten incarnations of Vishnu. He appeared during the great flood to save the Vedas.

Maya 16 – 'that which is not', or illusion. An important concept that describes the illusory nature of this world.

Mimamsa 119 – literally 'enquiry. One of the six darshans, though Vedanta is also called the 'later school of enquiry'.

Mirabai 147 – a famous woman saint whose poems and songs are still popular today.

Moghul 114 – the Muslim dynasty that ruled much of India from 1526 until about 1857.

Mohan Malaviha 142 – member of the Arya Samaj and co-founder of the Hindu Mahasabha.

Moksha 18 – liberation, specifically from the bondage of repeated birth and death.

Mridanga 93 – literally 'body of clay'; a two-headed drum, used in religious music more than in classical.

Mrigari 40 – a vicious hunter who turned saint and demonstrated the principal of ahimsa, non-violence.

Mundan 77 – the head-shaving ceremony, one of the main rites of passage for children.

Murari Babu 145 – popular saint famous for his public recitations on the Ramayana.

Murugan 50 – a name for Kartikeya, particularly popular in South India.

Naga 53 – the serpentine residents of the subterranean heavenly planets who are sometimes worshipped.

Nasik 72 – pilgrimage town on the River Godavari; site of one of the smaller Kumbha Melas.

Namakarana 77 – the name-giving ceremony performed shortly after birth.

Namaskara 95 – 'I pay my obeisance unto you' – a term of greeting usually accompanied with folded palms.

Namaste 95 – an alternative for 'namaskara'.

Namdev 139 – poet-saint appearing in the Das Kuta Vaishnava tradition.

Narada 131 – famous rishi (sage) who acts as the messenger of the devas (gods). He wrote several important texts.

Narayana 52 – a name of Vishnu, particularly his form in the spiritual realm.

Narmada 74 – one of the seven sacred rivers, flowing in central India.

Nastika 118 – 'unorthodox'; generally refers to schools which reject the Vedic canon, such as Buddhism and Jainism.

Nataraja 52 – 'the king of dancers'; a name for Lord Shiva, especially as he dances to destroy the material cosmos.

Nathapatnis 135 – prominent sect of Shaiva ascetics.

Nathdwar 134 – town in Gujarat focused on the worship of Krishna; an important centre for the Pushti Marg tradition.

Nathji 134 – a form of Krishna lifting Govardhana Hill. The main deity now resides in the town of Nathdwar, Gujarat.

Natya Shastra 92 – text on dance and the performing arts written by the sage Bharata Muni.

Nava-rasa 91 – the nine 'moods' of music as codified and explained by Bharata Muni. Rasa means 'taste' or 'flavour'.

Navaratri 67 – literally 'nine-nights'. The festival in honour of Devi usually celebrated in the evenings with dance.

Nayanars 135 – Shaivite poet-saints of Southern India who flourished in South India between about 700 and 1,000 CE.

Nimbarka 134 – a theologian and founder of one of the four Vaishnava sampradayas (disciplic successions).

Niti Shastra 131 – books of popular wisdom; they include the Hitopadesh, the Panchatantra and the Chanakya Shloka.

Nitya 43 – eternal; the five 'nitya karmas' refer to the five duties that cannot be given up.

Nrisimhadeva 67 – the half-man/half-lion incarnation of Vishnu who saved his devotee, Prahlada.

Nyaya 121 – logic, and one of the six orthodox schools of thought (darshans).

Om (Aum) 95 – the most important mantra for Hindus, often considered to represent the Supreme.

Padma 95 – lotus, an important symbol. it is often used metaphorically to describe beauty e.g. lotus eyes, or lotus feet.

Panchama 104 – 'the fifth varna', the untouchable class. Panch (pronounced more like 'punch') means five.

Panchatantra 131 – a anthology of fables featuring mainly animals as heroes and villains.

Pandapur 128 – most important centre for the Das Kuta Vaishnava sampradaya in Maharastra.

Pandu 120 – emperor of Greater India, husband of Kunti and father of Arjuna and his four brothers.

Papa 12 – sin, or activities that degrade (it is usually pronounced so that it rhymes with 'harp').

Paramatman 114 – the Superself, or Supersoul. God situated within the heart.

Parashara 125 – great sage, the father of Vyasa (Badarayana). He wrote many of the core texts on astrology.

Parashurama 116 – the sixth incarnation of Vishnu. With his axe he destroyed the irreligious members of the royalty.

Parvati 49 – the wife of Shiva, and daughter of the Himalayas. A benign form of Devi.

Patanjali 120 – author of the yoga sutras and founder of the corresponding darshan (school of thought).

Pradakshina 59 – circumambulation, an important feature of worship.

Pradhana 120 – the unmanifest stage of matter (prakriti).

Prajapati 53 – 'progenitor'; the higher beings who were responsible for populating the world.

Prakriti 14 – material energy in its manifest state.

Pramukhi Swami 144 – current spiritual head of the Swami Narayana Mission.

Pranam 95 – obeisance, usually offered by placing together the palms and bowing the head.

Prasad 98 – literally 'mercy'. It refers to any item sanctified by offering to God, most often sanctified food.

Pratyaksa 121 – direct perception; one means of obtaining knowledge.

Pravachan 58 – a talk or lecture on spiritual subjects; for some, an important act of worship.

Prayag 71 – site of the Maha (great) Kumbha Mela every twelve years.

Prema 28 – love, specifically of God; an important term within the bhakti traditions.

Puja 56 – ritualistic worship, most often of the installed murti.

Punya 12 – pious activities; actions that elevate the soul.

Purana 130 – literally "very old". The texts containing the many popular religious stories, sometimes called myths.

Puri 98, 71 – (1) a flat bread fried in oil or ghee, (2) a holy town in Orissa on the East Coast of India.

Purohit 64 – a priest who performs ritualistic ceremonies; often a brahminical surname also.

Purusha 34 – person, though specifically male; sometimes used to refer to the soul and sometimes God.

Purusha Shukta 124 – prayer about creation found in the Rig Veda.

Purva Mimamsa 119 – 'the earlier school of enquiry', often called simply Mimamsa (one of the six darshans).

Pushti marg 144 – 'the path of nourishment'; the process followed by the mainly Gujarati followers of Vallabha.

Radha 50 – the chief of the gopi girlfriends of Krishna. Vaishnavas often consider her part of the Godhead.

Raga 93 – a particular musical scale used in classical music, which is usually played impromptu.

Raja (astanga) yoga 127 – one of the four main yogas, the path of meditation and mystic power.

Raja 44 – 'king'. Often kings and holy men are addressed as 'Maharaja' – 'great king'.

Raja-guna 14 – the second of the three material qualities; the quality of passion or ambition, exemplified by royalty.

Rajas 14 – an abbreviated form of raja-guna (see above).

Rajneesh 139 – late guru who attracted many Western disciples; also known as Osho.

Rajputs 141 – a name for the warriors (kshatriyas) from Rajastan.

Raksha Bandana 67 – one of the main festivals when sisters tie a rakhi, bracelet, on the wrist of their brothers.

Rakshasa 53 – a race of man-eaters known for their ability to change form.

Rama 129 – usually considered the seventh avatar of Vishnu (or sometimes of Krishna). Also called Ramachandra.

Rama Carita Manas 133 – a popular version of the Ramayana written in Hindi by Tulsidas.

Rama Mohan Roy 140 – the founder of the Arya Samaj, one of the most important reform movements.

Rama Nama Satya Hai 80 – a mantra often chanted at funerals and meaning, "the name of Rama is truth".

Rama rajya 111 – 'the reign of Rama', adopted by many Hindu reformers as a symbol of the social ideal.

Ramakrishna 141 – a famous spiritual teacher from Bengal.

Ramanuja 138 – one of the most important Vaishnava theologians, and founder of Shri Vaishnavism.

Ramayana 129 – 'the journey of Rama'; the shorter of the two Hindu Epics.

Rameshbai Oza 139 – popular speaker who offers public recitations, mainly from the Bhagavat Purana.

Rameshvaram 72 – an important pilgrimage site in South India.

Rangoli 94 – a pattern made by Hindu ladies and girls, mainly in South India.

Rantideva 99 – a legendary king famous for his hospitality.

Rasa 93 – literally 'juice'; refers to the relationships defined in the performing arts and later in ontological theology.

Rasa-lila 34 – the dance that Krishna performs with his girlfriends, the gopis (cowherd girls).

Rashtriya Svayamsevak Sanga 140 – an influential cultural organisation with nationalistic tendencies.

Ratha-yatra 69 – a chariot (ratha) festival originally from Puri but now popular in many cities world-wide.

Ravana 129 – a king of the Rakshasas. He lived on Shri Lanka, kidnapped Sita and was killed by Rama.

Rig Veda 124 – the foremost and possibly earliest of the four Vedas.

Rishi 132 – sage; specifically the seven great sages of ancient times.

Rudra 52 – an angry form of Shiva, particularly prevalent during the Vedic period.

Sabji 96 – a preparation made from vegetables, usually spiced.

Sadhana 120 – spiritual discipline, such as chanting mantras, observing vows, etc.

Sadharana- Dharma 81 – general moral duties for all members of Hindu society.

Sadhu 85 – a pious or saintly person. Often used to refer to sannyasis.

Sahajanand Swami 144 – founder of the Swami Narayana Mission, considered by many followers an incarnation of God.

Sama Veda 124 – one of the four Vedas; it explains the melodies to be used in ritual sacrifice.

Samadhi 114 – the final stage of yoga, when the mind is perfectly focused on one point.

Samhita 124 – one of the four sections of the Vedas.

Sampradaya 31 – a disciplic succession, a line of gurus and disciples for disseminating spiritual knowledge.

Samsara 10 – the perpetual cycle of birth and death. The process of suffering in this way.

Samskara 76 – 'mental impression'; it refers to the various rites of passage.

Sanatana-dharma 24 – the eternal religion, the eternal function of the soul; often preferred to the term 'Hinduism'.

Sanatanist 126 – those who believe in Sanatana-dharma; used often today to denote eclectic worship instead of sectarian.

Sankhya 120 – one of the six darshans; it analyses matter in detail and also identifies the atman beyond matter.

Sarasvati 90 – goddess of learning & the arts; also a sacred river, now dried up; some say it still runs underground.

Saree 96 – the most popular traditional dress for Hindu women.

Sati 105 – one incarnation of Shiva's wife, Parvati. After her, the act of a wife's entering the funeral pyre of her husband.

Sattva-guna 14 – the highest of the three material qualities, characterised by goodness.

Satyagraha 141 – 'grasping the truth'; a term coined by Gandhi whilst in South Africa.

Satya-yuga 32 – the first of the four universal ages; also called Krita Yuga.

Savitri 146 – a young lady immortalised for her devotion towards her husband.

Seva 24 – service, a key Hindu principle/value; the soul's Sanatana-dharma, fully expressed through bhakti.

Shabda 115 – 'sound'; shabda brahman means 'spiritual sound', often considered the best means of obtaining knowledge.

Shaiva Siddhanta 129 – personalistic school of Shaivism, prevalent in South India.

Shaiva/Shaivite 117 – a worshipper of Shiva.

Shakta 96 – a follower of Shakti, the goddess.

Shakti 49 – a generic term to refer to the female deity, especially the consort of Shiva.

Shariraka Bhasya 125 – commentary on the Vedanta Sutras by Shankara.

Shastra 30 – scripture; used particularly of some texts e.g. the dharma-shastras.

Shibi 40 - legendary king renowned for his self-sacrifice and ideal leadership.

Shilpa Shastra 101 – one of the four Upavedas, dealing with architecture.

Shiva 48 – one of the trimurti, three principal deities. He is in charge of tama-guna. Some consider him the Supreme.

Shravana Kumar 41 – a legendary boy celebrated for his devotion to his elderly parents.

Shree Vallabha Nidhi 128 – UK organisation following the path of Pushti Marg.

Shri Bhasya 119 – commentary on the Vedanta Sutras by Ramanuja.

Shri Lanka 129 – the island reputed in the Ramayana to have been the kingdom of the tyrant Ravana.

Shri Rangam 132 – centre for one of the two main branches of the Shri (Vaishnava) Sampradaya.

Shri Sampradaya 138 – the preceptoral succession in which Ramanuja appeared and headed by Lakshmi.

Shri Vaishnavas 134 – one of the four main Vaishnava sampradayas, headed by Shri (another name for Lakshmi).

Shrikantha 132 – 13th century Shaivite theologian.

Shripati 132 – 14th century Shaivite theologian.

Shruti 122 – 'that which has been heard'; one of the two main sections of Vedic texts and considered of divine origin.

Shuddhadvaita 138 – 'qualified non-dualism', the philosophy expounded by Ramanuja and his sampradaya.

Shudra 82 – the fourth varna; a member of that varna, an artisan or labourer.

Siddhi 114 - 'perfection'; refers specifically to the eight mystic powers, such as the ability to become very light.

Siksha 31 – formal initiation taken from a guru (spiritual teacher).

Sindhu 113 – an important river now in Pakistan and called the Indus. Some believe that Hinduism had its roots here.

Sita 129 – the wife of Rama and heroine of the Ramayana.

Skanda 50 – one of the two sons of Shiva and Parvati; also called Murugan, Kartikeya and Subrahmaniam.

Smartas 137 – one of the four main denominations; they worship five deities.

Smriti 122 – 'that which is remembered'; the second category within the Hindu texts.

Soma 53 – a name for the Moon. Also, a celestial beverage used in Vedic sacrifice.

Somnath 70 – important place of pilgrimage for Shaivas, in Gujarat.

Surdas 139 – a blind musician famous for his songs, mainly in praise of Krishna.

Surya 50 – the Sun, worshipped by the Smarta traditions and also by the chanting of the Gayatri mantra.

Sushruta Samhita 101 – text yielding much information on Ayurvedic medicine.

Sutra 125 – literally 'thread'; an aphorism that can be unpacked almost unlimitedly to yield profound truths.

Svastika 95 – a popular Hindu symbol which was unfortunately adopted by the Nazis.

Svetashvatara Upanishad 134 – one of the Upanishads, considered canonical for many Shaivites.

Swami – 'controller' – a title used for sannyasis, who must control their senses. Goswami is an alternative.

Swami Narayana Mission 144 – a Vaishnava sampradaya, very popular amongst Gujarati Hindus in the UK.

Tagore, Devendranatha 140 – prominent Bengali reformer and father of the poet and writer, Rabindranatha.

Tamah-guna 14 – the lowest of the three material qualities, typified by ignorance, darkness and inertia.

Tamas 14 – a shortened version of tamah-guna (*see above*).

Tansen 93 – famous musician; one of the 'nine jewels' of the court of Emperor Akbar.

Tantra (1) 136 – a form of ritualistic Hinduism in which Shakti is worshipped, often together with Shiva.

Tantra (2) 123 – a category of texts, usually connected to goddess worship.

Tara 146 – wife of Vali; one of the five 'virtuous women' of Hinduism.

Tilak 132 – a clay mark applied to the forehead and denoting the particular affiliation of the worshipper.

Tirtha 72 – literally 'ford'. A holy place, where one can cross over to the other side i.e. attain liberation.

Tirthayatra 72 – pilgrimage

Tirupati 60 – a holy place in Andhra Pradesh. The temple of Venkata is perhaps the wealthiest in the world.

Tithi 68 – the lunar day, a thirtieth part of the lunar month, by which festival dates are calculated.

Treta-yuga 32 – the second cosmic age in the cycle of four.

Trimurti 48 – the three main deities, Brahma (the creator), Vishnu (the sustainer) and Mahesh, or Shiva (the destroyer).

Trishul 95 – a trident, the emblem associated with Siva and carried by many sannyasis devoted to him.

Tukarama 139 – a bhakti saint of Maharastra in Western India.

Tulsi 47 – a plant sacred to Vaishnavas, and from which their beads are usually made.

Tulsidas 139 – a bhakti saint famous for his rendering of the Ramayana.

Udupi 134 – sacred town in South India and head-quarters of the Madhva sampradaya.

Ujjain 72 – one of the four sites of the Kumbha Mela; it is on the River Shipra.

Upamana 115 – analogy; in Nyaya it is considered one of the four means of attaining knowledge.
Upanayana 78 – 'coming near', referring to the sacred thread initiation ceremony.
Upanishad 125 – one of the four sections of the Vedas. They are highly philosophical and identified with Vedanta.
Upasana 122 – a generic word for worship
Upasana kanda 122 – 'the worship section'; one of the three broad categories of scriptural content.
Upavedas 124 – four texts, supplementary to the Vedas and explaining traditional arts and sciences.
Utsava 67 – festival or celebration; one of the five nitya-karmas (essential duties).
Uttara Mimamsa 119 – 'the later school of enquiry'; another name for Vedanta.

Vaidika Dharma 122 – alternative to the term 'Hinduism'; it denotes the followers of the Vedas and their supplements.
Vaikunthaloka 138 – 'the place of no anxiety'; a name for the abode of Vishnu; the Kingdom of God.
Vaisheshika 121 – one of the six darshans, atomic theory as propounded by Kanada.
Vaishnavas 134 – the worshippers of Vishnu; generally accepted as the biggest of the four main denominations.
Vaishno Devi 71 – sacred cave dedicated to the three goddesses, Lakshmi, Kali and Sarasvati.
Vaishya 82 – a member of the third varna, the farming and mercantile community.
Vallabha 139 – founder of the Pushti Marg sampradaya, popular amongst many Gujaratis.
Vallabha 144 – theologian who founded the Pushti Marg sampradaya and taught the doctrine of purified monism.
Vali 140 – Varana (monkey) king and brother of Sugriva; killed by Rama for stealing sugriva's wife.
Valmiki 129 – the criminal-turned-sage who wrote the original Ramayana.
Vamana 110 – the fifth of the ten incarnations of Vishnu. He appeared as a brahmin dwarf to trick King Bali.
Vanaprashta 85 – the third order of life, or a member of that ashrama, the forest dweller.
Varanasi 71 – perhaps the most famous holy town, on the Ganges. It is also called Kashi and Benares.
Varna 26 – the largest social unit, originally as part of a meritocracy but now usually based on birth.
Varnashrama Dharma 26 – social system with different duties allocated to four classes and four stages in life.
Varuna 53 – god of the waters, akin to Neptune. More prominent during the Vedic period.
Vasista 132 – one of the seven great rishis; he had an ongoing dispute with Vishvamitra.
Vastu 99 – the science of sacred space, equivalent to the Chinese Feng-Shui.
Vayu 53 – the deity in charge of air and the wind. His offspring, such as Hanuman, tend to be physically very strong.
Veda 124 – literally "knowledge"; specifically one of the four Shruti texts that form the basis of sacred Hindu literature.
Vedangas 124 – texts supplementary to the four Vedas.
Vedanta 125 – the conclusion of the Vedas; one of the six darshans, often considered the most respectable.
Vedanta Sutra 125 – important aphorisms containing the essence of Hindu theology.
Vedic 124 – 'connected to, or derived from, the Vedas. Specifically, the period when the four Vedas were compiled.
Vidura 120 – saintly brother of Pandu and Dhritarastra, and well-wisher of the five Pandavas.
Vikrama 68 – a famous king after whom some Hindus date the years (i.e. according to the 'Vikrama era').
Vishishtadvaita 138 – the doctrine of 'qualified non-dualism' propounded by Ramanuja.
Vishnu 48 – one of the trimurti; the sustainer. Often identified with the Supreme Deity.
Vishnuswami 134 – forerunner of Vallabha and founder of one of the four Vaishnava sampradayas.
Vishva Hindu Parishad (VHP) 142 – a movement aimed at bringing about worldwide co-operation between Hindus.
Vishvamitra 132 – although born in a kshatriya family, he became a powerful brahmin.
Vishvanatha 69 – a name of Shiva; the most important temple in Varanasi.
Vithobha 139 – another name for Vitthala (see below).
Vitthala 139 – a famous form of Vishnu in the Maharastriyan town of Pandharpur.
Vivaha – the wedding ceremony, one of the important rites of passage.
Vivekananda 79 – disciple of Ramakrishna who widely popularised advaita Vedanta and propounded a neo-Hinduism.
Vraj 69 – the region around Mathura and Vrindavana, especially sacred to the worshippers of Krishna.
Vrata 86 – vow; women especially take vows, often related to fasting. Vows are also taken at initiation.
Vrindavana 41 – an important holy town close to Mathura and the place of Krishna's childhood and youth.
Vyasa 30 – also called Badarayana; an important sage credited with writing many important texts.

Yajna 113 – ritual sacrifice, prevalent during the Vedic age but still performed today especially through the havan.
Yajnavalkya 125 – sage and author of some important texts which form part of the Dharma Shastra.
Yajur Veda 124 – one of the four Vedas.
Yama 53 – the deity in charge of death and the awarding of punishment to the sinful. Also called 'dharma-raja'.
Yamuna 74 – a tributary of the Ganga, it flows through Vrindavana and is especially sacred to Krishna worshippers.
Yoga 44 – union, most specifically with the Supreme; any practice aimed at such realisation.
Yogi 44 – one who performs yoga. The feminine is sometimes 'yogini'.
Yudhisthira 126 – eldest of the five Pandava brothers and later emperor of greater India.

Useful Contacts

Teacher Support Services

This book and the entire 'Heart of Hinduism' teachers' pack comes with full teacher support. For free advice and for further information (temples visits, guest speakers and INSET) please contact:

ISKCON Educational Services, Hilfield Lane, Aldenham, Herts., WD25 8EZ U.K.
Tel: +44 (0)1923 – 859578
Email: ies@pamho.net
Website: www.iskcon.org.uk/ies/
For IES representatives in other locations, please consult "The Heart of Hinduism" CD-Rom, or ring on the above number.

Further possible useful contacts are as follows:

Faith Community Organisations

Ramakrishna Vedanta Centre,
Bourne End, Bucks, Sl8 5lG
Tel: 01628 526 464 fax: 01628 532 437
Email: vedantauk@talk21.com
website: www.vedantauk.com

The Education Department,
Shri Swaminarayan Mandir,
105 – 119 Brentfield Road,
Neasden, London NW10 8JP
Tel: 020 8965 2651 fax: 020 8965 6313
Email: admin@swaminarayan-baps.org.uk
Website: www.swaminarayan.org

Dr. N. Prinja,
The Vishva Hindu Parishad,
28, Glastonbury Avenue, Hale,
Cheshire, WA15 8QB

Mr. Vipin Aery,
The National Council for Hindu Temples,
c/o The Santana Mandir,
Weymouth Street, Leicester, LE4 6FP
Tel: 07958-464072

Dilip Lakhani,
www.btinternet.com/~vivekananda/schools.htm
Email: hindu@btinternet.com

Indian Arts and Culture

Dr. Nanda Kishor,
The Bharatiya Vidya Bhavan,
4a Castleton Rd, London W14 9HQ
Tel: 020 7381-4608

For Academic Advice

The Oxford Centre for Vaishnava and Hindu Studies,
13-15, Magdalen Street, Oxford, OX1 3AE
Tel: 01865-304300

Artefacts

Popats Stores, 52 Ealing Road,
Wembley, Middlesex, HA0 4PY
Tel. 020 8902-4182

ISKCON Educational Services (*see left*)

Religions in Evidence, Monk Road, Alfreton, Derbyshire, DE55 7RL. tel: 0800-318686

Articles of Faith Ltd., Resource House, Kay St., Bury, BL9 6BU. tel: 0161-736-6232

Illustrators (mainly children's books)

Ananta Shakti, tel: 020 8953-1023

Authors/writers

Anita Ganeri, tel: 01943-816790

Krishna Dharma, tel: 01923-856145

Rasamandala Das
Email: rasamandala.acbsp@pamho.net

Websites

http://www.hindunet.org/
A general site
http://www.reetirivaz.com/righ3.asp
A general site
http://www.iskcon.org/
from ISKCON (a Vaishnava tradition)
http://www.himalayanacademy.com/
from the publishers of "Hinduism Today"
(a Shaivite tradition)

More website addresses are included on "The Heart of Hinduism" CD-Rom.

The publishers cannot guarantee the accuracy of the information provided through these sites, or that these contact details are still current.

This book, and "The Heart of Hinduism" Teaching Pack is distributed by:
Veda Education,
Chintamani, Wall Hall Cottages,
Aldenham, Herts. WD2 8AS
England, U.K.
Website: www.heartofhinduism.org

Index